GRANTS FOR LIBRARIES

A How-To-Do-It Manual

Stephanie K. Gerding
Pamela H. MacKellar

HOW-TO-DO-IT MANUALS FOR LIBRARIANS

NUMBER 144

NEAL-SCHUMAN PUBLISHERS, INC.
New York, London

Published by Neal-Schuman Publishers, Inc.
100 William St., Suite 2004
New York, NY 10038

Printed and bound in the United States of America.

The paper used in this publication meets the minimum requirements of American National Standard for Information Sciences—Permanence of Paper for Printed Library Materials, ANSI Z39.48-1992. ∞

Library of Congress Cataloging-in-Publication Data

Gerding, Stephanie K.
Grants for libraries : a how-to-do-it manual / Stephanie K. Gerding, Pamela H. MacKellar.
p. cm.—(How-to-do-it manuals for librarians ; no. 144)
Includes bibliographical references and index.
ISBN 1-55570-535-9 (alk. paper)
1. Proposal writing in library science—United States—Handbooks, manuals, etc. 2. Library fund raising—United States—Handbooks, manuals, etc. 3. Proposal writing for grants—United States—Handbooks, manuals, etc. I. MacKellar, Pamela H. II. Title. III. How-to-do-it manuals for libraries ; no. 144.
Z683.2.U6G47 2006
025.1'1—dc22 2005027980

To Bruce and Alex MacKellar, and Marian Herd
Pam MacKellar

To Patrick Gerding;
My dream of publishing this book would not have been possible without my husband and his endless love, encouragement, and housework.

To Caroline Rawlins:
My mother has said that if she were not so hard on me, I never would have accomplished as much as I have. I agree and thank her for the strength, example, and love she has given me.
Stephanie Gerding

CONTENTS

LIST OF FIGURES

FOREWORD

Perhaps there were halcyon days of well-funded library and cultural institutions that predated my 35 years in the workaday world. Certainly, libraries have had patrons: Carnegie, Mellon, and Bill and Melinda Gates, to name just a few whose financial investment in our institutions has impacted our work in very real and meaningful ways. Since the early 1970s, libraries, along with their sister cultural and other community and nonprofit organizations, have not received adequate funding to do the work that their communities need and desire.

Each of the cultural professions, certainly librarianship, has professional training that is often required of practitioners by local and state authorities. Library schools and other professional programs across the country strive to prepare individuals for the realities that must be faced in the workplace on the first day, in the first decade, and throughout a career that may span many decades. It is not realistic to assume that any academic program of even 2 year's duration can prepare one for all circumstances or requirements, including knowledge of grant project planning and proposal writing.

That is what makes *Grants for Libraries: A How-To-Do-It Manual*—written for practitioners, by practitioners—is so very critical to the continuing education in our profession and those of our cultural partners. Most of us have struggled with fund-raising and grant proposal writing. There are so many ways to do it incorrectly, to sabotage, albeit unwittingly, one's effort. There are time-tested techniques, procedures, plans, and processes that are helpful—this book brings many of the best practices and models into one place. *Grants for Libraries* is one of the most useful conveyances of information yet developed and a crucial aspect of continuing professional development.

I hope when you read this book, you will find the help you need and succeed with its lessons. Please let us know your stories. We all share a love of our institutions and our work. What helps one helps all.

I am very grateful that Stephanie chooses to spend her work time with the Arizona State Library. My thanks to both Stephanie and Pam for the time and effort—and for the caring—evident on every page. My thanks to Neal-Schuman for their entire "How-To-Do-It" series. As State Librarian of Arizona, I am proud to recommend this particular "How-To" to the library community.

GladysAnn Wells
State Librarian
Arizona State Library
Archives and Public Records

PREFACE

Grants are always important to libraries—and in times of budget cuts and shortages, they are increasingly essential to fund new initiatives and sustain services. Unfortunately, library schools don't usually teach Grant Writing 101, and it's rare for a book on this subject to specifically take a library-centric approach. As a result, many grant applications are poorly written. We have read applications that are so unclear that it is impossible to determine what the project is and what exactly is being proposed. We hope *Grants for Libraries: A How-To-Do-It Manual* solves your writing problems, rewards you with approved proposals, and generates new sources of funding for your initiatives.

Librarians and information professionals are often surprised to learn that they possess many of the skills necessary to be successful grant writers. They already benefit from the ability to research, synthesize, package, and summarize information; a commitment to reach out and assess community needs; and a cooperative, collaborative professional attitude. What is needed is the synthesis of these skills and the practical knowledge of the grant process cycle. *Grants for Libraries* provides all the tools and instruction you will need to win financial awards for your institution. The text features worksheets, examples, templates, and checklists presented in an easy-to-follow, step-by-step grant process cycle.

PURPOSE AND AUDIENCE

We created this manual for anyone interested in grants and libraries. Our expertise stems from experience in every aspect of grant work. Each of us has been involved with both receiving and donating funds and each has both authored and evaluated proposals. We have worked for library nonprofits and state library agencies, and have received grant funding from government and private agencies. We presented workshops around the country and found that our process works for public, academic, and school libraries.

PERSPECTIVE AND ORGANIZATION

The foundation of *Grants for Libraries* is unique because it emphasizes strategic planning and goal setting. This not only simplifies the work and effort you have to put into the process but ensures that your work is directly linked to your library's larger mission and vision.

The material is arranged in three consecutive pieces. Part I features a full review of the grant process, complete with filled-out worksheets, examples, templates, and checklists. Part II features real-life success stories that demonstrate the process in practice and will motivate you to employ Part III as a workbook to create your own grant proposal. All of the tools at the end of the book are reproduced on the CD-ROM.

Part I thoroughly examines "The Grant Process Cycle."

Chapter 1, "Making the Commitment and Understanding the Process," outlines the steps necessary to successfully obtain grants. This chapter also provides an overview of the commitments that must be made by a library that is seeking these funds. You cannot consider grants just as free money. Acquiring them requires planning, resources, accountability, and sustainability. Grants also bring in more than funds—they establish valuable partnerships, resolve community needs, and increase community support.

Chapter 2, "Planning for Success," demonstrates why it is essential to have a strategic plan and community involvement in place before beginning grant work. We help your library get on track with guidance to develop a successful plan and furnish a sample from the Exemplar Library, the fictitious library we use to show our process throughout the book.

Chapter 3, "Discovering and Designing the Grant Project," covers one of the most creative and enjoyable parts of the process—developing the project. By developing worthwhile projects that implement your strategic plan and solve community needs, you can prove to funders why you should receive a grant. We show you how to develop project ideas and goals, outcomes, objectives, action steps, timelines, budgets, and evaluation plans. The included Project Templates will be invaluable when it is time to begin writing.

Chapter 4, "Organizing the Grant Team," helps you form a team of key individuals who will share the workload while increasing the likelihood of success. We share our thoughts on what makes a successful grant writer. Too many libraries fail to apply simply because they feel they don't have staff with the necessary skills. We explain how many of the everyday library skills can be leveraged in the grants process. There is also valuable information on using volunteers and professional grant writers. To get your team off to a solid start, we provide the basics for your first meeting.

Chapter 5, "Understanding the Sources and Resources," pulls together a wealth of information that will help you explore, locate, and select grant opportunities. This chapter explains the basic types of funding sources, including those specifically earmarked for libraries. It also looks at online and print resources you can use to research options or keep current on announcements.

Chapter 6, "Researching and Selecting the Right Grant," guides you in the selection of the right funder for your project. You will learn how to assess the awarding institution and identify those whose purpose most closely matches your library's project. A useful Keyword Selection Template uses your strategic plan's goals and objectives as a starting point in your search, and the Funder Summary Worksheet keeps your research findings organized.

Chapter 7, "Creating and Submitting the Winning Proposal," integrates the planning and research components with the actual writing process. Many applications request the same basic structure and elements—cover letter, proposal summary, organizational overview, statement of needs, project description, methodology, budget, evaluation, and appendix. We explain these components and provide planning and proposal templates that will allow you to easily adapt, modify, and replicate content for multiple grants. We also cover how to tell the story of your target audience and grant concept. We provide checklists to ensure that you have a thorough and clear proposal, which could make the difference between a winning proposal and a rejection letter.

Chapter 8, "Getting Funded and Implementing the Project," explains what happens after you send off your proposal. Find out what to do next, whether your proposal was accepted or rejected. We include an explanation of the most common reasons grants are turned down, details on customary grant report requirements, and steps for beginning your project implementation.

Chapter 9, "Reviewing and Continuing the Process," helps libraries evaluate their process and improve their plan for the next grant. Repeating the cycle will be easier as your experience grows and will be more rewarding as you learn from your previous attempts. We include questions to facilitate a review session and ways to keep your grant skills up-to-date through professional development and other collaborative opportunities.

Chapter 10, "Answering Five Essential Questions," lists the top five questions that your library must be able to answer to be successful with grant seeking. The five topics are (1) organizational capacity, (2) fulfillment of a community need, (3) sustainability, (4) relationship building, and (5) evaluation. This assessment will help you and your institution determine your potential for success.

Throughout the chapters you will find references to the *Grants for Libraries* Tool Kit and CD-ROM, which includes checklists, worksheets, and templates for you to examine and complete. We provide completed versions throughout; you will also find blank, reproducible versions in Part III and on the CD-ROM.

Part II, "Library Grant Success Stories," features sixteen examples of funded projects. If you need a little help with brainstorming creative ideas or want to get advice from other librarians who have weathered the storm, we have compiled inspiring stories from different types of libraries of various sizes from around the country. These selections include best practices and help bring together what you have just learned in the ten-step process. Photographs of grant projects in action are also included.

Part III, "The Grants for Libraries Tool Kit and CD-ROM" contains checklists, worksheets, and templates for you to examine and complete.

- Tool A includes a Grant Partnership Agreement worksheet and a Making the Commitment Checklist.
- Tool B contains a Library Planning Checklist and links to sample Library Strategic Plans.
- Tool C features six templates and a worksheet that will prove invaluable for discovering and planning your grant project. Templates for Project Action Steps, Project Timelines, and Grant Budgets are included.
- Tool D consists of a Keyword Selection Worksheet helpful for researching grants, a Funder Summary Worksheet for keeping track of funder information, and links to Funding Resources for Libraries.
- Part of Tool E, due to its length, is only available on the companion CD-ROM. It provides a Grant Proposal Template, a final checklist, and a variety of Example Requests for Proposals and Grant Announcements. We also include several proposals for successfully funded grant projects. These will prove invaluable for modeling, evaluating, and improving your own submissions.
- The complete *Grants for Libraries* Bibliography and Glossary are replicated on the CD-Rom.

All these are reproduced as Microsoft Word documents on the companion CD-ROM. You can complete the templates on your computer and save them as your own or print them out and fill them in by hand. Having these materials electronically will also facilitate your team's use of the tools.

GOOD LUCK AND HAVE FUN!

We know that grant work can seem intimidating, and our hope is that *Grants for Libraries: A How-To-Do-It Manual* will make it less of a mystery and more of an enjoyable adventure. Your journey may include a little fear but remember that writing a successful grant is achievable and that our Grant Process Cycle is easy to follow and will set you up for success. We believe that as librarians, we are ahead in the grant process—we know how to research; we are experts at partnering and collaborating; we are aware of our communities' needs; and we have a wealth of creative ideas for serving our users and furthering the pursuit of knowledge. When you put these pieces together in the right context of a grant proposal, you are sure to find success.

We wish you the very best of luck! Please let us know about your successes at librarygrants@earthlink.net. We'd love to include your story in our next book.

ACKNOWLEDGMENTS

PAM MACKELLAR

Thank you to Dr. Sherry Allison, who was a mentor to me as I learned to write my first large federal grant proposal. She was always available to provide guidance and advice when I needed it the most. Thanks to Patty Wolfe Hasselbring, who taught me more than I ever imagined there was to learn about proposal writing and who I can still hear saying, "It's all about the people, not the money." My sincere thanks to those who submitted grant success stories for this book. You have made a great contribution, providing real-life stories that will inspire others. Many thanks to Stephanie Gerding, who played a large part in creating the opportunity for me to coauthor this book with her. Your friendship means a lot to me.

STEPHANIE GERDING

Thank you to Pam MacKellar for writing this book with me and dealing with my constant torrent of new ideas, which she agreeably terms creativity. Most of all thank you for your friendship; it means a lot to me, too. I'd also like to thank the technology that made this book so much easier to write. Thank you, laptops, Internet, and fast printers! One last thank-you to all the librarians who submitted their grant success stories to us. They were a joy to read and will be helpful to many aspiring grant writers.

1 THE GRANT PROCESS CYCLE

1 MAKING THE COMMITMENT AND UNDERSTANDING THE PROCESS

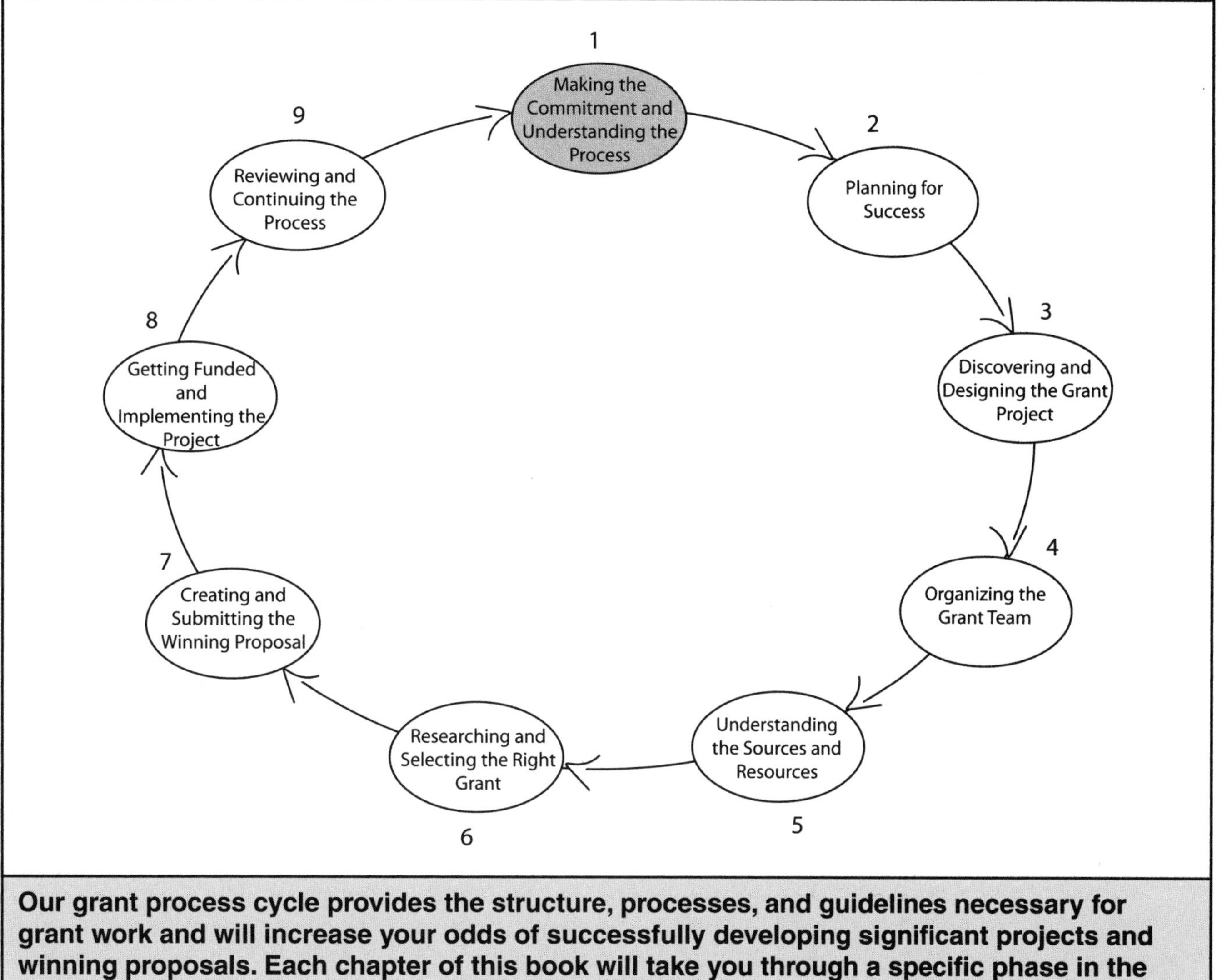

Our grant process cycle provides the structure, processes, and guidelines necessary for grant work and will increase your odds of successfully developing significant projects and winning proposals. Each chapter of this book will take you through a specific phase in the cycle.

OVERVIEW OF THE GRANT PROCESS CYCLE

"... One of your main tasks as an effective grant seeker is to be a master of information. You gather it, synthesize it, and make it available to funders and coworkers in the right format at the right time" (Brown and Brown 2001, 23). What could be easier for a librarian?

Successful grant work is the result of planning, organizational capacity, fulfillment of community needs, sustainability, relationship building, and evaluation. Grants are not just free money that will magically solve your library's budget problems. This book covers proposal writing and grant research but also focuses on the planning process necessary to have a successful project and a justly awarded grant. It is a holistic process that must include all facets of the library's planning and as many staff as possible. It is also a rational process based on project management principles. We will cover the entire grant process and help you develop core grant proposal components, useful for all applications.

1. MAKING THE COMMITMENT AND UNDERSTANDING THE PROCESS

There are skills necessary for grant work, but all can be learned, and many are ones that most library staff already have developed. Anyone who can research appropriate funders and grants, connect with the library's community, create a justifiable, well-planned project, and effectively write and communicate can be successful with the grant process. However, there is one other important requirement for success with grants. There must be a strong commitment throughout the entire process. Library leadership and grant coordinators must be committed to the entire process: the planning, the project development, the research, the writing, the implementation, and the follow-up.

2. PLANNING FOR SUCCESS

As part of this process, we encourage you to constantly refer to your library's strategic plan. If your library doesn't have a plan, make it a priority to develop a planning process before applying for grants. If this isn't possible, your library should at least have a written mission statement that can be used as a basis for project development decisions. The reason a strategic plan is encouraged is that it provides the framework that is needed for the grant process to be effective. Having a library plan in place will help prevent the mistake of creating new, yet unplanned or unneeded, projects for your library only because grant funding is available. If every grant project is developed from the goals and objectives in your library's plan, it will eliminate the possibility of creating projects or programs that aren't relevant to your library's mission or your community's needs. A plan also answers many of the questions that are found in the Requests for Proposal (RFP) that charitable organizations rely on to determine their grant awards. A library with a strategic plan is a more dependable and organized applicant. A plan demonstrates to funders that their money will be used responsibly and not just wasted on a hastily developed new idea.

Your library must also know the community's needs before applying for grants. Discover the true needs of your community and what makes your library's efforts meaningful and important. This will be very helpful when you begin to develop your project ideas and when you demonstrate need in a grant proposal. Chapter 2 covers planning and methods for needs assessments in more detail and includes a sample strategic plan of the Exemplar Library, the fictitious library we use to demonstrate our process throughout the book.

3. DISCOVERING AND DESIGNING THE GRANT PROJECT

Chapter 3 covers a step-by-step method for development of grant projects. This is often one of the most creative and enjoyable parts of grant work. Every project should be worthwhile and be a solution to an identified community need. Your project should never develop when reading grant stipulations. Projects are the implementation arm of your strategic plan and should be designed before beginning your research of funders and grant opportunities. The slickness or length of an application is seldom a critical factor in determining who will receive a grant. Rather, it is the project that counts. When projects are based on community needs, funders can understand the reasons that the project is important and relevant for funding. If funders can't determine why you are developing a project, there is no way they are going to be supportive. Learn how to plan your project by developing action steps, timelines, budgets, and evaluation plans. The included Project Planning Worksheet will be invaluable when it is time to begin writing your grant proposal.

4. ORGANIZING THE GRANT TEAM

Once you have identified a viable project that fulfills a need in your community, you will be ready to form and organize a grant team. This team should comprise representatives from library leadership, community advisers and partners, grant researchers, grant writers, staff members who will plan and implement the grant project, and subject matter experts. The size of your grant team will correlate with the size of your library. These key individuals will help minimize the workload while increasing the likelihood of success. One of the first things you will learn is what qualities are necessary for an ideal grant writer. Some libraries are reluctant to apply for grants due to the misconception that they have no employee with the necessary skills. You may be surprised to find that many of the needed abilities are ones that are developed in everyday library work. The responsibilities and skills of these team members are also covered. Helpful tips will make certain that your first grant meeting is a hit.

5. UNDERSTANDING THE SOURCES AND RESOURCES

This step of the cycle is often an easier one for librarians since it involves research. The two major types of funding sources are explained. Also included is how to find current funding opportunities in both online and print formats, including those geared specifically for libraries. The good news is that with the increase of electronic information, it is easier to find grant announcements and help with researching your options.

6. RESEARCHING AND SELECTING THE RIGHT GRANT

This chapter overviews locating applicable and viable grant opportunities for your specific project. Once you know the sources and resources covered in Chapter 5, next you must research and select the right funder and the right grant. Selecting the right grant necessitates knowing what funders are interested in supporting and knowing how closely their mission matches that of your library. Learn how to increase your search results with a useful Keyword Selection Worksheet that will use your strategic plan's goals and objectives as a starting point. Keep your research findings organized with the Funder Summary Worksheet.

7. CREATING AND SUBMITTING THE WINNING PROPOSAL

Once you reach this part of the grant cycle, your planning work will be complete, and writing the proposal will involve refining your ideas into the stipulations requested by the funders. Most grant proposals have the same basic structure and requirements. The common components include cover letter, proposal summary, organizational overview, project description, statement of needs, project description, methodology, budget, evaluation, and appendix. Some parts of the proposal are narrative and involve telling the story of the grant project and people it will serve. We provide checklists to ensure you have a thorough and clear proposal that could make the difference between a winning proposal and a rejection letter.

8. GETTING FUNDED AND IMPLEMENTING THE PROJECT

It may be weeks or months before you receive notification that your grant application has been accepted. You may be contacted by the funder with questions or requests for more information. Find out what to do whether your proposal was accepted or rejected. Included is an explanation of the most common reasons grants are turned down. If you are funded, the implementation process begins. You will need to revisit your timeline and budget and make any appropriate updates. We include details on customary grant report requirements. Don't forget to celebrate this great accomplishment with the entire grant team.

If you need a little help with brainstorming creative ideas for your project or want to get advice from other librarians who have completed grant projects, we have compiled inspiring success stories from libraries around the country. This selection of best practices offers you a chance to see how award-winning programs have been developed, funded, and implemented.

9. REVIEWING AND CONTINUING THE PROCESS

Grant work is an ongoing process, so the cycle should be repeated. This is the time to look back and then move forward with the knowledge you've learned from your first completion of the grant process cycle. Facilitate a review session with your grant team with provided questions and keep your relationships with partners and funders thriving. There are many professional development opportunities related to grants for libraries, so keep up-to-date by attending workshops, subscribing to electronic lists, networking, and researching new opportunities.

IMPLICATIONS TO CONSIDER

There are both advantages and disadvantages to applying for, and receiving, grants. Sometimes it may not be worth the effort and requirements necessary to apply. There may be too many hoops to jump through, you may not be able to fulfill the stipulations requested in the RFP, or your library may not have the support necessary for implementation. The funding must be worth the time, effort, and resources needed. These resources include not just the staff time spent planning a project and writing a proposal but the time to be spent in implementation and evaluation of the project as well.

All grants have costs for the submitting library. Sometimes this is obvious, such as matching funds or staff time, but there is also the impact of assigning a key staff member to the duration of the project, the building space and supporting materials needed, or the impact of neglecting existing essential activities while focusing on the new project.

THE IMPORTANCE OF PARTNERSHIPS AND COLLABORATIONS

"Collaborations spread the workload and multiply the ideas" (Reuben Hoar Library Success Story, see page 190).

Many funders request or require that partners or collaborators are involved in your grant project. The basic reason for this is that they realize that the greater the number of people at the table, the higher the probability of success. All funders want their grant money to be used for successful projects rather than squandered on mistakes or lack of implementation skills.

All of our communities have problems, real needs that the library can help fulfill. The most urgent of these problems require a concerted team effort that will bring together the contributions of many talented individuals and responsible organizations. As has been said before, "None of us is as smart as all of us." By combining resources of several entities, the library is better positioned to solve community problems.

For a partnership to work, there must be common goals, mutual responsibilities, shared rewards, and plenty of communication. You will find that there are many organizations in your community that share the same goals as your library, whether it be eradicating illiteracy, helping teens develop into accomplished individuals, or bridging the digital divide. Sharing the workload and the resources is, of course, a good thing, but this is where the communication comes in handy. There should definitely be a project director or someone designated to represent each partner. A partnership agreement or memorandum of understanding (MOU) can be used to specify the details of your partnership in writing. This can help avoid many common difficulties that collaborators often encounter. A sample partnership agreement is included in the Grants for Libraries Tool Kit on page 199 and on the CD.

MAKING THE COMMITMENT

Can your library really commit to the grant application and implementation process? The library leadership (director, board) and any staff that will have responsibilities tied to the grant or grant project should be involved in the decision. Most grants will have not only benefits but also obligations and in some cases maybe even specific constraints or drawbacks that need to be considered. If your project does not fulfill the funder's guidelines, you are wasting your organization's time and funds by preparing a hopeless grant application. Of course, you are also wasting the funder's valuable time. This is not the best way to build a relationship with a potential funder.

"After the grant was received, we had some difficulty allowing enough staff time to carry out publicity and planning activities" (Highland Park Public Library Success Story; see page 172).

Ask yourself the following questions before you begin a grant proposal:

- Does the funder have restrictions or requirements that would shape or affect our grant project in an unacceptable or undesirable way?
- Can we continue the project if grant funds are discontinued? What would be the effect on our clients or organization if the project were stopped abruptly?
- Should we propose a new project when we really need money for present programs?
- Would this project take too much time and attention away from core library programs?

Don't think that small grants aren't worth the effort. Large grants can be more difficult to obtain, and smaller grants may fit your scope and intent better. One grant officer said they would love to give huge grants, but sometimes smaller grants are more appropriate for certain projects and libraries. There are a lot of small grants that are available from local funders, and many have fewer strings attached than those from larger nonprofits or government agencies.

SPECIFIC COMMITMENTS

The grant process cycle is ongoing, which means the commitments must be ongoing as well. Some of these commitments should be made before the library decides to pursue grant funding. Others cannot be made until you have designed your grant project and researched and selected the appropriate funder's grant. At that time you should revisit these commitments. Your library must be able to commit to accountability, effective communication, meeting community needs, planning, partnerships, evaluation, sustainability, and following the grant guidelines.

The following questions will help you determine if you can really make the commitment. They are also available as a Checklist in the Grants for Libraries Tool Kit on page 200 and also as a downloadable file on the CD-ROM.

Commit to Accountability

- Will the grant project definitely support your library's vision and mission?
- Will your library leadership support the project?
- Will the library director commit the necessary resources to the project/grant?
- Will the library staff have the time needed to complete the application process and to implement the grant project?
- Will the grant team have all the necessary supplies, equipment, services, and space?
- Can the library follow through on the promises made in the grant proposal?
- Will the library spend the funds as specified and keep accurate accounts?
- Will you make sure there are not other organizations in your community already doing your project and filling the need?
- Will all grant reports be filed on time?

Commit to Effective Communication

- Will your proposal be as clear, concise, and honest as possible?
- Will your goals, objectives, and activities be clearly identified and understandable?
- Will you be able to convey that your library and the project are important?
- Will you ask for what you really need?
- Will all the library staff, board members, leadership, partners, and volunteers be continually informed about the grant?
- Will you ask the funder if the library's grant project clearly fits their interests?
- Will you use all your contacts?

Commit to Meeting Community Needs

- Will your library identify the needs of your community?
- Will your analysis include enough information to educate and inspire the funder?

- Can statistics be used to quantify the problems identified?
- Can stories and cases be used regarding specific patrons or programs that illustrate the needs?
- Will your grant project focus on solutions to meeting community needs?
- Will you identify a target audience for your grant project and involve representatives in the planning process?

Commit to Planning

- Does your library have a strategic plan? Will you review it before writing your grant?
- Will you have a project plan that includes goals, objectives, and activities and is based on your strategic plan?
- Will you set deadlines?
- Will you organize your materials (research, grant materials, etc.)?
- Will you have a budgetary goal?
- Will you have a method to track tasks and contacts?

Commit to Partnerships

- Will you cultivate a strong relationship with your grant's funder?
- Will you develop the appropriate collaborations to leverage resources, share expertise, and support the project?
- Will you determine what groups in your community share your library's vision and goals and approach them as partners?
- Will you invite community members to focus groups and planning sessions?
- Will you complete a partnership agreement outlining goals, responsibilities, and benefits?

Commit to Evaluation

- Can your library clearly identify what success is in respect to the grant project?
- Will you have an evaluation plan or logic model to determine if your project has met its goals?

- Will you be able to identify what impact your project achieves and what difference the project makes?
- Will you identify outcomes for the project? Will your project have meaningful results that cause a change in people's behavior, attitudes, skills, condition, or knowledge?
- Will you have a benchmark plan designed to measure each outcome?

Commit to Sustainability

- Will your project be completed?
- Will your project be supported by leadership after grant funds are depleted?
- Will you plan a funding strategy to continue your project after grant funds are depleted?
- Is your project reliant on a single person?
- If your project involves hiring new staff members, will their positions be maintained after the grant period ends?

Commit to Following the Grant Guidelines

- Will you check and double-check all instructions?
- Will you answer all questions and complete any required narrative sections?
- Will you compile all allowable attachments, including letters of support?
- Will you obtain all the required signatures?
- Will you submit the grant on time?

INCREASE YOUR ODDS

Hopefully this long list of commitments hasn't made grant work seem too daunting. It is a process, and once you've gone through it the first time, it really does get easier. Here are some quick tips that will increase your odds of obtaining grant funds.

1. Read this book.
2. Know what you can and can't do.

3. Identify your community's greatest needs.
4. Know what you want to do.
6. Plan an amazing project and put it in writing.
5. Create a team or teams.
7. Network, collaborate, and partner.
8. Do your research.
9. Know how you are going to evaluate throughout the cycle.

ADDITIONAL BENEFITS

The good news is that once you complete the grant process cycle, most libraries find that they have achieved more than they had expected. There are often additional benefits beyond the grant funds. If you follow the guidelines in this book, you will increase community support and find new partners and collaboration opportunities. You may even see an increase in the library's local budget and an increase in library use. If your library has made these commitments, you are now ready to continue the grant process cycle.

Success Story: "The Friends of the Library were so impressed with the impact that [the grant project] had on the students that they donated money to continue the program after the grant period ended" (Des Plaines Public Library; see page 168).

2 PLANNING FOR SUCCESS

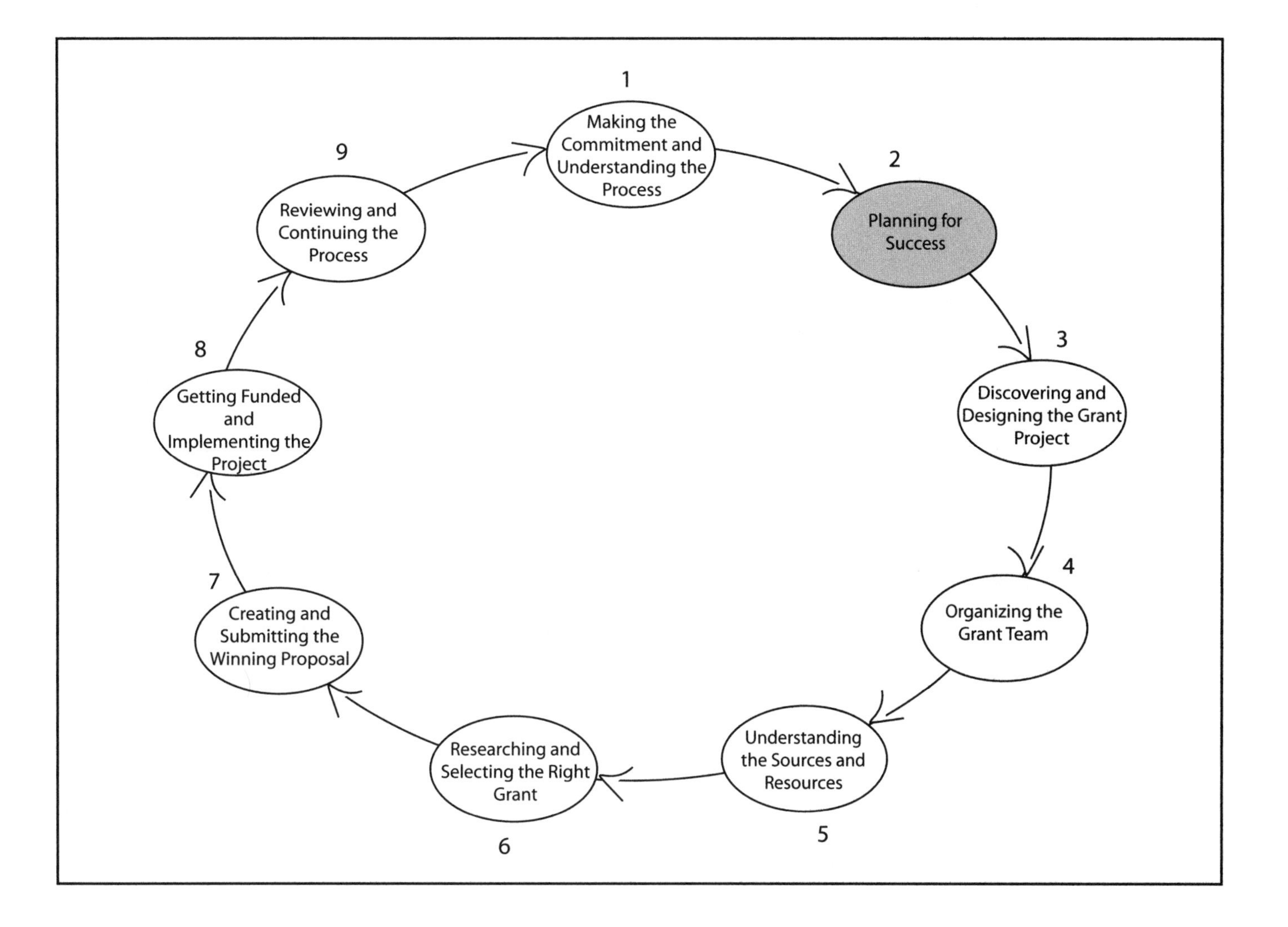

OVERVIEW

Chapter 2 focuses on strategic planning, which builds a foundation for your grant projects. Chapter 3 will take you to the next step of planning your specific project.

The focus of a strategic plan is usually on the entire organization, while the focus of a project plan is typically on a particular service, program, or product. Both types of planning are essential to successful grant proposals. First you must know what you do and why you do it. Essentially, this means you need to know your library's mission and vision, its purpose, and the true needs of its community. Then you can establish how you are going to meet those needs. Plans are the foundation upon which proposals are written and provide the framework for project development. Libraries with plans have much greater prospects for a successful future and often are able to achieve their community's biggest aspirations.

Planning helps you determine and prioritize exactly what you want to accomplish, and parts of strategic plans and project plans can be used directly into your grant proposal.

If your library doesn't have a strategic plan, how do you even know that you need grant funds? You should never create new projects for your library just because a grant is available. The process of obtaining grant funding should directly tie into your strategic plan. You will find that the main components for grant proposals and the inspiration for grant projects are easily found in a well-developed strategic plan. Just by examining your library's mission statement, you can gain essential information that will be helpful when searching for funders.

If you ignore your strategic plan, you may soon find that your library suffers from mission creep. If you aren't familiar with this term, it means that your organization's mission changes due to external factors such as money or outside influences. For example, if your library mission is focused on literacy, you should seek funding for literacy projects. If you submit a grant application to fund a project entitled *Cake Decorating for Teens*, based on the fact that you know a funder wants to support teen cooking classes, your library's mission may "creep" into focusing on teen cooking classes and resources rather than literacy. Teens in your area really have a need for literacy classes, which means the cake-decorating grant does not support your community in the best way possible. Your mission has changed to fit the guidelines of the funder rather than the needs of your community. Funding for hiring tutors or purchasing homework resources would be a better match for your mission.

"If you don't know where you're going, it doesn't matter which way you go," said the Cheshire Cat in Alice in Wonderland. If libraries do not understand their purpose, audience, and what they are trying to achieve, it will be very difficult to be successful.

There are many resources you can refer to that will be helpful in implementing a planning process for your library. The bibliography section of this book includes helpful recommendations, and the *Grants for Libraries* Tool Kit has links to a few good example library plans available on the Internet. It is true that strategic planning does not happen overnight. It should be a deliberate activity conducted by the library director, staff, board, and community participants. But if your library doesn't have a plan yet, it should at least have a mission statement. Your grant committee should be able to extrapolate and outline brief goals and objectives from the mission statement.

STRATEGIC PLANNING

Simply put, strategic planning determines where an organization is going over the next year or more, how it's going to get there, and how it'll know if it got there or not. Strategic planning will help guide the course for the future, establish new partnerships, form creative and innovative relationships between stakeholders, and ultimately better address the needs of your community. A community-wide strategic planning process will benefit from the wisdom of a diverse array of participants and ensure greater likelihood of success.

Successful planning is an ongoing process that has no beginning and no end. Strategic planning is a powerful tool. It is used to guide a library to improve itself, to prioritize, to ensure that all staff are working toward the same goals, and to assess and adjust the library's course in response to changing situations. Strategic planning is a deliberate effort to determine the appropriate decisions and actions that shape and guide what a library is, what it does, and why it does it. The grant cycle process involves planning because it involves intentionally setting goals, choosing desired outcomes, and developing an approach to achieving those outcomes. Funding is just one part of the picture.

Benefits of Strategic Planning

1. Creates a clear definition of the library's purpose; this focus leads to efficiency and effectiveness.
2. Produces a commonality of vision and mission that bridges staff and library leadership.
3. Establishes realistic goals and objectives consistent with the mission.
4. Determines the library's priorities to the community based on the greatest needs.
5. Ensures the most effective use of the library's resources (staff, budget, etc.).
6. Provides a basis for ongoing evaluation, measurement of progress, and informed improvement.
7. Provides a clear blueprint for the future.
8. Informs staff and management for decision making that is responsible and productive.
9. Strengthens responsible accountability to governing authorities and the public.
10. Increases staff morale and job satisfaction as informed partners.

A strategic plan should not be static. Once developed, it should not be imprinted with gold leaf and placed in a safe. Changes will happen that will need to be incorporated. When a major change or improvement is needed, you should revisit and update the plan. Major changes may include planning for a new or remodeled building or creating a new political arrangement, such as combining city libraries into a county system or dealing with budget cuts. Strategic planning stresses the importance of making decisions that will ensure the organization's ability to successfully respond to changes in the environment.

Whether or not you complete a strategic plan is your option. Many governmental and nonprofit funders are requiring a plan to be submitted as part of grant applications. For example, if your library wants to be eligible to apply for grants from many state libraries under the federal Library Services and Technology Act (LSTA) program or other federal- or state-funded grants, then you may be required to complete a library plan. Also, libraries and schools are required to have an approved technology plan to participate in the federal Universal Service Fund program, commonly known as the E-Rate program.

CREATING A STRATEGIC PLAN

Formulating missions, goals, and objectives is an involved and continual process. As a librarian, your first reaction may be that you don't have the time or the resources to accomplish this. In actuality, planning can save a lot of time and resources and so enable your library to accomplish more with less.

If your library cannot afford the luxury of assembling an entire planning committee, then at the very least include the library director, library board, and staff representatives. If possible, invite governing officials, library volunteers, and patrons to public planning meetings. In a small library, strategic planning might take place as part of quarterly or monthly board and staff meetings; with a larger library the planning committee can make progress reports to the board and meet more frequently.

There are a variety of perspectives, models, and approaches used in strategic planning. The way that a strategic plan is developed depends on many factors, such as the library leadership, the culture of the library, the complexity of the library's environment, the size of the library, and the expertise of the planners. Large urban libraries may hire outside consultants to coordinate the planning process, while smaller libraries often oversee the process internally.

The Public Library Association's community-based planning process, *Planning for Results*, provides a great planning structure for grants. This type of plan is not at all limited to public libraries, as every library serves a community, whether it is a neighborhood, campus, corporation, or school. It has proven successful with all sizes of libraries, as well as museums, churches, and schools. This process is based on involving a community committee and prioritizing the library's services. Funders often favor organizations that incorporate community awareness and involvement. Libraries have repeatedly confirmed how important the process of completing this type of plan has been in their local efforts to gain recognition, funding, and staffing for accomplishing the goals and objectives set out in their plans.

Don't be concerned about the "perfect way" to conduct strategic planning. If you do some research, you will find there are many models and thousands of books written on the best method of planning. Among the variety of strategic planning models, there are those that are based on goals, issues, and scenarios and those that are organic. Planning typically includes several major activities or steps in the process. Although there may be many different ways to identify these steps, there are many that are common to most strategic plans. They might not be conducted in the same order, and they may have different methods for writing goals and objectives, but usually the core elements are similar. Once you start strategic planning, you'll soon find your own particular approach or favorite method to complete the process. Don't be afraid to modify a planning process or combine two or three methods to create one that works for your library.

COMMON PLAN ELEMENTS

There are common elements found in most strategic plans. There is a complete sample plan at the end of this chapter. This is a 3-year, goal-based plan of the Exemplar Library, the fictional library that we use as an example for this book. Most plans range from 3 to 5 years. Any further into the future and it becomes increasingly difficult to incorporate imminent changes in the library infrastructure, community, technology, and so on. Plans vary in length from the more succinct ones, which are four to eight pages in length, to others considerably longer and more detailed.

At minimum, the strategic plan should include the following elements:

1. Vision Statement
2. Mission Statement
3. Community and Library Profiles
4. Needs Assessment
5. Goals

6. Objectives
7. Activities

Start with focusing on the library's vision and mission. Then identify the key background information on your community and library. Next, conduct a needs assessment to determine how well your library is serving your community and what improvements can be made in terms of services and programs. Finally, establish goals to work toward the vision, objectives to achieve the goals, and specific activities that will be the implementation part of the plan. The objectives and activities will determine what grants projects you develop.

VISION STATEMENT

The vision depicts an ideal future for the community and should be the motivating force for a library's strategic plan. Vision statements are inspiring and easily communicate the dream that drives your library's day-to-day efforts. Before you start developing your plan, your vision will tell you what the successful implementation of your strategic plan will look like.

Visioning must be a participatory process. A vision won't be effective if it's handed down from a single library leader or administrator. To achieve a shared community vision, key stakeholders and interested community members will need to spend time together talking about their ideas and listening to each other. As you incorporate everyone's ideas, the vision is likely to evolve and grow stronger. Indeed, you will increase your community's ownership of the vision and commitment to achieving it.

Example Vision Statements

The *Exemplar Library*: This is a vital community center that understands and responds to the community's essential needs, informs and inspires its members, and is significant to all.

The University of Texas at Austin Libraries: We will provide a community of learners with unfettered access to a universe of information, enabling all to enrich their lives and transform their worlds (www.lib.utexas.edu/vprovost/mission.html).

Volusia County Law Library (VCLL): The vision of the Volusia County Law Library is to communicate and facilitate meaningful access to the resources and services provided by the VCLL and to remain a vital, responsive, highly utilized, and integral part of the community (www.vclawlib.org/mission.htm).

MISSION STATEMENT

The mission is a broad statement of the role or purpose of the library. It identifies whom the library serves and justifies its existence. All the library staff should be able to connect their specific responsibilities to the mission. It should inspire their actions and give them an understanding of what the library is working to achieve. The library community should also be able to identify the library's purpose and the services it offers by reading the mission.

Mission statements should be brief but powerful and easy to understand. While some mission statements comprise many paragraphs, some are just one sentence. Mission statements should be broad. They should not need to be rewritten when new initiatives or directions are undertaken. They should be free of language that may discourage potential funders or partners from participating. Often funders will evaluate a potential grant recipient by how well their mission statement aligns to their own.

The mission should answer the following questions:

1. What are the basic purposes for which we exist?
2. Whom do we serve?
3. What basic community needs are we meeting and with what services?
4. What makes our purpose unique and distinguishes us from others?
5. Is our mission in harmony with our community?

Example Mission Statements

Exemplar Library: The mission of the Exemplar Library is to provide community members with an unbiased social and intellectual gathering place that includes resources and opportunities to enrich and fulfill their lifelong learning, informational, and leisure needs.

Fayetteville Public Library: Our mission is to provide citizens with access to information, kindle the imagination of children and adults, and encourage lifelong learning and achievement for all (www.faylib.org/information/vision_mission.asp).

Swansboro Elementary School Library: It is the mission of the Swansboro Elementary School Library to function as the nucleus for creating a foundation for a community of lifelong learners by focusing on the needs of the students. This will be accomplished through a learning environment that promotes information literacy and has as its foundation a creative, energetic library/media program, literature-rich resources, and intellectual and physical access to information (http://richmond.k12.va.us/schools/swansboro/our_media_center.htm).

ORGANIZATIONAL VALUES

While we didn't include Organization Values or Library Service Responses as one of the six common elements in strategic plans, they are helpful, and we encourage you to integrate them into your planning process.

Values define the set of beliefs and principles that guide the library. They relay what is important about the way the library conducts business, serves the community, works with partners, appreciates staff members, and is represented to the world. Values can be single words (such as integrity, trust, teamwork) or short phrases. They define what is respected and what is not and often carry a great deal of emotional connotations. They should drive the priorities of staff and leadership and how they perform and make decisions. They are the basis of the ethical standards that govern how a library interacts with staff, customers, vendors, and competitors.

A values statement is essential to good strategic planning because values underlie the decision-making process. Ignoring the cultural values of an organization is detrimental to strategic planning because, regardless of the plan, major and minor decisions alike will always align with the culture but not necessarily with the mission. Identifying and incorporating the values into the planning process will assure that goals, objectives, and strategies will be achievable. These values can be identified through a group exercise with the entire library staff or through surveying of staff.

Example Values

Arizona State University Libraries' Core Organizational Values (www.asu.edu/lib/library/ulsp/ul2000/values.htm). During the strategic planning process, more than 100 staff members participated in sessions in which they identified the core values held by the libraries. The following draft statement of core values is the product of this critically important activity:

As a service organization, we value:

- the educational process of which we are an integral part.
- friendly, helpful, superior service to our user community.
- generosity: providing open access to all our resources.

- technology in the service of people.
- the diversity of our resources and collections.
- inclusiveness: outreach to all our users.

In the process of getting our work done, we value:

- work of high quality that results in satisfied customers.
- the competence, knowledge, efficiency, expertise, and diversity of skills that foster superior quality.
- the development of our staff and their skills.
- professionalism at all levels.
- innovation, creativity, and risk-taking.
- flexibility and adaptability.

As a community, we value:

- cooperation, teamwork, esprit de corps.
- open communication.
- respect and trust among members.
- idealism and vision.
- the diversity that makes us strong.

Monroe County Public Library in Indiana Values (www.monroe.lib.in.us/general_info/mission_statement.html)

- Equitable access to information, ideas, and creative works.
- Intellectual freedom and diversity of opinion and cultures.
- Lifelong learning and the love of reading.
- Responsiveness to community demands.
- Excellence in service.
- The library as a welcoming place for all.
- Effective and efficient delivery of library services.
- Responsible stewardship of public resources.
- Partnerships to advance the library's mission.

Ann Arbor District Library Values (www.aadl.org/about):

- Excellence in customer service.
- Providing, supporting, and advocating access for all.
- Acting with initiative, creativity, and flexibility.

- Working together, with enthusiasm and optimism, to reach goals.
- Responsible stewardship of resources.

COMMUNITY AND LIBRARY PROFILES

We need to look at our environment and truly understand our library and community before we do any planning. A preliminary step to conducting a community needs assessment is developing a community profile.

Changes in politics, society, and economics impact our libraries. Libraries are in the business of providing information and must respond to the changes in their communities, keeping up with new and different community needs, and reaching out to new populations. An analysis of the community will reveal important information that the library director, staff, and board should know about, including what people need and expect from their library. The library can then respond by redefining its mission and roles and reallocating the collection, services, and programs to more accurately match the current needs.

Community Profile

A community profile is a brief description about the population and area served by the library. This may already be done by your city, university, or other local organization. If so, it is fine to use that information instead of creating your own profile. This is usually done every 3 to 5 years.

If you do need to develop your own community profile, you will need to gather specific information about the library's service area and the people it serves. The profile will document changes and new trends in people's lifestyles, interests, family and business pursuits, recreational activities, and social, civic, and educational concerns and will help the library reallocate its resources to provide what the community needs and expects.

This information can reveal major phases in a community's existence, whether they are growth, stagnation, rebirth because of outside forces (new businesses, new populations), or the need for dramatic change to remain viable and economically strong. The two major influences to be examined are the environment and the population. You may include these aspects of your community:

- Setting: environment, geography, climate, and recreational opportunities.
- Growth and development.
- Local government.
- Business and industry.

- Communications.
- Educational facilities.
- Cultural opportunities.
- Local organizations and civic groups.
- Population characteristics (age groups, race and language, educational levels, occupation and income levels, household size).

Library Profile

The Library Profile will be specific to your institution. It is a component often asked for in a grant application and sometimes called an Organizational Overview. The library's history, service population, achievements, primary programs, current budget, leadership, board members, and key staff members should all be included. Answer the questions, Who are we? and What do we do?

The Library Profile should include basic information but can also incorporate recent changes and interesting details such as:

- History.
- Service Population.
- Achievements.
- Primary Services, Programs, Collections, and Facilities.
- Current Budget and Resource Reallocations.
- Leadership and Staff.
- Cultural Diversity Initiatives.
- Technology Infrastructure.
- Collaboration and Partnerships.
- Proof of Significance.
- New Laws and Regulations.

NEEDS ASSESSMENT

A needs assessment will determine how well the library is serving its community and what other services or resources it can provide in the future. Identifying the needs or problems of your community is an important part of your information-gathering process. In order to determine the preferences and perceptions of those most affected by your work, involve the community in all stages of the grant cycle process. Needs assessments can later serve as a benchmark for your progress.

Needs assessments or needs statements are often asked for in grant applications and are an excellent way to prove the necessity of your proposed grant projects. You should always determine a need before you create a project. It will tell the funder why your project is necessary and who will benefit from the project. The grant project will be part of the solution to the need.

> ***Example Needs Statement:***
>
> Exemplar includes an underserved population of students whose test scores as well as their general knowledge of library research are below desired levels. These students will benefit from increased exposure to libraries and increased levels of instruction in information literacy and research skills.

It is important to involve your community and use assessment methods to identify true community needs. This means you should get input from all segments of your community, not just the politicians and leaders but farmers, teens, recent immigrants, and all large groups present in your community. The Las Vegas Clark County Library District (LVCCLD) did just that. *Library Journal* reported LVCCLD Director Dan Walters as saying, "We hired consultants who conducted both English- and Spanish-language telephone surveys in order to get at nonusers. The Latino community indicated that they would use the library much more if our collections were more diverse. This year we will circulate more than 200,000 items in Spanish." The system strives for diversity in language and format, including videos, DVDs, and audiobooks (Berry 2003).

Results of a needs assessment study can be used to determine:

- How the collections and technologies can be used to meet community needs.
- Who is using the library and how to reach nonusers.
- What are the most and least desired services and programs.
- Whether the facility and parking are acceptable.
- How the community is changing.
- What staffing and library hours changes are needed to accommodate the community.

The first step in performing a needs assessment is to decide who will oversee the project. A needs assessment can be carried out by outside consultants, library volunteers, or library staff. Your available resources, time frame, and comfort level with performing research may influence your decision. It is best to use a combination of these methods. For example, you might hire an outside consultant to help you set up the needs assessment study and design surveys but then use volunteers to actually complete a telephone survey and staff to interview community leaders.

- ***Outside consultants*** will have expertise in how to conduct research studies. They provide objectivity by offering an outsider's view. Since consultants are experienced at performing research, this option makes better use of your limited time. The primary disadvantage to using outside consultants is often the cost.
- ***Volunteers*** are another possibility. Volunteers are free and save library staff time. However, they may present a biased interpretation of what the community needs. It is important to select volunteers who reflect a broad array of the community and who have experience in performing needs assessments. Volunteers will also need to be trained and managed, so some staff time will also be involved.
- ***Library staff*** can also perform needs assessments. While library staff are less expensive than hiring outside consultants, they may be inexperienced in needs assessments or not have time to perform a needs assessment on top of their regular library responsibilities. However, a basic needs assessment can be done through interviews and basic research, as outlined in the following section.

The second step in performing a needs assessment is to decide what you want to learn about your community and what kind of information you plan to collect. For example, will you perform a broad-based study or one that is focused on a particular area or issue? Some of the categories of information you might be interested in collecting include historical, demographic, economic, social, cultural, educational, and recreational. Some libraries perform a SWOT (Strengths, Weaknesses, Opportunities, and Threats) analysis or other strategic method to identify the challenges and opportunities facing their community and library. Then they prioritize the issues and use the needs assessment to focus on addressing those specific issues.

Collecting the Data

Now that you have decided on the types of information you want to collect about your community, you need to determine how to collect that information. You can collect data by interviewing key community leaders in the community, holding a community forum, researching demographic data from public records and reports, and performing surveys. It is best if you can use more than one of these data collection methods.

Interviews

By interviewing key members of your community, you can get a better understanding of their impressions of the needs of the community. Interviews may also yield future partners that could support grant projects. However, this method provides subjective data since it is based on opinions that may not reflect the needs of the entire community. You can gain a lot of valuable information just by talking with the leaders in your community. If there is a target audience you are interested in, such as Spanish-speaking members of your community who aren't using the library, you can contact leaders who work with that specific community, such as church officials, health care workers, or teachers. If you have two staff members to assign to this task, they could split up and each conduct five interviews, or they could go together so that one could take notes while the other asks the questions. A volunteer could even help with note taking.

Focus Groups

Focus groups can provide very honest and useful information. Members can be selected by age, gender, occupation, or social interests, and groups can be organized into manageable numbers. If the participants are comfortable, they may give very helpful feedback. You will need to have a facilitator for each group, and organizing and scheduling focus groups can take a lot of time. This information is also subjective, and it could be time-consuming to compile the data as well.

Community Forum or Town Meeting

A community forum involves holding a group event and inviting your entire community. This can provide a lot of good information, give visibility to your library, and even raise its status within the community. However, these forums require a lot of planning and publicity. The majority of the attendees will probably be active library users, rather than those who do not use the library. This can make it difficult to determine the needs of the entire community. Another disadvantage of this method is that it tends to provide subjective and impressionistic data about the community's needs. Also, the less vocal and participatory segments of your community may not be represented.

Public Records

A more objective method of data collection is to use public records to research secondary data such as the social indicators or demographics of your community. A well-known source that is reliable and available for county- or city-level analyses is the U.S. Census Bureau. Using these records, you have access to such community information such as ages, genders, languages spoken, education levels, income levels, and marital statuses.

Surveys

Surveys can be distributed by mail, phone, in the library, or online. While mailed surveys are the most expensive option and get low response rates, the mailed survey method requires very little time to implement and is easy to coordinate. Some utility companies will include library surveys with their bills for no charge, so this is an option to explore for public libraries. There are several online surveys that are available for free or little cost. These are easy to develop and implement. Take a look at Survey Monkey (www.surveymonkey.com) or Zoomerang (www.zoomerang.com). Both have free versions for smaller surveys.

Information gathered from surveys is only as good as the questions asked. If you are performing the needs assessment yourself, you might want to consult an experienced surveyor as you design the questions. The shorter a survey is, the easier it will be for a busy customer to complete. Be sure to provide confidentiality to your survey participants. Reassuring your participants that their survey responses will be kept confidential and anonymous might help improve your response rates, especially in a small community.

Using Community Feedback

In order to make use of the information you have collected, the results have to be interpreted and evaluated. When the data analysis is complete, prioritize the responses. At the end of this process, the findings should be compiled and shared with the library leadership, staff, and the community. This can be done through meetings, public displays, or articles on your library Web page or in the local newspapers. Of course, once you have broadcast these needs, make sure that the library will be able to follow up on the top priorities.

LIBRARY SERVICE RESPONSES

Library Service Responses were created by the Public Library Association (PLA) and are used in the community-based planning process outlined in *The New Planning for Results*. They are used to prioritize library services and programs that match the community needs identified through a visioning process. By doing this, libraries can choose to do a few things very well instead of spreading energy and resources among too many efforts to be really effective. It is better to meet a few needs of your community than to miss the mark and not help solve any of the community issues. *The New Planning for Results* includes more detailed information.

Library Service Responses

Basic Literacy	Current Topics and Titles
Business and Career Information	Formal Learning Support
Commons	General Information
Community Referral	Government Information
Consumer Information	Information Literacy
Cultural Awareness	Lifelong Learning
	Local History and Genealogy

See the Exemplar Library Plan on page 35 for an example of the Library Service Responses selected by their Community Planning Committee.

GOALS

One of the main functions of a strategic plan is to establish clear goals and realistic strategies to achieve those goals. Goals are broad, general statements describing a desired condition or future toward which the library will work. They are the path to achieving the vision of the library and part of the solution toward fulfilling the needs identified in the needs assessment. We encourage libraries to set their sights high when it comes to goal setting. Some libraries are really compiling only a checklist of what they know will be achieved, rather than pushing themselves to go beyond the norm. If a goal is never accomplished, it shouldn't be viewed as a failure; it just means that a review should occur, that changes may be needed for success, or perhaps that it should just be viewed as a learning experience.

Some goals may be short-term, while others will cover a multiyear period. Achieving a goal may mean changing the services or programs offered by the library. All goals should be written in positive language.

Example Goals from the Exemplar Library's Strategic Plan

Community members are aware of the importance and purpose of the library's resources and services.

The Exemplar Library's facilities are comfortable and accessible and efficiently accommodate the changing needs and interests of our community.

> The Exemplar Library's resources and services reflect diverse community needs and interests, are easily assessed, and meet the information needs of the customers.

OBJECTIVES

Objectives are written for each goal but may also relate to more than one goal. Objectives are short-range and more focused than goals. The acronym SMART is often used as a way to remember the important elements in writing objectives. SMART stands for Specific, Measurable, Achievable, Realistic, and Time-Bound. Check each objective you write to make certain it meets these conditions. Objectives are the way the library measures its progress toward reaching a goal. For that reason, it must be very clear what the objective will accomplish and how the objective will be measured.

Statements of objectives should include:

1. A specific, realistic, and achievable end result (for example, to increase the number of teens as registered borrowers).
2. The method of measurement (for example, by 40 percent).
3. The time frame (for example, March 2007).

When you combine these elements, your objective is that the number of teens who have library cards will increase by 40 percent by March 2007.

> ***Example Objectives from the Exemplar Library's Strategic Plan***
>
> By 2008, 50 percent of the community will be able to name three primary resources or services offered by the library, excluding the customary circulation of books.
>
> The number of community organizations that use library meeting rooms will increase 10 percent each year over the next 3 years.
>
> By 2007, 85 percent of the people who reserve an item will receive that item within 4 weeks, if it is available from the publisher.
>
> Each year at least 5,000 community members will attend programs sponsored by the library, and 90 percent of those people who complete evaluation forms will rate the programs highly.

ACTIVITIES

Part of the strategic planning process is to develop a series of activities or strategies you can use to reach the goals and objectives. These activities will form the basis for many of the library's actions and resource allocations for the period covered by your overall plan. At this point in strategic planning, you will need to be very specific about what will be done. This is sometimes called project planning and involves detailing everything necessary for effective implementation of the project, including identifying action steps, allocating resources, creating timelines, determining the budget, and establishing evaluation methods. Of course, as you plan for these activities, you are also planning possible grant projects. The specifics of grant project planning and evaluation are covered in the next chapter, "Discovering and Defining the Grant Project."

This can be a creative process done by a committee. Brainstorm the activities necessary for accomplishing individual goals and objectives or combinations of goals and objectives from your library's strategic plan. There should be a direct link between your objectives and your activities. You might find that a single activity addresses more than one goal or objective. Also, some activities might help accomplish more than one objective.

For example, possible activities that address Goal 1 and the corresponding objectives from the Exemplar Public Library's Goals and Objectives:

Goal

Community members are aware of the importance and purpose of the library's resources and services.

Objective:

By 2008, 50 percent of the community will be able to name three primary resources or services officered by the library, excluding the customary circulation of books.

Activities

1. Develop a public relations plan and marketing strategy.
2. Increase visibility by pursuing mutually beneficial partnerships with other libraries, government and community agencies, media outlets, educational institutions, businesses, and other organizations.
3. Develop curriculum and implement classes to highlight the library's resources to the business community.

4. Create and implement an Information Technology Public Awareness campaign to promote the library's technological services to community and business leaders and the general public.
5. Improve communication about library services with all community members.
6. Develop and implement a community evaluative survey.

MONITOR AND UPDATE THE STRATEGIC AND PROJECT PLANS

Regularly revisit your plans and evaluate whether the goals are being met and whether action steps are being implemented. Perhaps the most important indicator of success of the library is positive feedback from the community concerning services, programs, and resources. Having established clearly defined outcomes and outputs will provide a feedback mechanism to evaluate program performance and will influence future planning, resource allocation, and operating decisions. The next chapter covers creating and measuring outcomes.

Funders appreciate strategic plans and project plans because they demonstrate that your project ideas are realistic and prove that the library is capable of responsibly handling funds and implementing projects. It also provides evidence that the library monitors, evaluates, and measures progress toward goals.

Use the following checklist to help identify areas of improvement in your library's planning process. This checklist is also available in the Grants for Libraries Tool Kit on page 202 and as a file on the CD-ROM.

> Success Story: "The most important element of a successful grant: A well planned project that indicates to the funder that it can be carried out with success" (Highland Park Public Library; see page 172).

LIBRARY PLANNING CHECKLIST

____ Does your library have a clear mission statement?

____ Have you clearly defined what the library does?

____ Are your goals obtainable and supportive of your library's mission?

____ Are your objectives clear, measurable, and tied to goal achievement?

____ Do you regularly evaluate your objectives to be certain progress is being made?

____ Have you selected a strategy for collecting data on your community and library?

____ Are statistics aggregated to allow for easy retrieval of necessary information?

____ Are statistics kept that are seldom or never used?

____ Can you list the strengths of your library?

____ Are you aware of key weaknesses in your library?

____ Are you involving library staff and community members in the planning process?

____ Did you communicate the final plan to staff, leadership, and community members and respond to their concerns?

____ Is the timetable for implementation of your library's plan accurate?

____ Have you designated specific dates for assessing progress toward goals?

EXEMPLAR LIBRARY STRATEGIC PLAN

VISION

The Exemplar Library is a vital community center that understands and responds to the community's essential needs, informs and inspires its members, and is significant to all.

MISSION

The mission of the Exemplar Library is to provide community members with an unbiased social and intellectual gathering place that includes resources and opportunities to enrich and fulfill their lifelong learning, informational, and leisure needs.

LIBRARY SERVICE RESPONSES TO THE COMMUNITY

With the Exemplar Library's Vision and Mission statements as a starting point, the Community Planning Committee, made up of members representing the community, established four service priorities for library services, which they felt will best meet the needs of the community:

> **Current Topics and Titles** Community members will have materials and services available to meet their information needs on current, high-interest topics and to provide satisfying recreational experiences.
>
> **General Information** All community members will be able to get answers to their personal and work questions.
>
> **Lifelong Learning** All community members will have materials, programs, and services to support their personal growth and self-education.
>
> **Commons** All community members will have a place where they feel comfortable, can meet and interact with others in the community, and can participate in programs and public discourse about issues of interest.

GOALS, OBJECTIVES, AND ACTIVITIES

Based on the four service priorities selected by the Community Planning Committee, the Library Board adopted eight goals designed to meet anticipated community needs. Each goal has specific objectives and activities designed to achieve these objectives.

Goal 1. Community Members Are Aware of the Importance and Purpose of the Library's Resources and Services.

Objective 1.1

By 2008, 50 percent of the community will be able to name three primary resources or services offered by the library, excluding the customary circulation of books.

Activities

1. Develop a public relations plan and marketing strategy.
2. Increase visibility by pursuing mutually beneficial partnerships with other libraries, government and community

agencies, media outlets, educational institutions, businesses, and other organizations.

3. Develop curriculum and implement classes to highlight the library's resources to the business community.
4. Create and implement an Information Technology Public Awareness campaign to promote the library's technological services to community and business leaders and the general public.
5. Improve communication about library services with all community members.
6. Develop and implement a community evaluative survey.

Objective 1.2

Outreach to new community members will increase 50 percent by 2007.

Activities

1. Develop a public relations plan and marketing strategy.
2. Place informational materials in all phone bills and welcome packets.
3. Work with local realty companies and housing authorities to distribute information on applicable library programming.
4. Develop and implement an evaluation survey for new community members.

Goal 2. The Exemplar Library's Facilities Are Comfortable and Accessible and Efficiently Accommodate the Changing Needs and Interests of Our Community.

Objective 2.1

By 2007, 90 percent of organizations that use library meeting space will indicate that the space met or exceeded their expectations.

Activities

1. Create a checklist of safety, cleanliness, and comfort guidelines to be used monthly for evaluation purposes.

2. Meet with community focus groups to determine their meeting space needs.
3. Designate a library volunteer who is available to assist groups using meeting spaces during the event.
4. Develop and implement a library meeting space satisfaction survey.

Objective 2.2

The number of community organizations that use library meeting rooms will increase by 10 percent each year over the next 3 years.

Activities

1. Partner with other community stakeholders to redesign the library to be an integrated community center.
2. Create flexible spaces that by their size, furnishings, and orientation encourage exploration, innovation, and customization in all modes of information exchange, including individual and collaborative.
3. Track usage statistics of meeting room space.

Objective 2.3

By 2008, 80 percent of library customers will feel comfortable using the library.

Activities

1. Agree on minimum standards and an implementation program to ensure the library provides a safe, ADA (Americans with Disabilities Act) compliant environment for staff and customers.
2. Improve interior signage to ensure easy location of assistance and location of materials.
3. Reshape library spaces into new environments that support different learning styles (quiet rooms, group study areas, and computer labs), streamline use, and enable customers to make more effective use of library space.
4. Identify appropriate benchmarks for the technology needed and provide the resources to ensure that this level is sustained.

5. Build and operate a library café staffed by the Friends of the Exemplar Library.
6. Develop and implement a library user satisfaction survey.

Goal 3. The Exemplar Library's Resources and Services Reflect Diverse Community Needs and Interests, Are Easily Accessed, and Meet the Information Needs of the Customers.

Objective 3.1

By 2007, 85 percent of the people who reserve an item will receive that item within 4 weeks, if it is available from the publisher.

Activities

1. Purchase a copy of any title with at least three holds.
2. Develop efficient ways to reallocate Technical Services staff resources to allow more staff time for ordering and processing materials. This could include a new automated answering system and/or additional staffing.
3. Develop a plan to accelerate processing of resources.

Objective 3.2

From 2006 to 2008, an increased 20 percent of library customers will indicate they found something that met their needs during their visit to the library.

Activities

1. Reallocate funds to support areas of the collection that have heavy use and buy multiple copies of popular titles to meet customer needs.
2. Increase the number of Internet stations available for the public, with at least two Express Internet stations limited to 30 minutes of use.
3. Develop subject-specific workshops, geared toward targeted audiences, such as teachers, businesspeople, or home schoolers, offering both individual and group options, and include off-site locations.
4. Develop standardized research guides on popular topics.

5. Revise the current information literacy program and provide customer training in critical inquiry, including evaluation of Web sites.
6. Provide individual and group instruction for adults, teens, and children on the use of the online catalog and online reference databases.
7. Create interesting and topical displays of materials.
8. Survey library customers when leaving the library as to whether they found something that met their needs.

Objective 3.3

In 2007, annual circulation of print and media materials will increase by 15 percent; circulation will continually increase by 5 percent each year thereafter.

Activities

1. Develop and utilize a responsive collection development plan.
2. Improve visual appeal and access to new materials.
3. Increase number of popular titles/copies available for circulation and expand collections that have the highest circulation statistics.
4. Revise the loan period of feature videos and DVDs.
5. Increase advertising/marketing of library collections.
6. Review processing work flow to ensure new materials are on the shelves as quickly as possible.
7. Make personalization features of the library's automated catalog available to library users.
8. Develop innovative reader's advisory services related to promoting reading and popular materials; include staff training opportunities on delivering reader's advisory services.

Goal 4. The Library Is Responsive to the Community through the Expansion and Introduction of Specialized Services.

Objective 4.1

In 2008, at least 85 percent of community members will find library services valuable and applicable to their interests and needs.

Activities

1. Conduct focus groups and interviews with public and staff to determine the vital, relevant, and effective library services that meet community needs to be compiled into a report by March 2006.
2. Cooperate actively with other libraries and community agencies in order to share resources and broaden the scope of the library's services without duplication of effort.
3. Utilize appropriate technologies to maintain and improve library operations and services.
4. Evaluate current library services and reallocate resources to support those identified in focus groups and interviews.

Objective 4.2

Each year at least 5,000 community members will attend programs sponsored by the library, and 85 percent of attendees will rate the programs highly.

Activities

1. Locate prior statistics for program attendance.
2. Conduct a needs assessment to determine the programs of most value to the community through interviews and focus groups of library users, nonusers, and leaders in the community.
3. Create and expand programming and services targeted to specific groups and age levels, such as new parents, fathers as caregivers, and intergenerational program efforts.
4. Offer special topic adult/teen educational and do-it-yourself programming.
5. Plan a publicity campaign to aggressively market library programs.
6. Develop evaluation and data collection instruments.
7. Offer programs at remote sites in the community.

Goal 5. The Library Attracts, Develops, and Retains Quality Staff with Specialized Skills, Knowledge, and Abilities to Assist Library Customers.

Objective 5.1

Staff turnover will not exceed 15 percent per year, beginning in 2007.

Specific Activities

1. Create an environment that motivates staff to achieve high levels of performance and productivity.
2. Develop and implement an internal communication plan defining means by which information is shared among library staff.
3. Allow staff to rotate responsibilities based on skill or preference.

Objective 5.2

Each year, 90 percent of staff will report that they are greatly valued, informed, and well trained.

Specific Activities

1. Improve promotion and compensation policies and procedures for staff.
2. Analyze the library positions against others in the community to ensure market equity for similar skill sets.
3. Define a common set of competencies to be achieved by all staff and allow cross-training opportunities.
4. Provide basic technical support training to staff to resolve difficulties related to the increasing use of electronic information resources.
5. Hire a dedicated technical support librarian who is able to resolve technology problems.
6. Identify one staff per ten computers to troubleshoot equipment and share information with other staff so that a common body of knowledge exists to resolve basic equipment issues.
7. Develop and implement an anonymous staff survey instrument.

Objective 5.3

By 2008, 90 percent of community members will indicate they experience exceptional service from library staff.

Specific Activities

1. Include reference and customer service training as part of new staff orientation programs; existing staff should attend at least once every 3 years.
2. Offer periodic training on the use of electronic resources.
3. Offer training on how to deal with customer service issues.
4. Promote professional development by enabling staff to participate in professional organizations and to attend professional conferences and workshops.

Goal 6. Spanish-Speaking Members of the Community are Able to Find Resources and Opportunities to Pursue Their Own Learning and Meet Their Individual Information Needs.

Objective 6.1

By 2007, evaluate and improve the library's ability to serve Spanish-speaking customers.

Activities

1. Research and evaluate library readiness, including multilingual signage, staff skills concerning cultural awareness, interpreters, pathfinders, materials, and so on.
2. Allocate funds to support areas of the collection concerned with English as a second language and Spanish materials.
3. Provide staff training on cultural awareness, sensitivity, and service.
4. Revise current library policies that impact delivery of services.

Objective 6.2

Coordinate at least six programming activities per year in meeting room facilities outside the library for members of the Spanish-speaking community.

Activities

1. Draft a document of requirements for meeting venues.
2. Contact meeting venues and gather policies, fees, and schedules.
3. Select six meeting venues within the city limits and schedule a program or activity of interest to Spanish speakers.
4. Coordinate programs, including curricula, speakers, registration, and marketing.

Goal 7. The Library Successfully Serves the Lifelong Learning, Informational, and Leisure Needs of the Mature Adult Population in the Community.

Objective 7.1

By 2008, at least 40 percent of the total older adult population will be registered library borrowers.

Activities

1. Research population statistics to determine number of older adults present in community.
2. Include optional designation on registration card indicating older adult status.
3. Examine registration policies to determine if there are barriers that could be eliminated.
4. Develop a plan to distribute library cards and lend materials in areas of heavy use by older adults.
5. Conduct a needs assessment to determine lifelong learning, informational, and leisure needs of the mature adult population.
6. Incorporate results of needs assessment into library programming, services, and material selection.

Objective 7.2

Participation in programs geared toward the baby boomer adult population will increase by 80 percent by 2008.

Activities

1. Organize and sponsor a Baby Boomer Fair, which will include entertainment, seminars, and informational tables.
2. Identify and contact appropriate business and community organizations and offer space for a fair booth to inform and attract those looking for help and advice regarding enjoying the upcoming retirement years.
3. Organize speakers for seminars on health and wellness, retirement, financial and legal issues, relationships and stress in retirement, working in retirement, leisure and volunteer pursuits, Social Security, and health insurance.

3 DISCOVERING AND DESIGNING THE GRANT PROJECT

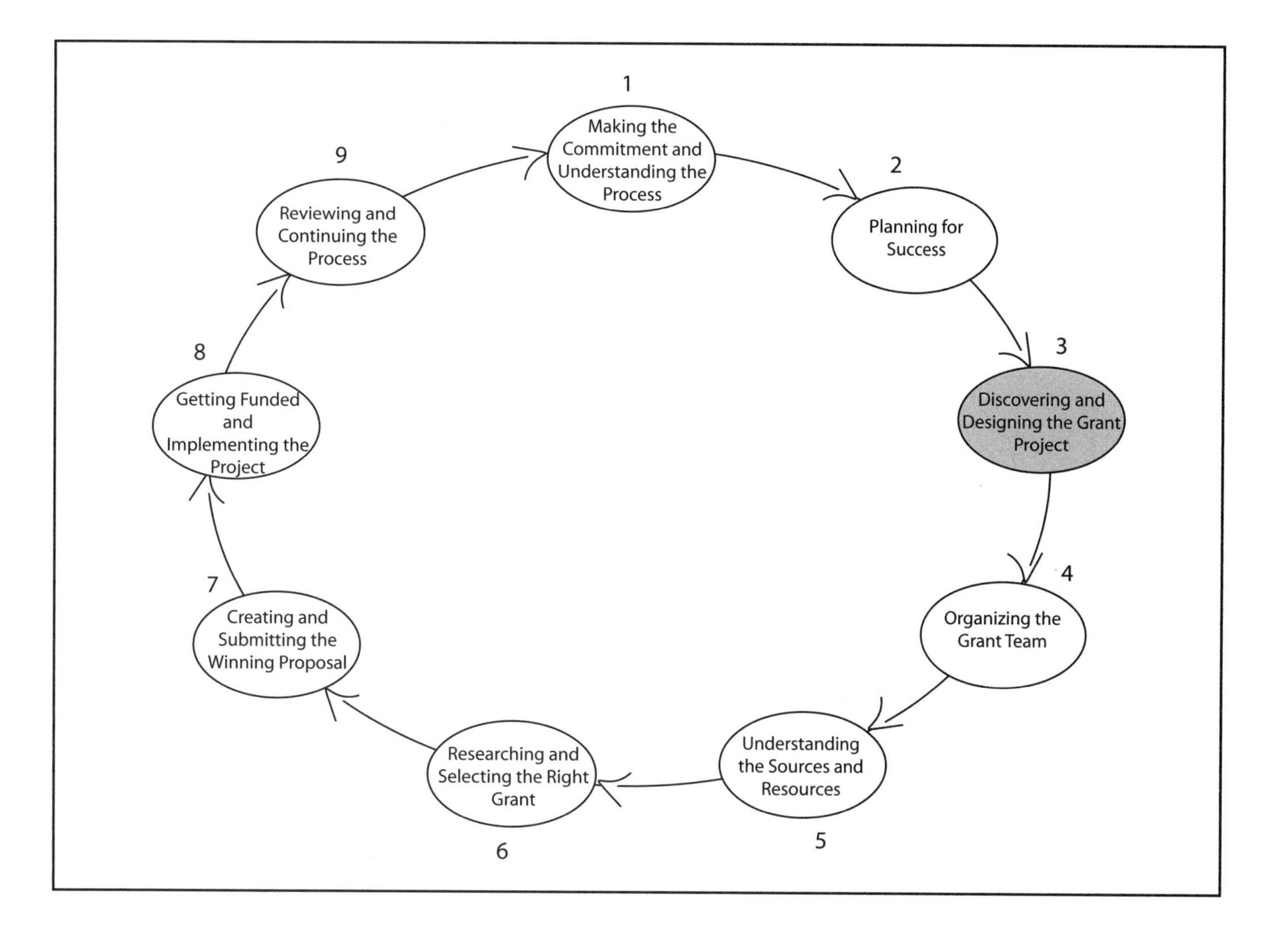

In Chapter 2 we discussed the planning process where you, community members, partners, and stakeholders participated in assessing and analyzing the needs of your organization and your community, and you devised a strategic plan to meet those needs. You looked at the gaps between the current state of what your library offers and the desired results, and you decided which gaps you want to address in the period covered by your plan.

Then you developed and defined goals and specific, measurable, achievable, realistic, and time-bound objectives and activities designed to close these gaps.

WHAT DOES PROJECT PLANNING HAVE TO DO WITH GETTING GRANTS?

Discovering and designing your grant project and proposal writing are closely linked. Proposal writing does not stand alone or separate from project planning. As you define your project, you will be designing—and sometimes even writing—your proposal. By planning your project before sitting down to write your proposal, you are ensuring that your project comes from the desire to meet real needs in your community, that you are working within the vision and mission of your organization, and that your project is an integral part of your strategic plan.

Attempting to write your grant proposal before planning your project puts the primary focus on getting the dollars, not on implementing a project that meets your community's needs. If you approach proposal writing this way, you may end up with a grant that does not address the needs of your community or that is not tied to your organization's mission or planned path. Project planning based on your library's strategic plan not only orients you in the existing plans and mission of your organization but ensures that you are working to better the lives of people in your community.

It is essential that your projects are rooted in your plan, as this is the groundwork and the foundation you have built to serve your community and its specific needs. Ideally, you have already done this planning, so all you need to do is pull the plan out and start from there. This is not the time to begin thinking about organizational goals. If you have not done your strategic planning, consider stopping here and taking the time to do it. Going through the organizational planning process first will save you lots of time and headaches in the end. It will also ensure that you are developing projects that are in sync with your mission and that will benefit your community and ensures that you are including potential partners. Creating the plan first will decrease the chances that your project will have no real benefit to the community, is not in line with your organizational goals, and is not including potential partners.

Your community needs assessment identified the areas needing change or improvement, or the problems to be solved in the community. You already have the solutions—or goals, objectives, and activities—that you have identified for the period covered by the plan, you have solicited community input and the participation of stakeholders, and you have established relationships with potential partners.

WHAT IS A GRANT PROJECT?

For the purposes of this book, "grant project" is defined as a project of any kind for which you will be writing a proposal to seek grant funding from an outside source. In other resources you may see a grant project also referred to as a "grant program." A grant project can be an equipment project, a capital project, a planning or implementation project, a research project, a model demonstration project, or a project for operating expenses, to name a few. At this point we are concentrating on discovering and designing your potential projects. Later we will think about identifying what kind of project you have developed for the purposes of seeking a funding source. You will discover your grant projects by beginning to work with the goals, objectives, and activities in your strategic plan.

With your strategic plan in place, you now have what you need to design grant projects that are directly related to the plan. Because they come straight from your plan, these grant projects will inherently be mission-driven and will be designed to meet identified needs in your community.

THE PROJECT PLANNING PROCESS

STEP 1: CLARIFY YOUR LIBRARY'S GOALS, OBJECTIVES, AND ACTIVITIES

Placing your library's goals, objectives, and activities into a chart will help you to see them clearly. It will also serve as a starting point for project planning team members to understand them, and it will quickly orient those on your project planning team who may not be very familiar with the library's strategic plan. Figure 3-1 shows the Exemplar Library's goals, objectives, and activities taken from the example strategic plan developed in Chapter 2.

Use the Strategic Plan Goals, Objectives, and Activities Template in the Grants for Libraries Tool Kit on page 203 to chart your organization's goals, objectives, and activities from your plan.

Goals from Strategic Plan	Objectives from Strategic Plan	Activities from Strategic Plan
Goal 1 Community members are aware of the importance and purpose of the library's resources and services.	**Objective 1.1** By 2008, 50% of the community will be able to name three primary resources or services offered by the library, excluding the customary circulation of books.	1. Develop a public relations plan and marketing strategy. 2. Increase visibility by pursuing mutually beneficial partnerships with other libraries, government and community agencies, media outlets, educational institutions, businesses, and other organizations. 3. Develop curriculum and implement classes to highlight the library's resources to the business community. 4. Create and implement an Information Technology Public Awareness campaign to promote the library's technological services to community and business leaders and the general public. 5. Improve communication about library services with all community members. 6. Develop and implement a community evaluative survey.
	Objective 1.2 Outreach to new community members will increase 50% by 2007.	1. Develop a public relations plan and marketing strategy. 2. Place informational materials in all phone bills and welcome packets. 3. Work with local realty companies and housing authorities to distribute information on applicable library programming. 4. Develop and implement an evaluation survey for new community members.
Goal 2 The Exemplar Library's facilities are comfortable and accessible and efficiently accommodate the changing needs and interests of our community.	**Objective 2.1** By 2007, 90% of organizations that use library meeting space will indicate that the space met or exceeded their expectations.	1. Create a checklist of safety, cleanliness, and comfort guidelines to be used monthly for evaluation purposes. 2. Meet with community focus groups to determine their meeting space needs.

Figure 3-1. Goals, Objectives, and Activities from the Exemplar Library's 2006–2008 Strategic Plan

Goals from Strategic Plan	Objectives from Strategic Plan	Activities from Strategic Plan
		3. Designate a library volunteer who is available to assist groups using meeting spaces during the event. 4. Develop and implement a library meeting space satisfaction survey.
	Objective 2.2 The number of community organizations that use library meeting rooms will increase by 10% each year over the next 3 years.	1. Partner with other community stakeholders to redesign the library to be an integrated community center. 2. Create flexible spaces that by their size, furnishings, and orientation encourage exploration, innovation, and customization in all modes of information exchange, including individual and collaborative. 3. Track usage statistics of meeting room space.
	Objective 2.3 By 2008, 80% of library customers will feel comfortable using the library.	1. Agree on minimum standards and an implementation program to ensure the library provides a safe, ADA-compliant environment for staff and customers. 2. Improve interior signage to ensure easy location of assistance and location of materials. 3. Reshape library spaces into new environments that support different learning styles (quiet rooms, group study areas, and computer labs), streamline use, and enable customers to make more effective use of library space. 4. Identify appropriate benchmarks for the technology needed and provide the resources to ensure that this level is sustained. 5. Build and operate a library café staffed by the Friends of the Exemplar Library. 6. Develop and implement a library user satisfaction survey.

Figure 3-1. Goals, Objectives, and Activities from the Exemplar Library's 2006–2008 Strategic Plan (*Continued*)

Goals from Strategic Plan	Objectives from Strategic Plan	Activities from Strategic Plan
Goal 3 The Exemplar Library's resources and services reflect diverse community needs and interests, are easily accessed, and meet the information needs of the customers.	**Objective 3.1** By 2007, 90% of the people who reserve an item will receive that item within 4 weeks if it is available from the publisher.	1. Purchase a copy of any title with at least 3 holds. 2. Develop efficient ways to reallocate Technical Services staff resources to allow more staff time for ordering and processing materials. This could include a new automated answering system and/or additional staffing. 3. Develop a plan to accelerate processing of resources.
	Objective 3.2 From 2006 to 2008, an increased 20% of library customers will indicate they found something that met their needs during their visit to the library.	1. Reallocate funds to support areas of the collection that have heavy use and buy multiple copies of popular titles to meet customer needs. 2. Increase the number of Internet stations available for the public, with at least two Express Internet stations limited to 30 minutes of use. 3. Develop subject-specific workshops, geared toward targeted audiences, such as teachers, businesspeople, or home schoolers, offering both individual and group options, and include off-site locations. 4. Develop standardized research guides on popular topics. 5. Revise the current information literacy program and provide customer training in critical inquiry, including evaluation of Web sites. 6. Provide individual and group instruction for adults, teens, and children on the use of the online catalog and online reference databases. 7. Create interesting and topical displays of materials. 8. Survey library customers when leaving the library as to whether they found something that met their needs.

Figure 3-1. Goals, Objectives, and Activities from the Exemplar Library's 2006–2008 Strategic Plan (*Continued*)

Goals from Strategic Plan	Objectives from Strategic Plan	Activities from Strategic Plan
	Objective 3.3 In 2007, annual circulation of print and media materials will increase by 15%; circulation will continually increase by 5% each year thereafter.	1. Develop and utilize a responsive collection development plan. 2. Improve visual appeal and access to new materials. 3. Increase number of popular titles/copies available for circulation and expand collections that have the highest circulation statistics. 4. Revise the loan period of feature videos and DVDs. 5. Increase advertising/marketing of library collections. 6. Review processing work flow to ensure new materials are on the shelves as quickly as possible. 7. Make personalization features of the library's automated catalog available to library users. 8. Develop innovative reader's advisory services related to promoting reading and popular materials; include staff training opportunities on delivering reader's advisory services.
Goal 4 The library is responsive to the community through the expansion and introduction of specialized services.	**Objective 4.1** In 2008, at least 85% of community members will find library services valuable and applicable to their interests and needs.	1. Conduct focus groups and interviews with public and staff to determine the vital, relevant, and effective library service that meet community needs, to be compiled into a report by March 2006. 2. Cooperate actively with other libraries and community agencies in order to share resources and broaden the scope of the library's services without duplication of effort. 3. Utilize appropriate technologies to maintain and improve library operations and services. 4. Evaluate current library services and reallocate resources to support those identified in focus groups and interviews.

Figure 3-1. Goals, Objectives, and Activities from the Exemplar Library's 2006–2008 Strategic Plan (*Continued*)

Goals from Strategic Plan	Objectives from Strategic Plan	Activities from Strategic Plan
	Objective 4.2 Each year at least 5,000 community members will attend programs sponsored by the library, and 85% of attendees will rate the programs highly.	1. Locate prior statistics for program attendance. 2. Conduct a needs assessment to determine the programs of most value to the community through interviews and focus groups of library users, nonusers, and leaders in the community. 3. Create and expand programming and services targeted to specific groups and age levels, such as new parents, fathers as caregivers, and intergenerational program efforts. 4. Offer special topic adult/teen educational and do-it-yourself programming. 5. Plan a publicity campaign to aggressively market library programs. 6. Develop evaluation and data collection instruments. 7. Offer programs at remote sites in the community.
Goal 5 The library attracts, develops, and retains quality staff with specialized skills, knowledge, and abilities to assist library customers.	**Objective 5.1** Staff turnover will not exceed 15% per year, beginning in 2007.	1. Create an environment that motivates staff to achieve high levels of performance and productivity. 2. Develop and implement an internal communication plan defining means by which information is shared among library staff. 3. Allow staff to rotate responsibilities based on skill or preference.
	Objective 5.2 Each year, 90% of staff will report that they are greatly valued, informed, and well trained.	1. Improve promotion and compensation policies and procedures for staff. 2. Analyze the library positions against others in community to ensure market equity for similar skill sets. 3. Define a common set of competencies to be achieved by all staff and allow cross-training opportunities. 4. Provide basic technical support training to staff to resolve difficulties related to the increasing use of electronic information resources.

Figure 3-1. Goals, Objectives, and Activities from the Exemplar Library's 2006–2008 Strategic Plan (*Continued*)

Goals from Strategic Plan	Objectives from Strategic Plan	Activities from Strategic Plan
		5. Hire a dedicated technical support librarian who is able to resolve technology problems. 6. Identify one staff per 10 computers to troubleshoot equipment and share information with other staff so that a common body of knowledge exists to resolve basic equipment issues. 7. Develop and implement an anonymous staff survey instrument.
	Objective 5.3 By 2008, 90% of community members will indicate they experience exceptional service from library staff.	1. Include reference and customer service training as part of new staff orientation programs; existing staff should attend at least once every 3 years. 2. Offer periodic training on the use of electronic resources. 3. Offer training on how to deal with customer service issues. 4. Promote professional development by enabling staff to participate in professional organizations and to attend professional conferences and workshops.
Goal 6 Spanish-speaking members of the community are able to find resources and opportunities to pursue their own learning and meet their individual information needs.	**Objective 6.1** By 2007, evaluate and improve the library's ability to serve Spanish-speaking customers.	1. Research evaluation criteria to be used, including multilingual signage, staff skills concerning cultural awareness, interpreters, pathfinders, materials, and so on. 2. Allocate funds to support areas of the collection concerned with English as a second language and Spanish materials. 3. Provide staff training on cultural awareness, sensitivity, and service. 4. Revise current library policies that impact delivery of services.
	Objective 6.2 Coordinate at least six programming activities per year in meeting room facilities outside	1. Draft a document of requirements for meeting venues. 2. Contact meeting venues and gather policies, fees, and schedules.

Figure 3-1. Goals, Objectives, and Activities from the Exemplar Library's 2006–2008 Strategic Plan *(Continued)*

Goals from Strategic Plan	Objectives from Strategic Plan	Activities from Strategic Plan
	the library for members of the Spanish-speaking community.	3. Select six meeting venues within the city limits and schedule a program or activity of interest to Spanish speakers. 4. Coordinate programs, including curricula, speakers, registration, and marketing.
Goal 7 The library successfully serves the lifelong learning, informational, and leisure needs of the mature adult population in the community.	**Objective 7.1** By 2008, at least 40 percent of the total older adult population will be registered library borrowers.	1. Research population statistics to determine number of older adults present in community. 2. Include optional designation on registration card indicating older adult status. 3. Examine registration policies to determine if there are barriers that could be eliminated. 4. Develop a plan to distribute library cards and lend materials in areas of heavy use by older adults. 5. Conduct a needs assessment to determine lifelong learning, informational, and leisure needs of the mature adult population. 6. Incorporate results of needs assessment into library programming, services, and material selection.
	Objective 7.2 Participation in programs geared toward the baby boomer adult population will increase by 80% by 2008.	1. Organize and sponsor a Baby Boomer Fair, which will include entertainment, seminars, and information tables. 2. Identify and contact appropriate business and community organizations and offer space for a fair booth to inform and attract those looking for help and advice regarding enjoying the upcoming retirement years. 3. Organize speakers for seminars on health and wellness, retirement, financial and legal issues, relationships and stress in retirement, working in retirement, leisure and volunteer pursuits, Social Security, and health insurance.

Figure 3-1. Goals, Objectives, and Activities from the Exemplar Library's 2006–2008 Strategic Plan (*Continued*)

STEP 2: PULL TOGETHER A PROJECT PLANNING TEAM

Next, convene a project planning team of creative thinkers that includes library staff, community members, potential partners, local businesspeople, and other stakeholders. Include people from the library staff and potential partner organizations who you think may be participating in implementing a community project in which the library could be a partner. If you are in a large organization, you may want to create more than one project planning team, one for each organizational goal. These teams will include different people with different areas of expertise or community involvement depending on the goal with which they are working. If you are in a small library, a team of two people may be sufficient. Try to include one person from outside the library, preferably from another organization or agency in your community or a potential partner or a prominent business leader. It is sometimes difficult to think creatively about new project ideas when you are trying to do this with a team consisting of all library staff who see each other and deal with the same issues every day.

More about Including Potential Partners

It is very important to include potential partners from the very beginning of the project planning process. Ideas from potential partners are invaluable as you discover new projects. These people tend to look at things from a different angle, and they may even tell you about related activities they are already doing in the community that you may not know about. This information can help to shape the project planning process and is likely to save you time and effort in the long run. By including potential partners from the community in your project planning, you will decrease your chances of developing an idea that has already been planned or is already being done by another organization or agency in your community. Additionally, partners can build on your ideas during the planning stages, bringing a dimension to your projects that you may never consider without their perspective, knowledge, talents, and resources.

> "The success of the project rested with the numerous partnerships formed with other organizations also interested in promoting xeriscape practices. Each entity advertised programs and provided their own particular expertise to strengthen it" (Rodeane Widom, Glendale Public Library, Glendale, AZ).

If your partners are participating in planning your projects from the beginning, you will not have to go out into the community later to convince them to join you in an idea that library staff has already planned. Also, if they are in on creating the project from the beginning, they will have ownership without lots of extra effort on your part. Funders across the board are looking for partnerships in grant applications. They know their dollars will go much further if more than one organization is involved in developing and implementing a project they fund. They also know that a project is more likely to be sustainable if more than one organization is involved.

Of course, it is impossible to predict who the ideal partners will be for your projects before you have even planned them. Use your best judgment based on what you know about your organization's goals and objectives, projects already going on in your community, other organizations doing activities in the community that might combine well with potential library projects, and business and organizational leaders who are likely to be good partners and with whom your library already has good relationships.

STEP 3: START THE PROJECT PLANNING PROCESS

It is important to facilitate the project planning process. Someone must lead the team through the process of discovering and designing the project. It could be a member of the library staff who was instrumental in the strategic planning process. If you have the funds, you could hire an outside consultant to facilitate this process. If you are a one- or two-person library, the whole staff can be involved in facilitating.

At the first meeting distribute copies of your library's Strategic Plan Goals, Objectives, and Activities Chart to all team members. (This is the Strategic Plan Goals, Objectives, and Activities Template in the Grants for Libraries Tool Kit on page 203 that you completed in Step 1.) The team's first task is to understand the library's vision, mission, service responses to the community, goals, objectives, and activities. For those team members who were not involved in the strategic planning process, it may be necessary to share some background information about the community needs assessment and how the goals were determined.

Make it clear to the team that their purpose is to plan one or more projects from the goals, objectives, and activities in the plan. These are projects that the library may work on over the next few years as ways to accomplish the goals established in the plan. If any of these projects require grant funding, they will become grant projects. You must design your grant project prior to seeking grant funding. Encourage brainstorming and creativity but keep the parameters of the projects you plan within the scope of the library's strategic plan.

The team's ultimate goal is to develop specific projects using the goals, objectives, and activities in your library's plan. Your goal is not to tackle all the elements in your plan by thinking of projects for them all. You may want to come up with one or several small projects rather than one large project. As you work with the smaller projects, try combining several. It is much easier to grow a project than to shrink it.

STEP 4: DISCOVER THE PROJECT IDEA AND GOALS

Make this a fun activity for the team. Have flip charts, colored index cards, markers, scissors, favors, or prizes for the best ideas, group activities, and so on. Move around. Brainstorm. Try dividing the larger group into small groups of three or four. Maybe you could assign each group a goal and then tell them they can draw from any objective or activity to accomplish the goal. Give team members permission to expand or alter the objectives and create new activities for the purposes of this process, as long as they still address reaching the goals and objectives stated in the plan. Try to remove any barriers that you think may be restricting this process without compromising the library's strategic plan. Remember to record all ideas and compile them in one document for team members to use in future meetings as they work through project ideas. Most of all, have fun!

Here are some example project ideas developed from Exemplar Library's goals, objectives, and activities that we identified in Step 1:

> **Project Idea 1: Information Technology You Can Use** Exemplar Library, in partnership with Sprague Electric Company, Grand Foods Public Market, and the Exemplar Social Services Agency will develop curriculum and offer classes to community members on the availability and use of information technology in the Exemplar Library.
>
> **Project Idea 2: Welcome to Exemplar: Information Technology at Your Library** Exemplar Library, in partnership with the Exemplar Welcome Wagon, will develop a marketing strategy and public relations campaign for reaching new residents with information about the library and the services it offers. Promotional items will be included in the Welcome Wagon packets delivered to newly occupied homes in Exemplar.
>
> **Project Idea 3: Using Information Technology in Your Government Office** In partnership with the city of Exemplar and the county of Superior, the Exemplar Library will develop and launch a campaign to increase awareness among city and county government employees about the information technology available through the library that could benefit them in doing their jobs.

Developing Project Idea 1: Information Technology You Can Use

Based on the Exemplar Library's goals, objectives, and activities, some goals for Project Idea 1, Information Technology You Can Use, might be:

> By offering classes on the availability and use of information technology in the library, this project will (1) assist the Spanish-speaking population in using information technology to find jobs; (2) assist the mature adult population in the community to find and use health and medical information using information technology; and (3) inform new

> community members about information technology available in the library and how to use it.

The above goals for Information Technology You Can Use would address the following Exemplar Library goals, objectives, and activities (see Figure 3-1):

> Goal 1: Community members are aware of the importance and purpose of the library's resources and services.
>
> Goal 3: The Exemplar Library's resources and services reflect diverse community needs and interests, are easily accessed, and meet the information needs of the customers.
>
> Goal 4: The library is responsive to the community through the expansion and introduction of specialized services.
>
> Goal 6: Spanish-speaking members of the community are able to find resources and opportunities to pursue their own learning and meet their individual information needs.

Exemplar Library objectives that could be addressed by Information Technology You Can Use are:

> Objective 1.1: By 2008, 50 percent of the community will be able to name three primary resources or services offered by the library, excluding the customary circulation of books.
>
> Objective 1.2: Outreach to new community members will increase 50 percent by 2007.
>
> Objective 3.2: From 2006 to 2008, an increased 20 percent of library customers will indicate they found something that met their needs during their visit to the library.
>
> Objective 4.1: In 2008, at least 85 percent of community members will find library services valuable and applicable to their interests and needs.
>
> Objective 4.2: Each year at least 5,000 community members will attend programs sponsored by the library, and 85 percent of attendees will rate the programs highly.
>
> Objective 6.1: By 2007, evaluate and improve the library's ability to serve Spanish-speaking customers.
>
> Objective 7.2: Participation in programs geared toward the baby boomer adult population will increase by 80 percent by 2008.

The following are some activities from the Exemplar Library's Strategic Plan that could be used or adapted for Information Technology You Can Use:

Increase visibility by pursuing mutually beneficial partnerships with other libraries, government and community agencies, media outlets, educational institutions, businesses, and other organizations.

Develop curriculum and implement classes to highlight the library's resources to the business community, the Spanish-speaking, older adults, and new community members.

Create and implement an Information Technology Public Awareness campaign to promote the library's technological services to community and business leaders and the general public.

Develop a public relations plan and marketing strategy.

Place informational materials in all phone bills and welcome packets.

Work with local realty companies and housing authorities to distribute information on applicable library programming.

Develop subject-specific workshops, geared toward targeted audiences, such as teachers, businesspeople, or home schoolers, offering both individual and group options, and include off-site locations.

Develop standardized research guides on popular topics.

Provide individual and group instruction for adults, teens, and children on the use of the online catalog and online reference databases.

Cooperate actively with other libraries and community agencies in order to share resources and broaden the scope of the library's services without duplication of effort.

Create and expand programming and services targeted to specific groups and age levels, such as new parents, fathers as caregivers, and intergenerational program efforts.

Project Goals

Every project must have a goal. The goal is the accomplishment you seek. Ask yourself what it is that you are seeking to accomplish. How do you want your services, situation, or community to change as a result of your efforts? It is important not to confuse goals with organizational mission or vision. The goal must be consistent with your mission and vision but at the same time be program-specific.

STEP 5: DEFINE PROJECT OUTCOMES

The Importance of Outcomes

"The purpose of the Laurelton Library Youth Empowerment Initiative is to provide a positive atmosphere at a neighborhood library where youth age 7–15 participate in activities that help them succeed in school and prepare for the future" (Maureen T. O'Connor, Queens Borough Public Library, Laurelton Branch Library). "Never make it about what the library needs. Always point to the end user and how they will benefit" (Becky Heil, Dubuque County Library, Farley, Iowa).

As you begin to discover your project ideas, it is important to think about outcomes. Outcomes are used to identify a change in behavior, attitude, or knowledge in the people served by the project, and they reflect the long-term impact a project is making toward solving a community problem or toward improving the lives of the people it serves. Most funders require applicants to state the outcomes of their project in the proposal. The fact that a library proposes to provide assistive technology, Spanish-language materials, after-school programs, information technology training, or any other number of services is nice, but the funder wants to know that those services will make a difference in the lives of the people who are served. You want to ensure that the project will address or solve a problem in the community by changing the behavior, attitude, or knowledge of the people served by the project. This not only is good practice but makes good sense.

As you do your preliminary project planning and throughout the planning process, continue to ask yourself these questions about project outcomes:

1. How will the project improve the lives of people?
2. How will people's behavior, attitude, or knowledge change as a result of the project?
3. How will the project help to solve a problem in the community?

"The project had to change the behavior of young people in the library, but it also had to address the way library staff was reacting to those youth" (Maureen T. O'Connor, Queens Borough Public Library, Laurelton Branch Library).

If you do not clarify your project outcomes from the outset, it will be impossible to build them in later, when you are preparing your grant proposal.

Now let's develop some desired outcomes for Information Technology You Can Use. Remember, outcomes identify a change in behavior, attitude, or knowledge in the people served by the project. As we think about outcomes for this project, we might want to focus on a particular part of the population or a specific segment of information technology. Some desired outcomes for this project idea might be:

1. The ability of Spanish-speaking community members to find jobs will be increased due to their knowledge and use of information technology.
2. The ability of mature adult community members to research health-related questions using information technology will increase their ability to make informed medical choices.
3. New community members will be knowledgeable about information technology available in the library, and they will know how to use it to improve their quality of life.

More About the Definitions of Outcomes and Objectives

Funders do not always use the same definitions when it comes to outcomes and objectives. The definitions for Goals, Outcomes, Objectives, and Activities or Action Steps can vary widely by funder. What one funder considers an outcome another may consider an objective. In some cases your goal may actually be an outcome. Remember that you are trying to identify a desired change and measure that change, regardless of what the funder calls it.

Outcomes and objectives present a unique challenge. It may be that these words are used as synonyms by one funder. Or it may be that the two terms have distinct meanings to a funder, and proposal writers who fail to recognize the difference may be unsuccessful by presenting this information incorrectly.

While the definitions of goals, outcomes, and objectives may vary by funder, you can manage these differences by investigating a little further. If a funder uses an example, follow it back to your own goals, outcomes, and objectives. If you are not sure about their definition, call the funder and ask.

STEP 6: PLAN YOUR PROJECT

Now it's time to plan your project. Start using the Project Planning Worksheet on page 207 in the Grants for Libraries Tool Kit as you develop your project ideas. Based on the planning we have done so far, try working on nos. 1–7. Make sure that these items tie back to your library's plan, vision, and mission. It is not necessary to complete the worksheet for each project idea at this point. Don't get bogged down in the worksheet. It is meant to facilitate the planning process, help you to work out some of the details, record your ideas, and test their feasibility. Use a new Project Planning Worksheet for each new project idea. Figure 3-2 illustrates a sample Project Planning Worksheet for Information Technology You Can Use.

STEP 7: DEVELOP PROJECT OBJECTIVES

You must design specific, measurable, achievable, realistic, and time-bound objectives that specifically address your project outcomes. You may find that you can use objectives already developed in your strategic plan; however, it is more likely that your project objectives will be a subset of the objectives in your library's plan.

> "You have written your goals and objectives for a non-librarian audience and they are realistic" (Kathy Dabbour, Oviatt Library, Northridge, CA).

For instance, how will you demonstrate that the ability of Spanish-speaking community members to find jobs is increased due to their use of information technology? You might determine that over the course of the project, the ability of the Spanish-speaking population served by the project

1. Project Description: Describe your project in one sentence. Include what you will do, where, why, and with whom.	**Information Technology You Can Use** Exemplar Library, in partnership with Sprague Electric Company, Grand Foods Public Market, and the Exemplar Social Services Agency will develop curriculum and offer classes to Spanish-speaking community members, mature adult community members, new community members, and the general community on the availability and use of information technology in the Exemplar Library.
2. Keywords: List keywords that describe your project.	Information technology Computers Curriculum Classes Training Community Library Public awareness Spanish-speaking people Mature adults Newcomers
3. Needs Statement: Describe the need in your community or the problem your project will address.	Lack of awareness of library's information technology services and resources among the Spanish-speaking community, the mature adult population, and new community members.
4. Target Audience: Identify target audience for the project.	Spanish-speaking community members, the mature adult population, and new community members.
5. Project Goals: What are the goals of the project?	Goals: By offering classes on the availability and use of information technology in the library, this project will (1) assist the Spanish-speaking population in using information technology to find jobs; (2) assist the mature adult population to find

Figure 3-2. Project Planning Worksheet Information Technology You Can Use

	and use health and medical information using information technology; and (3) inform new community members about information technology available in the library and how to use it.
6. Project Objectives: What are the specific changes you expect to make in your community or among the beneficiaries of your project? Articulate objectives for the project.	(1) An increase of 25% of the Spanish-speaking population will use information technology resources in the library to find jobs. (2) An increase of 25% of mature adult community members will use information technology in the library to answer their health and medical questions. (3) 50% of new community members will be aware of the library's information technology resources and how to use them.
7. Project Outcomes: What are the expected changes in people's behavior, attitude, or knowledge? How will the project improve the lives of people? How will the project impact a community problem?	(1) The ability of Spanish-speaking community members to find jobs will be increased due to their knowledge and use of information technology. (2) The ability of mature adult community members to research health-related questions using information technology will increase their ability to make informed medical choices. (3) New community members will be knowledgeable about information technology available in the library, and they will know how to use it to improve their quality of life.
8. Project Action Steps: List the steps required to make the changes listed above. Develop activities or strategies required to reach an objective. How are you going to solve this problem?	See **PROJECT ACTION STEPS WORKSHEET**
9. Resources Needed: List the resources you will need to accomplish the steps. What resources do you already have?	Computer lab Staff Telephones Copier Office supplies Projector

Figure 3-2. Project Planning Worksheet Information Technology You Can Use (*Continued*)

10. Project Budget: The cost of the project.	See **PROJECT BUDGET WORKSHEET**
11. Partners and Collaborators: List your partners on this project. Who else is addressing this problem in our community? Who is likely to partner with us on this project?	Sprague Electric Company Grand Foods Public Market Exemplar Social Services Agency
12. Evaluation: Describe how you will measure your success. How will things be different, or what will the improvement be?	See **EVALUATION PLAN WORKSHEET** Figure 3-7.
Form adapted from Project Profile/Planning Worksheet. JUST GRANTS! Arizona	

Figure 3-2. Project Planning Worksheet Information Technology You Can Use (*Continued*)

to find jobs using Internet resources will be increased by 25 percent. Or that 50 percent of the Spanish-speaking people who attend classes will create or update their résumés using computers in the library.

Look at your project outcomes, develop your project objectives, and record them on your Project Planning Worksheet. Later you will use these objectives to design your evaluation methodology.

STEP 8: DEFINE PROJECT ACTION STEPS

Now it is time to develop the action steps that are going to accomplish your project's objectives and produce the desired outcomes. Let's start by reviewing the sample project objectives and outcomes from the Project Planning Worksheet for Information Technology You Can Use.

Sample Project Objectives

1. An increase of 25 percent of the Spanish-speaking population will use information technology resources in the library to find jobs.
2. An increase of 25 percent of mature adult community members will use information technology in the library to answer their health and medical questions.

3. Fifty percent of new community members will be aware of the library's information technology resources and how to use them.

Sample Project Outcomes

1. The ability of Spanish-speaking community members to find jobs will be increased due to their knowledge and use of information technology.
2. The ability of mature adult community members to research health-related questions using information technology will increase their ability to make informed medical choices.
3. New community members will be knowledgeable about information technology available in the library, and they will know how to use it to improve their quality of life.

Here are a few possible project action steps designed to achieve the sample project objectives and outcomes:

1. Develop curriculum and implement classes to train Spanish-speaking community members about using information technology to find and secure jobs.
2. Develop curriculum and implement classes to educate mature adult community members about using information technology to answer their medical and health questions.
3. Partner with the Social Services Agency to market specific library services that may help unemployed Spanish-speaking persons find and secure jobs.
4. Create and implement an Information Technology Public Awareness campaign to promote the library's technological services to community and business leaders, medical and social services personnel, and the general public.
5. Partner with the Welcome Wagon to market information technology resources and services to new community members.

Note that these action steps are either taken directly from activities in Exemplar Library's Strategic Plan or adapted from activities in the plan, or they enhance activities already in the plan. If you create any new action steps that don't meet these criteria, make sure that they relate back to the goals and objectives in the strategic plan.

What are some action steps that might accomplish your project goal through your stated objectives and result in the outcomes you have identified? Use the Project Action Steps Template on page 210 in the Grants for Libraries Tool Kit to define your project's action steps. As you complete this form, think about who will be doing the action steps and enter the position name in the personnel column. In your grant proposal, the action steps and who will do them will become your methodology, strategy, or approach. This information also becomes the basis for your timeline.

Figure 3-3 illustrates some possible objectives, action steps that will help to achieve them, and what positions will be responsible for implementing the action steps for Information Technology You Can Use. Record your project's possible action steps on the Project Action Steps Template on page 210 in the Grants for Libraries Tool Kit.

Project Objectives	Personnel	Action Steps
In 12 months an increase of 25% of the Spanish-speaking population will use information technology resources in the library to find jobs.	Tech. Librarian	Develop curriculum.
	Library Assistant	Develop a public awareness plan and marketing strategy.
	Library Assistant	Create a brochure.
	Reference Librarian	Hold public awareness activities at unemployment office, social services, medical offices.
	Reference Librarian	Design pre- and postsurveys.
	Library Assistant	Implement pre- and postsurveys.
In 12 months an increase of 25% of mature adult community members will use information technology in the library to answer their health and medical questions.	Tech. Librarian	Develop curriculum.
	Library Assistant	Schedule classes/Reserve computer classroom.
	Circulation Clerk	Advertise classes.
	Library Assistant	Register people for classes.
	Tech. Librarian	Teach classes.
	Reference Librarian	Design pre- and posttests.
In 12 months 50% of new community members will be aware of information technology resources in the library.	Circulation Clerk	Create advertisement.
	Circulation Clerk	Advertise information technology resources and services in local newspaper.
	Water Department	Put advertising inserts in water bills.
	Reference Librarian	Offer incentives or prizes to winners of information technology "games."
	Library Assistant	Track computer usage.

Figure 3-3. Project Action Steps Example

STEP 9: CONSULT PREVIOUS PROJECTS, BEST PRACTICES, AND SIMILAR PROJECTS

As you are planning your project, read about other projects like yours that have already been done. Take notes and collect this research. Based on the experiences or products of others, you may want to alter your project. It makes sense to build on what others have done. If there are curricula already in place that will meet your project's needs, use them. If another community like yours had success reaching a similar target population, learn from its successes—and failures. Build this experience and research into your project plan. It will be more viable, be more likely to succeed, and have a better chance of being sustainable. Call or e-mail the manager of a project like the one you are considering to ask about his or her experiences.

Include this information in your grant proposal. It shows the funder that you are well informed about what has already been done in the field and that you are knowledgeable about best practices. Extrapolate your outcomes to the outcomes documented in the literature. For instance, "Based on the results of XYZ Library, we have chosen to take ABC approach in our community." The funder wants to know that you will not be doing something that has already been tried without success.

STEP 10: MAKE A PROJECT TIMELINE

Timelines are a project planning tool that can be used to represent the timing of tasks required to complete a project. They are easy to understand and construct, and they are used by most project managers to track the progress of a project.

Each action step takes up one row. Dates run along the top in increments of days, weeks, or months, depending on the total length of the project. The expected time for each task is represented by check marks or horizontal bars marking the expected beginning and end of the task. Tasks may run sequentially, at the same time, or overlapping. Include the personnel responsible for doing each action step. Use the Project Timeline Template on page 211 in the Grants for Libraries Tool Kit to create a timeline for your project.

In constructing a timeline, keep the tasks to a manageable number (no more than fifteen or twenty) so that the chart fits on a single page. If your project is complex, it may require subcharts and subtasks. This timeline can go directly into a grant proposal for this project.

Figure 3-4 illustrates a timeline using the action steps we developed for Information Technology You Can Use.

Action Steps	Personnel	Jan	Feb	Mar	Apr	May	June	July	Aug	Sept	Oct	Nov	Dec
Develop a public awareness plan and marketing strategy.	Library Assistant (LA)	✓	✓										
Create a brochure.	LA			✓	✓								
Hold public awareness activities at unemployment office, social services, medical offices.	Reference Librarian (RL)					✓	✓	✓	✓	✓	✓	✓	✓
Design pre- and postsurveys.	RL	✓											
Implement presurveys.	LA		✓										
Implement postsurveys.	LA											✓	✓
Create advertisement.	Circulation Clerk (CC)	✓											
Advertise information technology resources and services in local newspaper.	CC			✓	✓								
Insert brochure in water bills.	CC					✓							

Figure 3-4. Project Timeline Example

Action Steps	Personnel	Jan	Feb	Mar	Apr	May	June	July	Aug	Sept	Oct	Nov	Dec
Offer incentives or prizes to winners of information technology "games."	RL						✓	✓	✓				
Track computer usage.	LA	✓	✓	✓	✓	✓	✓	✓	✓	✓	✓	✓	✓
Develop curriculum.	Technology Librarian (TL)	✓	✓	✓									
Schedule classes/Reserve computer classroom.	LA	✓	✓										
Advertise classes.	CC			✓	✓	✓	✓	✓	✓	✓			
Register people for classes.	LA			✓	✓	✓	✓	✓	✓	✓	✓		
Teach classes and implement pre- and posttests.	TL			✓	✓	✓	✓	✓	✓	✓	✓		
Design pre- and posttests.	RL	✓	✓										
Manage Project	TL	✓	✓	✓	✓	✓	✓	✓	✓	✓	✓	✓	✓

Figure 3-4. Project Timeline Example (*Continued*)

STEP 11: DEVELOP A PROJECT BUDGET

Personnel Budget

For each project, figure out the required personnel and FTE from the timeline and the activity worksheet.

1. Select one position and determine the activities that position will do, for instance, for our sample project, Information Technology You Can Use:

   The Library Assistant will:

   - develop a public awareness plan and marketing strategy.
   - create a brochure.
   - implement pre- and postsurveys.
   - track computer usage.
   - schedule classes and reserve computer classroom.
   - register people for classes.

2. Determine the amount of time the position will be spending on these activities over the duration of the project and calculate the cost of the salary to cover that amount of time.

   For example, the Library Assistant will be doing the above activities throughout the entire 12-month period of the project, and we can estimate that this will take the Library Assistant an average of 8 hours a week. Since the Library Assistant works 40 hours a week, this is one-fifth, or .20 full-time equivalent (FTE) of the Library Assistant's time. The Library Assistant's full-time salary is $26,000 per year; therefore, the cost to the project for the Library Assistant's salary is $5,200.

3. Calculate the cost of benefits for your project personnel and make sure to add that cost to the project budget. Your personnel department will be able to tell you this figure.

   For example, if the cost of benefits is 23 percent of the employee's salary, for the Library Assistant, that is $5,980 per year. For a .20 FTE Library Assistant that is one-fifth of $5,980, or $1,196.

Therefore, the total cost to the project for the .20 FTE Library Assistant for the 12-month duration of the project is $5,200 (salary) + $1,196 (benefits) = $6,396.

Position	Salary	Benefits (23%)	Total
.20 FTE Library Assistant	$5,200	$1,196	$6,396
.15 FTE Reference Librarian	$6,000	$1,380	$7,380
.05 FTE Circulation Clerk	$900	$207	$1,107
.25 Technology Librarian	$10,000	$2,300	$12,300
TOTAL PERSONNEL COSTS	**$22,100**	**$5,083**	**$27,183**

Figure 3-5. Personnel Budget Example

Go through the same process for all project personnel. Then create a personnel budget for your project using the Personnel Budget Template on page 212 in the Grants for Libraries Tool Kit. Don't forget to include fringe benefit costs for all personnel and make sure to include or designate a project manager. Figure 3-5 shows a Personnel Budget for Information Technology You Can Use.

"Be realistic about what goals you can achieve in relation to staff, facility, additional resources needed" (Debra Mandel, Northeastern University Libraries, Boston).

A word of warning: If library staff will be working as project personnel, you must decrease their current job duties and responsibilities to allow for the additional project duties they will be taking on before they begin working on the funded project. For instance, if Library Assistants currently work a 40-hour week, they already have job duties that take 40 hours a week to do. You must take away some of those job duties (by delegating to someone else or hiring another staff person) so they can add the additional project duties. You cannot simply pile more work on a person who is already working a full-time job. This can be a setup for failure and will ensure that a staff person will not want to participate in any more library grant projects in the future. Expecting staff to assume additional work because a project is funded is a common pitfall that must be avoided.

Nonpersonnel Budget

Next, determine the cost for items other than personnel such as marketing, equipment, space rental, and supplies. Develop a Nonpersonnel Budget for your project using the Nonpersonnel Budget Template on page 213 in the Grants for Libraries Tool Kit. See Figure 3-6 for a sample Nonpersonnel Budget for Information You Can Use.

Combine a project budget by combining the two budgets and add the total costs from each to determine the total project cost. Record the total cost of your project in no. 9 on your Project Planning Worksheet.

"Anticipating expenses and developing a budget was complicated. We had the good fortune of corporate sponsorship funds to supplement the grant, so we were able to carry out all the activities and have a surplus of funds!" (Julia Johnas and Susan Dennison, Highland Park Public Library, Highland Park, IL).

Item	**Description**	**Cost**
Marketing		
Brochure	10,000 for $1,000.00	$2,000
Newspaper ads	$90 for quarter page × 6	$540
Equipment		
Projector		$2000
Copying Costs		
Handouts	5,000 @ $.03/copy	$150
Supplies		
Prizes		$100
Office supplies	$50/month × 12	$600
Printer cartridges	100 @ $30. each	$300
Paper	40 reams @ $2./ream	$80
Space Rental		
Computer classroom	600 sq.ft. @ $200/mo × 12	$2400
TOTAL NONPERSONNEL COSTS		**$8,170**
TOTAL PERSONNEL COSTS		**$27,183**
TOTAL PROJECT COST		**$35,353**

Figure 3-6. Nonpersonnel Budget Example

STEP 12: CREATE AN EVALUATION PLAN

You must now determine how you will measure the effectiveness of your project in reaching your stated objectives and outcomes. How will you measure your progress? How will you measure your success? How will you decide what adjustments need to be made to facilitate the success of your project as it progresses?

It is important to understand why you must conduct an evaluation and why an evaluation plan is a necessary part of your project plan. Projects are undertaken to have an impact. Evaluations are conducted to show the success of a project's impact, and they can also point out improvements you can make in the project design.

Kinds of Evaluations

Some funders prefer that you conduct evaluations throughout the life of the project rather than evaluating the project at its end. This will enable project staff to measure the success of the project while it is being carried out and to make any adjustments needed to ensure the project's success. This type of evaluation is known as formative evaluation, and it emphasizes the process that was conducted during the project.

Some funders ask for an evaluation at the very end of the project that reports the accomplishments. This is known as a summative evaluation and stresses the outcome of the project.

A quantitative evaluation obtains and analyzes data covering a large number of cases. Qualitative evaluations seek to collect data of greater depth on a smaller number of cases.

For some projects, you might want (or be required by the funder) to conduct both formative and summative evaluations. Don't limit your evaluation to the type required by the funder. Decide on an evaluation approach that serves the needs of the clients and that will best measure the success of your particular project.

Outcome-Based Evaluation (OBE)

Outcome-based evaluation (OBE), is a systemic way to determine if a program has achieved its goals. OBE is the measurement of results. It makes observations that demonstrate change, and it systematically collects information about specific indicators to show the extent to which a project achieves its goals.

OBE is an emerging evaluation methodology that government agencies and organizations are adopting for some of their programs—including library programs—and focuses on measuring the effect of a project on the people it serves (outcomes) rather than on services (outputs). OBE methods can be used at many points in a project to provide indicators of a project's effectiveness, and it provides a greater degree of public accountability. They give critical feedback about what is working, what needs to be changed, and how a program can be improved.

An outcome is a measure of change that benefits the people served by your project, such as achievements or changes in skill, knowledge, attitude, behavior, condition, or life status. Examples of outcomes are:

1. Library users will become aware of the electronic resources in the library.
2. People with disabilities will be able to use library resources because of assistive technology.
3. The ability of the unemployed to find jobs will be increased due to job-finding resources in the library.

Methods for Collecting Data for Evaluations

Your objectives will tell you the types of information you need to collect. Now you need to determine how to collect that information. Evaluation instruments can include questionnaires and surveys; interviews; documentation review; observation; focus groups; or case studies. It is important to use the proper evaluation instrument to measure your results. Decide what measurement instrument is most appropriate to get the strongest data specific to your project.

Questionnaires or Surveys You can get lots of lots of information quickly and easily from many people in a nonthreatening way using questionnaires and surveys. People can complete them anonymously, they are inexpensive to administer, and you can administer them to many people. It is easy for you to compare and analyze results, and you can get lots of data. Information gathered from surveys is only as good as the questions asked, so you might want to consult an experienced surveyor as you design the questions. However, there are many survey and questionnaire instruments that have already been designed that you can use as templates. The shorter a survey is, the easier it will be for a busy customer to complete. Be sure to provide confidentiality to your survey participants. Reassuring your participants that their survey responses will be kept confidential and anonymous might help improve your response rates.

Interviews Use interviews when you want to fully understand someone's impressions or experiences or learn more about their answers in surveys or questionnaires. Interviews give you the opportunity to get the full range and depth of information, they give you the opportunity to develop a rapport with the interviewee, and you can be flexible with your questioning. This method provides subjective data since it is based on opinions that may not reflect the true success of the project. It is a very time-consuming process, but it may yield future partners.

Documentation Review Use documentation reviews when you want an impression of how your project is operating without interrupting the project. This method comprises reviewing statistics, memos, minutes, and so on. Because this method does not measure changes in people's behavior, skills, knowledge, attitudes, condition, or life status, use it only as a supplement to instruments that do measure these things.

Observation By observing a project, you can gather accurate information about how it actually operates, particularly about the process. You view the operations of a project as they are actually occurring.

Focus Groups Focus groups allow you to explore a topic in depth through group discussion. They can provide very honest and useful information, you can get reactions to an experience or suggestion, and you can gain an understanding of common complaints. Focus group members can be organized into manageable numbers. If the participants are comfortable, they may give very helpful feedback. This is an efficient way to get key information about a project, and you can quickly and reliably get impressions. You will need to have a facilitator for each group, and organizing and scheduling focus groups can take a lot of time. This information is subjective, and it could be time-consuming to compile the data.

Case Studies Use case studies to fully understand or depict a customer's experiences as a participant in your project input, process, and results. This is a powerful way to portray to the outsiders the impact your project has had on individuals and may be the best way to convey something like change in condition of life. Case studies are very time-consuming, and they are difficult to collect, organize, and describe.

Writing an Evaluation Plan

You can incorporate outcome-based evaluation (OBE) into library planning and grant proposals by devising evaluation plans for your projects in the planning stage. This strategy naturally informs the library and community in measurable terms of the impact on customers as well as prepares the evaluation section of your grant application well before the deadline. Participants who follow this results-oriented approach to one particular library project will discover that, although it may require more time, energy, and resources, it can lead to more focused and successful programs and services. Once an initial project has been designed and implemented in this fashion, the methodology can be applied to other library projects. In the course of a few years, most of the significant projects will be measurable in terms of customer benefits.

The key to writing an evaluation plan is to first have objectives that are measurable—the two are intertwined. If the objectives are written in vague terms and can't be measured, the evaluation section will be vague and weak. With measurable objectives, the evaluation section will become a natural extension of the objectives and will be relatively easy to compose. It might help to think of objectives as the purpose of your project, the "things" that are left when the project is over. Usually, objectives are written in terms of increases and/or decreases. For example, specific types of skills, such as problem solving, will show an increase, while undesirable behaviors, such as truancy, will show a decrease.

If you have worked through the project planning process to this point, you already have all the information you need to easily develop an evaluation plan. Figure 3-7 shows a sample Evaluation Plan for Information Technology You Can Use. Use the Evaluation Plan Template in the Resources Section on page 214 to plan your project evaluation plan.

Goal	Outcome	Objective	Evaluation Method	Timeline
Community members are aware of the library's resources and services.	The ability of Spanish-speaking community members to find jobs will be increased due to their use of information technology.	In 12 months an increase of 25% of the Spanish-speaking population will use information technology resources to find jobs.	Surveys and interviews will be conducted with Spanish-speaking community members (1) prior to the implementation of the project and (2) at the conclusion of the project to determine the percentage of this population who use information technology to find jobs. Pretests and posttests will be administered to Spanish-speaking community members taking classes to determine their success in using information technology to find jobs.	February and November/ December
	The ability of mature adult community members to research health-related questions using information technology will enhance their ability to make informed medical choices.	In 12 months an increase of 25% of mature adult community members will use information technology in the library to answer their health and medical questions.	Surveys and interviews will be conducted with mature adult community members (1) prior to the implementation of the project and (2) at the conclusion of the project to determine the percentage of this population that uses information technology to answer health and	February and November/ December

Figure 3-7. Evaluation Plan Example

Goal	Outcome	Objective	Evaluation Method	Timeline
			medical questions. Pretests and posttests will be administered to mature adult community members taking classes to determine their success in using information technology to answer health and medical questions.	
	New community members will be knowledgeable about information technology available in the library, and they will know how to use it to improve their quality of life.	In 12 months 50% of new community members will be aware of information technology resources in the library.	Surveys of new community members will be taken prior to the implementation of the project and at its conclusion to determine the percentage of new community members who are aware of information technology resources in the library and whose quality of life has been improved as a result.	January–December

Figure 3-7. Evaluation Plan Example (*Continued*)

Key Considerations for Writing an Evaluation Plan

Consider the following questions when you are designing a project evaluation:

1. What is the purpose of the evaluation; i.e., what do you want to measure as a result of the evaluation?
2. Who are the audiences for the evaluation results, e.g., funders, government, board, staff, partners, other libraries, or potential partners?
3. What kinds of information do you need to measure your progress, the strengths and weaknesses of the project, impact on customers, or how and why the project failed?
4. What sources will you use to collect the information, e.g., staff, customers, program documentation?

5. How can the information be collected, e.g., questionnaires, interviews, observation, conducting focus groups?
6. When do you need the information?
7. What resources are available to collect the information?

Now record your evaluation methods in no. 12 of your Project Planning Worksheet.

Congratulations! Your Project Plan is complete.

4 ORGANIZING THE GRANT TEAM

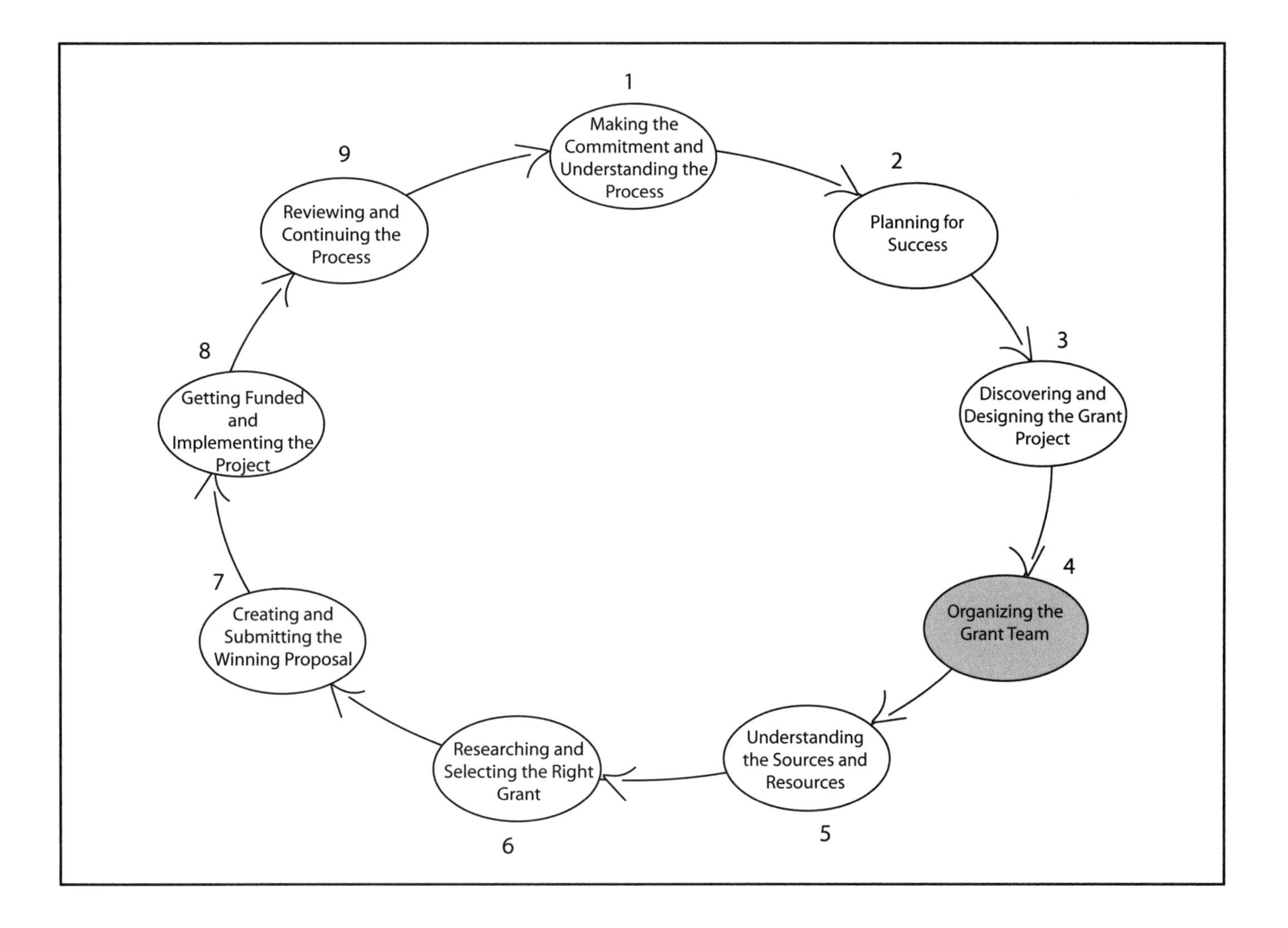

OVERVIEW

Your library has committed to grant work, completed the planning, including identifying the needs of your community, and developed a grant project. So now you are ready to form your grant team. As we discussed in Chapter 1, the library's leadership and staff must be committed to carrying out the planning and implementation of grant opportunities. Representatives from leadership and staff should be included on the grant team, especially staff who will be implementing the grant. Continuing the involvement of community members on planning or project committees can also be beneficial. Creating a small team with representatives from each of these groups will generate ownership, buy-in, support, implementation, follow-up, and sustainability of grant projects. Also, someone must be responsible for overseeing the entire process. Depending on the size of the library, you may have one or two people who have to perform all these roles, or your library may be large enough to have an individual person concentrate specifically on each task. The team is tasked with identifying grant sources, writing applications, and supporting the entire grant process.

Teams are always stronger than individuals, as the more people involved increases the number of skills and ideas, and the amount of energy, momentum, and time available. Teams enable multiple perspectives, a variety of experiences, and a broad skill set. As the old adage attests, many hands make light work. The more people who will brainstorm ideas, research funders and grants, check rough drafts, type, edit the finished proposal, and generally give freely of their opinions, the less daunting the tasks of the grant process.

SELECTING THE GRANT TEAM MEMBERS

Each member of the grant team should bring a unique quality that will benefit the whole team, such as superior writing abilities, storytelling experience, excellent editorial skills, excellent math or budget aptitude, a good eye for details, computer skills/background, ability to speak with funders, capability as a library champion, organizational skills, project or event management, and even a sense of humor. These team members will be vested in the grant process and will be more likely to become involved when the grant proposals are funded. Isolation is the nemesis of grant writing. Solicit help early on and throughout the process, and the ideas generated and the time saved will ensure success and lessen stress. Selecting the right number of people to complete the team is important. Keep the team as small as possible while still bringing in all the necessary skills. The smaller the group, the easier it will be to manage and keep focused on specific tasks.

POSSIBLE TEAM MEMBER TITLES

- Library Director/Leadership
- Staff and Board Representatives
- Grant Coordinator(s)
- Community Advisers
- Researcher(s)
- Writer(s)
- Implementation Team
- Subject Matter Experts
- Partners

RESPONSIBILITIES OF EACH TEAM MEMBER

Director/Leadership

These team members will act as sponsors to maintain support and encouragement for the project from the library; they should be representative of senior management. They can also help remove internal barriers and be spokespersons in support of the team. Examples include the library director or liaisons with county or city governing agencies.

Staff and Board Representatives

It is very important that the library board and staff are aware of the library's grant activities. This is crucial for maintaining buy-in and also for obtaining a united and supportive group. It is important that they are informed and, if contacted by the funder, that they can articulate the project and how it connects with the library's mission. They can also help establish relationships with partners or may know staff from funding agencies on a personal level.

Grant Coordinators

Grant Coordinators (one or two people) are responsible for the performance of the team and are the main point of contact with the funding organizations and partners. They will coordinate all grant tasks and promote good relationships and communications among all team members. They will ensure that all tasks meet the deadlines. In a larger library, they could be assisted by project directors. A project director would manage each specific grant project. Project directors must be self-motivated and devoted to the project idea. They should passionately support the project, be very organized, and be able to keep the big picture in mind.

Community Advisers

These are representatives of key stakeholder groups (for example, representatives from the population to be served by grant) who contribute their perspectives on project issues. It is important to make sure it is clear that they have an advisory role and are not charged with making decisions or representing the library without authority. Funders will be pleased that there is involvement from the population to be served by the grant, as this shows that the library is not acting in isolation from the community.

Researchers

Researchers will be responsible for researching sources of grants, compiling information regarding library information, and also investigating other related efforts by other community groups. They may also research possible partners. They will compile all information on specific grant opportunities and potential funders.

Writers

Writers will write and compile the actual proposal, from cover letter to narrative to evaluation. For some libraries, this may be a team effort, but one person should be responsible for the final compilation to ensure flow of the writing.

Implementation Team

These are the people who will be responsible for performing the project work—the front-line staff. They will implement and help monitor and evaluate the project. They need to know their responsibilities and that the library is committed to the project. What does the grant stipulate, and will they be willing to do it? This team may be headed by a Project Director.

Subject Matter Experts

Subject Matter Experts (SMEs) provide specialized expertise at various phases or steps of the project. This could be a systems librarian or other technology expert, as technology is often involved in library grants. Fiscal agents or whoever will be managing the awarded funds should also be included. They will understand current budget cycles and any stipulations regarding accepting grant funding. This isn't always as simple as you may think, and you will need to be certain your library can accept and utilize the funding. You never want to find out you can't receive funds after all your hard work. You may also have a legal expert to whom you can refer if necessary.

Partners

It is also helpful to include a representative from each of your partnering organizations. Involving such representatives early on will ensure that they are fully vested in the entire process and that they are aware of their role in any grant projects. One funder told us that after a library had been awarded their grant, they discovered that the library had not even contacted the partners they had named in their proposal who were essential to the grant project. When the partners were contacted, they declined to participate since they had not been consulted previously. Oops!

HIRING A PROFESSIONAL GRANT WRITER OR RESEARCHER

You may want to hire a professional grant writer if you don't have anyone with grant experience on your staff, or if you are just too busy. While it may seem cost-prohibitive to spend money on getting money, it could be useful to have someone with experience write a master proposal. You could then use this proposal as the basis for other proposals. The grant writer could take care of some of the more difficult sections of the grant, which are often asked for by all funders. Examples include the organizational background and overview, the community demographics, the description of needs, and evaluation methods. Or you could hire someone to do research on funding sources. Searching grant directories and databases does take time, and this could be another skill your organization could eventually develop internally.

There are several very important things to consider when seeking outside assistance with grants. The job of a grant consultant/writer is to assist those who are seeking the grant. Do not be tempted to have the grant writer plan, design, and write your proposal for you. This will result in a project that the grant writer supports but that may not be something you and your staff can or want to do. Hiring or relying on an outside grant consultant should not relieve the library of devoting time to planning a project and overseeing the design and writing of a proposal.

You will need to have planning meetings with your consultant. It is vital to the success of the future project that all stakeholders have input into the project being designed. Even if you hire a consultant, grant work still takes time. You will also need to review drafts of the proposal and give feedback along the way to ensure that the project represented fits the library's vision.

Remember that grant-writing consultants are professionals and skilled in the grant-writing business. Most outside consultants will require an hourly fee to write your proposal just as doctors, attorneys, and accountants charge for their expertise. Never pay a grant writer a percentage of the awarded grant. Most grants will not allow the cost of obtaining a grant to be included in the requested grant request. No grant writer is successful all the time, so avoid using any consultant who guarantees a successful proposal.

USING VOLUNTEERS

Instead of paying someone to write proposals or research grants, you could solicit volunteers. You may find you have a retiree in your community who has spent a career obtaining grants and would love to give back to the local library and community with his or her existing skills. Volunteers can do research, proofreading, or even writing of the proposal. Or you may have a college or university that requires internships. One high school in South Dakota even taught high school students to write grants for the libraries—and they were successful. In Angel Fire, New Mexico, a volunteer grant writer wrote almost one grant a month for a year for her small library and was awarded seven of the grants. She said the first one took the most time, but after that they took a lot less time, since some of the information could be replicated (Gerding 2003, 16).

You should interview volunteers just as you do paid staff, and you should have clearly written job responsibilities even for people who aren't paid. Review their writing samples and check references. The grant proposal will represent your agency, and you want someone credible.

Contacting your state library may be helpful as well. It may know of other libraries that have successful received grants from the same funder or that have implemented similar projects. Often state libraries distribute grants as well and may provide grant workshops free of charge.

TEAM MEMBERS' SKILLS

The following skills are needed for grant work. Don't worry if you are working on a grant by yourself and don't feel you are completely skilled in all these areas. We've often worked on grant proposals with just one or two primary people but additionally sought input from other individuals skilled in specific areas, for example, budgeting.

- Organizational Awareness: know your library
- Community Awareness: know your users
- Planning: creating goals, objectives, timelines
- Project Development: from problem to solution
- Project Management: overseeing the implementation
- Coordination: overall effort
- Initiative: do-it-yourselfers
- Information Gathering and Research: sources, funders needs, and so on
- Budget Development
- Partnership Building
- Writing
- Time Management
- Resource Management

GRANT TEAM MEETINGS

A team is a group of people with interdependence, aiming for a specific goal. So once you have identified the members of the team, you are ready to actually bring these individuals together to form a team. We don't just mean getting everyone together in one room. When having grant team meetings, keep in mind these five teamwork fundamentals identified in *Visualizing Project Management* (Forseberg 1996, 31).

FUNDAMENTALS OF TEAMWORK

- Common goals
- Acknowledged interdependency and mutual respect
- A common code of conduct

- Team spirit and energy
- Shared rewards

Your team will share the rewards of purpose, fulfilling the library's mission, sharing innovative ideas, and networking. A shared vision and a sense of belonging to an appreciated, valuable group can be very rewarding and can boost staff morale.

INITIAL INFORMAL MEETING

Team members need to know the team goals, and they should be able to put them in their own words. The grant coordinators should start with an initial informal meeting or conversation with each team member to discuss his or her skills and how those abilities will be used by the team. This is particularly useful in a large library, when working with people from areas of the library with whom you are less familiar. This meeting should also include determining how much time employees will have to devote to the team and what tasks and reports will be required. Keep the discussion upbeat and organized, explaining all facets of the grant work and project and their individual roles, while encouraging their ideas and input. Make sure they understand what the team will be doing and confirm that they want to be a part of the grant effort.

THE FIRST TEAM MEETING

Once the grant coordinators have met with each team member individually, the team should have their first meeting. This meeting should include a review of the budget, timeline, and available resources. Each person's responsibilities should be clearly identified, while making sure everyone knows that the process will not be micromanaged. By giving team members a degree of freedom in how they do their jobs, productivity will ultimately increase. There must be mutual respect for the team to be most effective. By sharing the strengths that each team member is bringing to the group, progress can be made toward this essential team element.

These meetings don't need to be formal or boring, but they should be organized, with a set agenda. This demonstrates that you value your team members' time. Bringing snacks and encouraging a warm environment will help with teamwork as well. Assign one person the task of preparing a summary of the meeting's goals, which should be distributed before the meeting. In addition to providing team members with a valuable reference, the prompt distribution of the summary will help convey the importance of the project. You will also want to maintain a written schedule or timeline for the project that can be adjusted and updated as work proceeds. You can establish common rules of behavior such as no interrupting, no gossiping, requiring a representative to be sent if the team member must miss a meeting, and acknowledging that all ideas will be listened to.

The team must be empowered and know that together they will produce something greater and more significant than could be achieved alone. Team members should work together and be willing to do what must be done to get the grant submitted on time. Each member must be committed and accountable for his or her actions, or lack of action. Don't forget to celebrate each milestone and thank each person for his or her individual contributions.

ONGOING GRANT COORDINATOR RESPONSIBILITIES

While Grant Coordinators may have existing job responsibilities, it is critical that they set aside a certain amount of time each week to fulfill their role as grant team leaders. Here are a few of the ongoing tasks they are responsible for:

- Monitor the progress of the grant team. It's critical that they are available to help team members when needed. They should check in with each participant periodically to see if they can provide guidance. This will help in solving minor issues before they become major problems that could jeopardize the project's success. The must track all due dates, tasks, and progress of individual responsibilities.
- Keep all leadership updated. It is easy to become so consumed with managing a team that you forget to let your own supervisors know how the initiative is progressing. Regular updates should be made to library leadership and board members.
- Communicate as much as possible. All team members should be provided with all the information they need. This may be in the form of training (research, writing proposals, etc.) or informational sessions led by other staff members who have worked on recent grants. The role of the finance department should be fully explained.

"We used the PLA Planning Process and the forms from Managing for Results to keep the planning team on track. Starting by analyzing community needs, having representation from target group, and moving through the process is an excellent way to keep things moving!" (Athens Regional Library System Success Story; see page 166).

The team should be able to identify and familiarize themselves with all resources, to brainstorm about possible departmental or community collaboration on grant projects, and have all the support they need.

IMPLEMENTATION

There is more funding available for projects than for operating expenses, so you must be certain that your library can afford the amount of staff time and expense that getting a grant requires. It isn't just depositing the check, after all. You must have the resources to carry out the project and to do the necessary follow-up and promotion. While writing a proposal takes time, implementing a project will take even longer. If you are overwhelmed with the time needed for the initial planning and design of a grant proposal, you may not have the time to devote to the project if the proposal is successful.

Some of the resources needed by the team include:

- Space; there must be a primary place for the team to organize materials and concentrate on writing, making phone calls to funders, and so on. This could range from a few file folders, to a closet (actually done by one librarian), to a separate office.
- Print and online resources; see Chapter 5 for recommendations of resources and Foundation Center Libraries that have grant collections.
- Computer for organizing research, performing searches, sending e-mail, and writing grant proposal.
- Copier, printer, postage meter, telephone.
- Ongoing professional development, including training and funder meetings, including time and travel expenses.
- Staff: the people who will be involved in the entire cycle.
- Time—maybe the most important resource.

Few libraries have full-time development staff that can devote their days to researching grants, contacting funders, writing proposals, and completing evaluations. Instead, most librarians wear many hats and find that grant seeking is just one of many responsibilities. One of the complaints we hear from librarians is that they wish they had more time. By forming a team to work on grants, you can gain a lot of time. If you have only one hour a week to devote to grants, you may find yourself staying up late at night, working extra hours to get your proposals in on time. But if you can gather a team of staff and/or volunteers who can each give one or two hours a week, the math is simple, and you suddenly have ample time. This team will build collaboration within your organization, and they also have the potential to increase their own leadership skills, which in turn can boost their confidence and commitment to the library.

5 UNDERSTANDING THE SOURCES AND RESOURCES

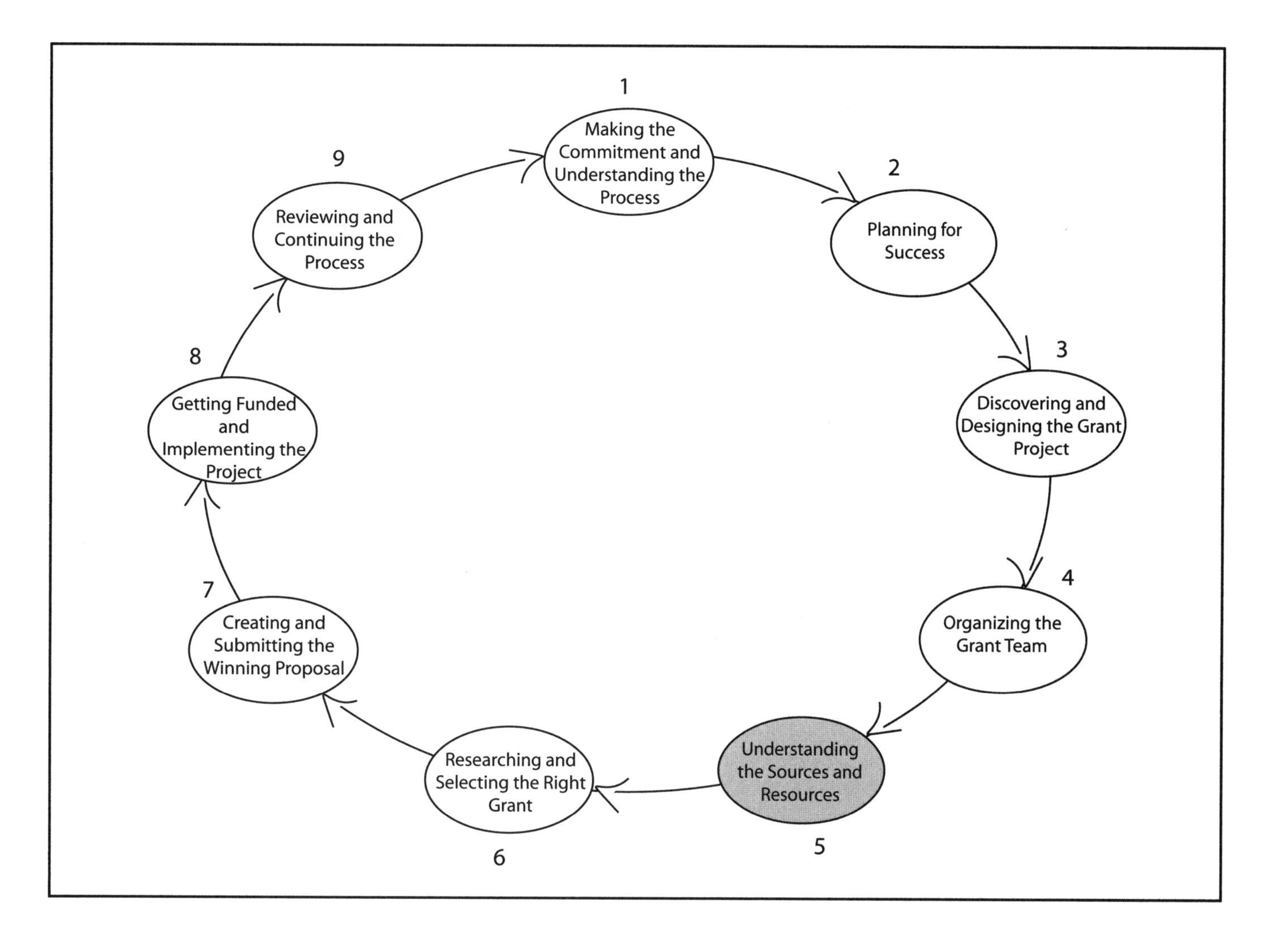

So far we understand and have made the commitment to the grant process, we understand the importance of planning, and we have planned our project. Now it is time to take a look at what types of funding sources there are and what kinds of resources we will be using to locate the grant that is just right for the project we have planned.

There are multiple funding sources that award grants. In this chapter we will first explain the two types of funding sources—government and private. Then we will provide a general overview of the resources you will be using to locate the funding opportunity that is most appropriate to your specific grant project.

TYPES OF FUNDING SOURCES FOR GRANTS

There are two basic types of funding sources: government and private. Within each type there are various categories (Figure 5-1).

Government	Private
• Federal Government • State Government • Local Government (County, City, Town, Village, Municipality)	• Foundations and Nonprofits • Corporations • Clubs and Organizations • Professional and Trade Associations

Figure 5-1. Types of Funding Resources

GOVERNMENT FUNDING SOURCES

Federal Government Sources

The federal government offers billions of dollars annually for research and development, facilities improvement, demonstration and model projects, and grants covering a broad range of educational and social reforms and initiatives designed to carry out the purposes established by legislation. There are hundreds of federal government grant programs managed by a wide variety of departmental bureaucracies. The federal government is the largest source of grant funding in the United States, and each governmental department, bureau, or office has its own unique and separate grant priorities and guidelines. Grant guidelines for federal government agencies are highly competitive and can be very complex. Examples of federal government sources are the Institute of Museum and Library Services, the U.S. Department of Education, and the National Library of Medicine.

State and Local Government Sources

Some federal funding is passed directly to states, counties, or local governments for their use or for redistribution. A local government entity may also acquire a grant of its own which requires others to perform part of its project's scope of work. In this case, the local government will issue a Request for Proposals (RFP) for services or products. State libraries are an example of state government sources.

PRIVATE FUNDING SOURCES

Foundations

Foundations exist to support specific ideals that inspired the creation of the foundation. Billions of dollars are granted annually by foundations to help schools, communities, libraries, and other nonprofit organizations reach their goals. Community foundations are foundations in communities that distribute funding for many different funders in the community, such as small foundations, businesses, corporations, organizations, or individuals.

Corporations

Corporations offer many opportunities in the form of partnerships, material resources, mentors, expertise, and funds to schools, communities, libraries, and other nonprofits. Corporations are generally looking to establish their names and relationships within the communities in which they operate. Commercial enterprises are driven primarily by their desire for public recognition.

Clubs and Organizations

Local clubs and organizations such as the Rotary Club, Civitans, Elks, and the Junior League provide support for local projects and programs. Motivated to help local communities through service, materials, and financial investments, these local opportunities are not widely advertised or promoted.

Professional Associations

Professional associations often make grant funds available to members of the association or organizations that carry out missions that are compatible with the interests of the professional organization.

RESOURCES FOR FINDING GRANT OPPORTUNITIES

The resources you will use to identify funding opportunities are available in a variety of formats. Grant opportunities are compiled and listed in printed directories, online databases, CD-ROMs, Web sites, print and electronic newsletters, and e-mail discussion groups. A general overview of the available resources follows. Remember that there may be resources specific to the topic of your project or your geographical region that are beyond the scope of this overview. Do the research necessary to find these resources.

You will use many resources in the course of your grant research. There is not one directory or database that will contain all the funding opportunities available to fund your project. Some of these resources are costly; however, you should be able to find them in your state library, a nearby college or university library, the reference collection in a nearby large public library, the Web, or your local community foundation.

GOVERNMENT FUNDING RESOURCES

In the past, the way to find federal funding opportunities was in the paper editions of the *Federal Register* and the *Catalog of Federal Domestic Assistance*. With the advent of the Internet, federal grant opportunities are now found mainly online. Some agencies are even discontinuing their notices for funding availability in the *Federal Register*. The Web sites of federal agencies often offer a listing of available grants frequently asked questions (FAQs), applications, guidelines, contact information, and more.

Federal Funding Resources

Catalog of Federal Domestic Assistance—www.cfda.gov *The Catalog of Federal Domestic Assistance* (CFDA) provides access to a database of all federal programs available to state and local governments; federally recognized Indian tribal governments; territories and possessions of the United States; domestic public, quasi-public, and private profit and nonprofit organizations and institutions; specialized groups; and individuals. The CFDA is disseminated electronically primarily via its Web site at www.cfda.gov.

Federal Register—www.gpoaccess.gov/fr/index.html The *Federal Register* is the official daily publication of U.S.

federal agency information, including presidential documents, agency meetings, rules, proposed rules, executive orders, proposed federal regulations, and notifications and announcements of grant opportunities by federal agencies and organizations. A new edition of the *Federal Register* is published every business day. You can find the printed editions of the daily *Federal Register* at your local Federal Depository Library or visit www.gpoaccess.gov/fr/index. html for the online version.

Grants.gov—www.grants.gov *Grants.gov* at www.grants .gov is the single access point for over 900 grant programs offered by the twenty-six federal grant-making agencies. Here you can electronically find and apply for competitive grant opportunities from all federal grant-making agencies. According to *Grants.gov,* "The grant community, including state, local and tribal governments, academia and research institutions, and not-for-profits, need only visit one Web site, Grants.gov, to access the annual grant funds available across the Federal government."

USDA's Notices of Funding Availability—http://ocd1.usda .gov/nofa2.asp Hosted by the USDA, this Web site allows you to see active federal government grant opportunities in all agencies by topic and agency.

State, County, and City Government Resources

LSTA (Library Services and Technology Act) Funding

Every year the federal government allocates LSTA (Library Services and Technology Act) funding to your state library for distribution throughout your state. The Library Services and Technology Act of 1996, a section of the Museum and Library Services Act, promotes access to learning and information resources of all types of libraries for individuals of all ages. LSTA outlines two broad priorities for this funding. The first is for activities using technology for information sharing between libraries and between libraries and other community services. The second is for programs that make library resources more accessible to urban, rural, or low-income residents and others who have difficulty using library services.

Through the legislation, the Institute of Museum and Library Services (IMLS) provides funds to State Library Agencies using a population-based formula. Applicants for this grant program must be one of the fifty-nine State Library Administrative Agencies. State libraries may use the appropriation to support statewide initiatives and services through competitive subgrant competitions or cooperative agreements to public, academic, research, school, and special libraries in their state. Check with your State

Library about the availability of LSTA funds through a subgrant or cooperative agreement. Many State Libraries announce LSTA subgrant opportunities and application guidelines on their Web sites, and some even have online applications and free grant workshops. LSTA funding has increased over the last several years, and continues to be a good potential source of funding for most libraries.

See the CD in this book for links to the State Library Agencies and LSTA opportunities through State Library Agencies.

State Humanities Councils, Arts Councils, Cultural Services Agencies, and Departments of Education

Also remember to investigate grant opportunities in other agencies in your state, county or city that may fund your project, such as the State Department of Education, and Humanities, Arts and Cultural Services Agencies. You can find your State Humanities Council at www.neh.gov/whoweare/statecouncils.html.

PRIVATE FUNDING RESOURCES

Foundations

The Foundation Center is the largest producer of directories and databases of grant-giving foundations. The center publishes print directories by subject, foundation name, geographic region, and grants previously funded. The subject directories cover topics such as arts and culture, children and youth services, education, environment and animal welfare, health, international, libraries and information services, religion, and social services.

Foundation Center Cooperating Collections

The Foundation Center's Cooperating Collections are free funding information centers found in libraries, community foundations, and other nonprofit resource centers in every state. Each collection consists of a core collection of Foundation Center publications, including *FC Search* CD-ROMs and a variety of supplementary materials and services in areas useful to grant seekers. Go to www.fdncenter.org to find the Foundation Center Cooperating Collection nearest you.

Print Resources

Foundation 1000 profiles include grant maker contact information, reviews of program interests, purpose and giving limitations statements, application guidelines, names of key officials, list of recent grants, and tables documenting funding patterns.

The *Foundation Directory* features key facts on the nation's top 10,000 foundations by total giving and provides over 51,000 descriptions of selected grants.

The *Foundation Reporter,* published by the Taft Group, provides important foundation contact, financial, and grant information. This resource covers the top 1,000 private foundations in the United States that have at least $10 million in assets or have made $500,000 in charitable giving.

Guide to U.S. Foundations, Their Trustees, Officers, and Donors contains data on all active grant-making foundations and the individuals who run them and provides current information on over 67,000 foundations. It also includes a list of the decision makers who direct U.S. active foundations.

Electronic Resources

The Foundation Center's database on CD-ROM, *FC Search,* includes over 76,000 foundations, corporate givers, and grant-making public charities; a grants file with more than 324,000 grants, linked to funders; a searchable index of over 352,000 trustees, officers, and donors; program descriptions and application guidelines; links to over 3,900 grant-maker Web sites; and more than 2,200 corporate Web sites.

> The *Foundation Directory Online* is available from the Foundation Center at several levels, from a package including a database of the nation's largest 10,000 foundations to one that includes over 76,000 foundations, corporate givers, and grant-making public charities and over 350,000 grant records (www.fconline.fdncenter.org/).
>
> The Foundation Center's database of grants and grant makers is also available through DIALOG (Files 26 and 27).
>
> The *Foundation Grants Index on CD-ROM* provides information on recently awarded grants of over 1,000 of the largest independent, corporate, and community foundations in the United States and features approximately 125,000 grant descriptions.
>
> *Prospector's Choice,* a CD-ROM product from the Taft Group, presents key financial information on more than 10,000 corporate and foundation giving programs. Data on up to fifty grants per profile are provided, as well as contact and application information, financial summaries, and biographies for giving officers.
>
> The Foundation Center's *RFP Bulletin* provides listings of Requests for Proposals (RFPs). Each listing provides a brief overview of a current funding opportunity offered by

a foundation or other grant-making organization, along with the date the RFP was posted and the deadline. You can sign up at http://fdncenter.org/pnd/rfp to receive the *RFP Bulletin* as a free, weekly e-mail newsletter.

Corporations

Corporations often create corporate foundations for the purpose of granting money for specific projects. Corporations also give directly to projects. The following resources cover both corporate foundations and corporate direct giving programs.

Print Resources

Corporate Foundation Profiles provides profiles on over 200 of the largest corporate foundations in the United States and provides information on how much money a foundation gives in specific categories and specific population groups.

The Taft Group's *Corporate Giving Directory: Comprehensive Profiles of America's Major Corporate Foundations & Corporate Giving Programs* provides profiles of the 1,000 largest corporate foundations and corporate direct giving programs in the United States. This reference includes coverage of the 100 biggest givers, the top 100 companies, and preselected giving lists and covers the top 10 corporate givers for the previous year. It provides biographical data on officers and directors that can help you in identifying contacts between the leaders in your organization and those in corporate foundations.

Corporate Philanthropy Report, issued by Aspen Publishers, is a useful periodical for keeping up-to-date on corporate giving.

You can search for corporate foundation funding and direct corporate giving in the Foundation Center's *National Directory of Corporate Giving,* which includes detailed portraits of close to 2,300 corporate foundations and 1,300 direct giving programs; application guidelines; key personnel; types of support awarded; giving limitations; and financial data including assets, annual giving, and the average size of grants; and over 6,500 descriptions of recently awarded grants.

The *National Guide to Funding for Libraries and Information Services* provides essential facts on approximately 800 foundations and corporate direct giving programs, with histories of awarding grants to libraries and information centers.

Electronic Resources

The *Foundation Directory Online* is available for a monthly fee from the Foundation Center at several levels, from a package including a database of the nation's largest 10,000 foundations to one that includes over 76,000 foundations, corporate givers, and grant-making public charities and over 350,000 grant records (www.fconline.fdncenter.org/).

The *Foundation Grants Index on CD-ROM* provides information on recently awarded grants of over 1,000 of the largest independent, corporate, and community foundations in the United States and features approximately 125,000 grant descriptions.

Prospector's Choice, a CD-ROM product from the Taft Group, presents key financial information on more than 10,000 corporate and foundation giving programs. Data on up to fifty grants per profile are provided, as well as contact and application information, financial summaries, and biographies for giving officers.

Make sure to investigate the Web sites of corporations operating in your geographic area, looking for links to "community involvement." Many corporations devote this part of their Web sites to explaining what they fund and how to apply. You may even find an online application that you can submit electronically.

Visit your local community foundation and ask to see the information it has about corporations in your area that fund local projects. You may find annual reports or other compilations that include descriptions of the corporation's granting interests and grant-making history. Don't forget to check local finding directories specific to your state or geographical region for corporate funding opportunities.

Clubs and Organizations

Funding opportunities available through local organizations are not widely advertised. This is where your networking and people skills will come in handy. Ask friends, neighbors, and family members who are involved in local organizations what their organizations support. Mention your idea or project to them and inquire about the possibility of presenting it to the organization. Ask if they know any other local organizations that support ideas or projects like yours.

Professional Associations

Investigate your state, regional, and special library associations, including divisions, special interest groups, and chapters. The American Library Association and Special Libraries Association offer grant and fellowship opportunities.

Community Foundations

Visit your local community foundation and talk to the staff there. Tell them about your project idea and ask if there are any grants through the community foundation that funds projects like yours. Establish a relationship with these people and check in with them periodically. When funding becomes available for projects like yours through the community foundation, the staff will contact you about applying. Community foundations often have solid collections of materials about writing proposals and print, electronic, and local directories of funding sources and offer classes for community members about their funding and resources. You will find extensive information about local corporations and foundations that you may not find collected in any other place. You can find your local community foundation using the Council on Foundation Web site: www.cof.org/Locator/index.cfm?menuContainerID=34&crumb=2.

LOCAL FUNDING DIRECTORIES

Your state and local funding directories are invaluable resources for finding foundations and corporations that limit their giving to your geographic area. Find your local directory in *State and Local Funding Directories: A Bibliography* at http://fdncenter.org/learn/topical/sl_dir.html.

RESOURCES FOR LIBRARY PROJECTS

Federal Agencies

Following are some federal government agencies that fund libraries, information clearinghouses, archives, and technical information services.

U.S. Department of Agriculture

Cooperative State, Research, Education, and Extension Service's unique mission is to advance knowledge for agriculture, the environment, human health and well-being, and communities by supporting research, education, and extension programs in the Land-Grant University System and other partner organizations. CSREES doesn't perform actual research, education, and extension but rather helps fund it at the state and local level and provides program leadership in these areas: www.csrees.usda.gov/fo/funding.cfm.

U.S. Department of Education (DOE)

The DOE is providing about $36 billion this year to states and school districts, primarily through formula-based grant programs, to improve elementary and secondary schools and meet the special needs of students. DOE is providing about $2.5 billion to help strengthen teaching and learning in colleges and other postsecondary institutions and about $3.3 billion to support rehabilitation, research and development, statistics, and assessment: www.ed.gov/fund/landing.jhtml?src= rt.

> *Office of Innovation and Improvement* makes strategic investments in promising educational practices through grants to states, schools, and community and nonprofit organizations. It also leads the movement for greater parental options and information on education.
>
> *Office of Elementary and Secondary Education* provides financial assistance to state and local education agencies for both public and private preschool, elementary, and secondary education. Working together with these and other education partners, the Office of Elementary and Secondary Education promotes and supports equal educational opportunities and educational excellence for all students.
>
> *Office of English Language Acquisition, Language Enhancement, and Academic Achievement for Limited English Proficient Students* administers programs designed to enable students with limited English proficiency to become proficient in English and meet challenging state academic content and student achievement standards.
>
> *Office of Postsecondary Education* directs, coordinates, and recommends policies for programs that are designed to provide financial assistance to eligible students; improve postsecondary educational facilities and programs; recruit and prepare disadvantaged students for postsecondary programs; and promote the domestic study of foreign languages and international affairs, research, and exchange activities.
>
> *Office of Special Education and Rehabilitative Services* assists in the education of children with disabilities and the rehabilitation of adults with disabilities and conducts research to improve the lives of individuals with disabilities regardless of age.

Office of Vocational and Adult Education (OVAE) works to ensure that all Americans have the knowledge and technical skills necessary to succeed in postsecondary education, the workforce, and life. Through the Preparing America's Future initiative's comprehensive policies, programs, and activities, OVAE is helping reform America's high schools, supporting America's community colleges, and expanding America's adult education programs. These efforts will transform the federal role, sparking state and local reform efforts.

Department of Health and Human Services

Administration for Children and Families (ACF) is a federal agency funding state, territory, local, and tribal organizations to provide family assistance (welfare), child support, child care, Head Start, child welfare, and other programs relating to children and families. Actual services are provided by state, county, city, and tribal governments and public and private local agencies. ACF assists these organizations through funding, policy direction, and information services: www.acf.hhs.gov/grants/index.html.

Health Resources and Services Administration

The Health Resources and Services Administration directs programs that improve the nation's health by expanding access to comprehensive, quality health care for all Americans: www.hrsa.gov/grants/default.htm.

National Library of Medicine (NLM)

The NLM provides the following grants and fellowships to organizations and individuals: research grants, awards supporting career development and training, fellowship programs at NLM; support for outreach initiatives to improve access and eliminate health disparities; and National Institutes of Health (NIH) programs and initiatives supported by NLM: www.nlm.nih.gov/grants.html.

Office of Juvenile Justice and Delinquency Prevention

The Office of Juvenile Justice and Delinquency Prevention supports states, local communities, and tribal jurisdictions in their efforts to develop and implement effective programs for juveniles: http://ojjdp.ncjrs.org/funding/funding.html.

National Endowment for the Arts (NEA)

This is a public agency dedicated to supporting excellence in the arts; bringing the arts to all Americans; and providing leadership in arts education. The NEA is the nation's largest annual funder of the arts, bringing great art to all fifty states, including rural areas, inner cities, and military bases: www .nea.gov/.

Institute of Museum and Library Services (IMLS)

The IMLS is an independent federal agency that fosters leadership, innovation, and a lifetime of learning. IMLS supports all types of libraries and archives from public and academic to research and school. IMLS grant programs help libraries bring people the information they want and can use. Through statewide initiatives and subgrants, nationwide competitions for leadership activities, and grants to improve Native American and Native Hawaiian library service, IMLS support reaches libraries in thousands of communities every year: www.imls.gov/grants/library/ index.htm.

National Endowment for the Humanities

The National Endowment for the Humanities is an independent grantmaking agency of the U.S. government dedicated to supporting research, education, preservation, and public programs in the humanities: www.neh .fed.us.

National Historical Publications and Records Commission (NHPRC)

The NHPRC is the outreach arm of the National Archives and Records Administration and makes plans for, and studies issues related to, the preservation, use, and publication of historical documents. The commission makes grants to nonfederal archives and other organizations to promote the preservation use of America's documentary heritage: www.archives.gov/ grants/index.html.

National Institute for Literacy

The National Institute for Literacy provides national leadership regarding literacy, coordinates literacy services and policy, and serves as a national resource for adult education and literacy programs: www.nifl.gov/nifl/grants_ contracts.html.
For links to these agencies' Web pages, where you can find information about current grant opportunities, see the CD-ROM inside this book.

Directories

Annual Register of Grant Support, published by Information Today, Inc., is a comprehensive directory that provides details on more than 3,500 major grant programs offered by private and public foundations, government agencies, corporations, unions, educational associations, professional organizations, community trusts, and other special interest groups of all types and sizes.

Library Grants Hotline is a newsletter published by the Quinlan Publishing Group that highlights government, foundation, and corporate grant opportunities for all types of libraries. Each entry includes eligibility guidelines, deadline, funds, contact information, and a description of the purpose of the grant.

Grant$ for Libraries and Information Services. (Annual). New York: Foundation Center. Provides descriptions of over 3,600 recent grants to libraries, archives, and information centers of $10,000 or more awarded by 633 foundations.

Grant$ for Information Technology. (Annual). New York: Foundation Center.

National Guide to Funding for Libraries and Information Services. (Annual). New York: Foundation Center. Provides essential facts on approximately 800 foundations and corporate direct-giving programs, with histories of awarding grants to libraries and information centers.

Constable, M. R. (1993). *Federal Grants and Services for Libraries: A Guide to Selected Programs*. Washington, DC: American Library Association.

Taft Group. (2002). *Big Book of Library Grant Money: Profiles of Private and Corporate Foundations and Direct Corporate Givers Receptive to Library Grant Proposals*. Chicago: American Library Association. Profiles foundations and corporate grant makers that have made grants to libraries or listed libraries as typical recipients.

Organizations

ALA Awards and Scholarships. Includes ALA General, Divisions, and Offices: www.ala.org/Template.cfm?Section=grantfellowship.

American Association of School Librarians Funding Opportunities: www.ala.org/aasl/resources/funding.html.

SLA Scholarships and Grants: www.sla.org/content/learn/scholarship/index.cfm.

Libraries for the Future provides programs at the national, state, and local levels, typically in partnership with libraries, library systems, foundations, and community-based organizations. They currently operate in more than 100 communities in twenty states: www.lff.org/.

Newsletters

Foundation & Corporate Grants Alert. New York: Aspen Publishers, Inc. 1993.
Aspen Publishers, Inc.
200 Orchard Ridge Dr., Ste. 200, Gaithersburg, MD 20878 United States
customer.service@aspenpubl.com
301-417-7500
800-638-8437
www.aspenpub.com

Grants for Libraries Hotline. United States. Quinlan Publishing Co., Inc. 2001.
Quinlan Publishing Co., Inc.
23 Drydock Ave., 2nd fl., Boston 02210-2387
info@quinlan.com
617-542-0048
800-229-2084
www.quinlan.com

Electronic Resources

The authors of this book maintain a Library Grants Blog at http://librarygrants.blogspot.com/, where they regularly post new grant opportunities for libraries.

6 RESEARCHING AND SELECTING THE RIGHT GRANT

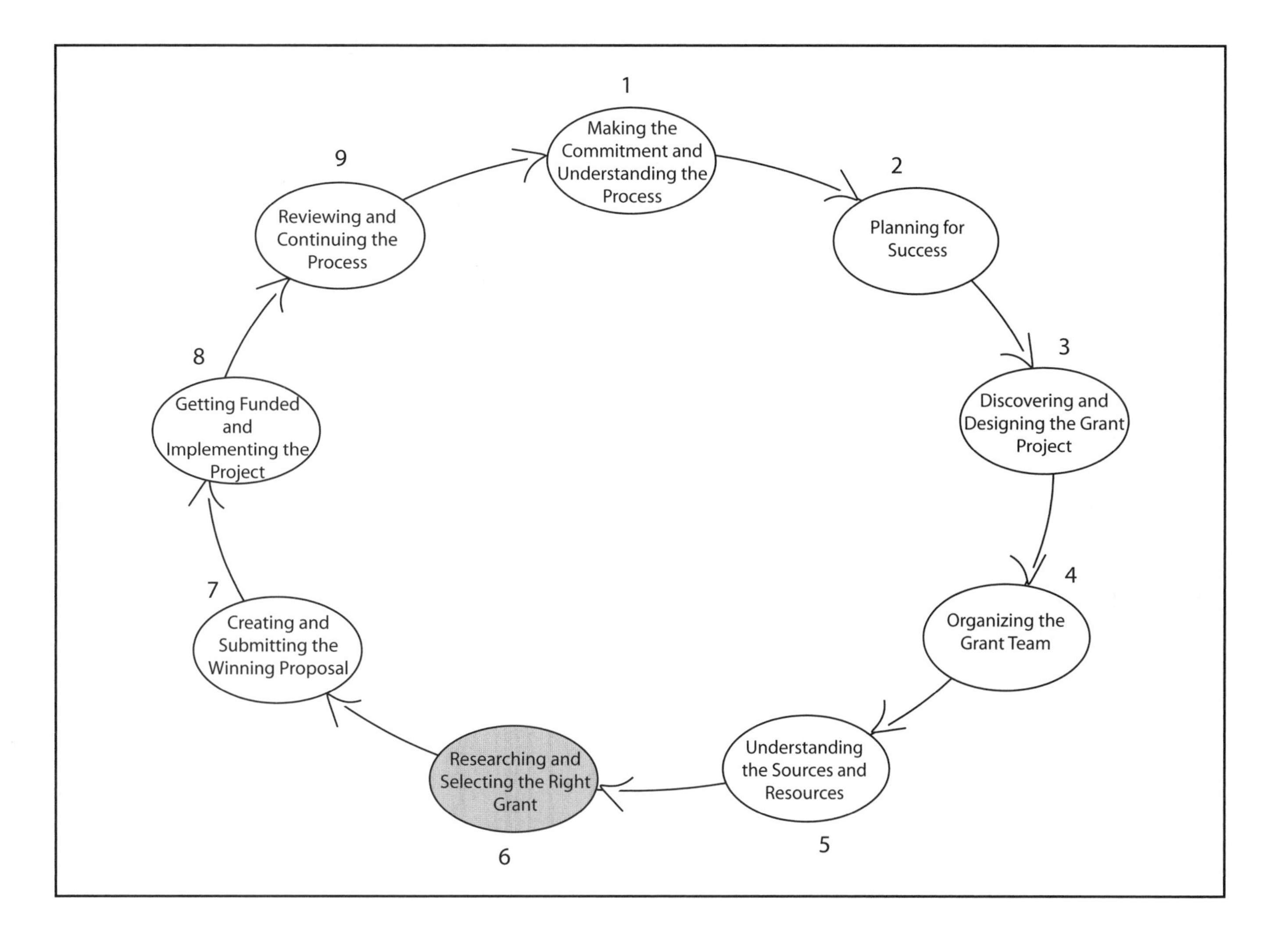

Now that you have a well-planned project, know about the different grant types and grant categories, and understand the resources available for identifying the grant funders, it is time to research and select funders looking to award grants for projects just like yours.

The first thing to do is to let everyone know that you are looking for funding and tell them about the project you want to fund. Tell staff, board members, the city council, family and friends, and local business leaders. You never know who might know someone on the board of a foundation who has just the funding you are seeking.

Here are some other things you can do to find the right funder:

- Do thorough Internet and library research.
- Read publications like newsletters, electronic discussion groups, journals, and local newspapers for new funding opportunities.
- Contact other libraries in your area that have received grants.
- Talk with funders about their interests and priorities.

INTERNET AND LIBRARY RESEARCH

"The more thoroughly you conduct your research, ask smart questions, and cultivate foundation contacts, the more your organization will stand out from the crowd." From "Finding Foundation Funders" by Andy Robinson in the March/April 2004 *Grassroots Fundraising Journal.*

Internet and library research is the easy part for us. We are librarians, and we have an advantage when it comes to doing research. We are trained to use reference materials, and we have the skills to find information, wherever it may be and however deeply it is buried. We're naturals at this. So let's put these valuable skills to work to get the grant that will improve our libraries and meet the needs of our communities.

Here are some tips for you to think about while doing your research:

- Translate your project into the language of the resources.
- Work from the general to the specific.
- Record what you find.
- Keep your research findings organized.

TRANSLATE YOUR PROJECT INTO THE LANGUAGE OF THE RESOURCES

"Think outside of the box and look at other, less traditional funding sources for libraries and library programs." Maureen T. O'Connor, Queens Borough Public Library, Laurelton Branch Library.

When identifying keywords describing your project, remove any mental barriers about libraries and what libraries traditionally do. Eliminate stereotyping and think big. Be generous and open-minded about choosing terms, rather than restrictive. Funders and compilers of resources may not even think "library" when they are writing profiles or defining areas of focus. For instance, if a funder is interested in awarding grants for children's performances, they may not know that many libraries have programs that include children's performances. In a case like this, "library" would not appear as a keyword in the entry, but "children," "theater," and "performance art" would.

If you searched only for "library," you would have missed this potential funder. Make sure to uncover each and every possible match by thinking broadly when it comes to keywords describing your project.

Keep up this kind of thinking when you are choosing resources to search. Of course, you will want to use the *National Guide to Funding for Libraries and Information Services* and *Grants for Libraries and Information Services*; however, don't overlook other subject guides such as the *National Guide to Funding in Arts and Culture* if your project involves an art exhibit or cultural performance. Look at *Grants for the Physically and Mentally Disabled* if persons with disabilities will benefit from your project. Thoroughly search for local or lesser-known specific funding resources that may help you in your search for a grant. Examples of these are the *National Directory of Foundation Grants for Native Americans* and the *Directory of Building and Equipment Grants*.

Spend some time with each resource to understand the unique terms it uses and how each term is defined in that resource. For instance, a grant opportunity usually appears in the *Federal Register* as a "Notice of Funding Availability." Be clear on how a resource defines kinds of grants and use exactly those terms to narrow your search. Kinds of grants may include equipment, operating, planning, research, program, demonstration, or model. A resource usually includes definitions of terms in a glossary, appendix, or user's guide.

WORK FROM THE GENERAL TO THE SPECIFIC

Broad Research

First, record the goals, objectives, and activities of the project you want to fund on a Keyword Selection Worksheet. Take this information directly from the Project Planning Worksheet you completed in Chapter 3. Then bring together your grant team to develop a comprehensive list of keywords that describe your project. Think of broad, specific, and related terms. Start with general keywords like "library," "libraries," or "information." Or use words more specific to your project, yet still broad, like "technology," "resources," "services," or "instruction." Use the keywords you already identified on your Project Planning Worksheet. Think of variations on words and synonyms.

Do a brainstorming activity together or work in small groups. Team members might be given 10 minutes to write down the keywords on their own copy of the Keyword Selection Worksheet first. Record the keywords your team agrees to and write them on a single worksheet, which you will be using throughout your research to keep you on track and headed in the right direction. Figure 6-2 is an example of a completed Keyword Selection Worksheet for the project we designed in Chapter 3, Information Technology You Can Use. See page 215 in the Grants for Libraries Tool Kit for a Keyword Selection Template you can use for your own project.

Use these keywords to do your broad research in all probable general resources you can find, such as national directories and grant databases for government, foundation, corporate, and local funders.

Narrowing Your Search

As you narrow your research, you will use more specific resources such as local directories, online databases, or CD-ROM databases. Databases allow you to combine multiple fields in one search. Local funding directories list funders who limit their grant giving to your geographic area. Local directories also include corporate giving programs and small corporate grants that may not appear in the national directories.

Record What You Find

> "Understand the grantors' requirements and be sure that your proposal fits their interests." Leslie A. Massey, Clermont County Public Library, Batavia, Ohio.

From the time you begin your research, you will make a Funder Summary Worksheet (see page 216 in the Grants for Libraries Tool Kit) for each potential funder you identify. To make decisions whether or not a funder is a good match, you will need to use your Keyword Worksheet to compare the funder's purpose; field of interest or focus; and the type of support the funder gives to the keywords describing your project. When you are done with your research, you will have a healthy pile of Funder Summary Worksheets representing "good matches" for grants.

KEEP YOUR RESEARCH FINDINGS ORGANIZED

Look carefully through your Funder Summary Worksheets and separate those that are questionable. If, as you look at these worksheets again, you determine that some are definitely not good matches, file them. They were close enough for you to start a worksheet, and they may be on-target for a future project. If you have questions on some or need further clarification on a whether or not a funder may be interested in a project like yours, contact funder. By now you are very familiar with the foundation, agency, or corporation, so you will be asking intelligent, informed questions. Use this initial contact to develop a rapport with the contact person. These people are usually happy to answer your questions and work with you, and they will be pleasantly surprised at how much you already know from the research you have done. After this contact, you will place the worksheet in the "go" or "no-go" pile.

The worksheets in the "good matches" pile represent the funders you will approach. Start a separate file for each funder. Here you will keep your worksheet, record of contact, phone notes, application materials, proposals submitted, correspondence, and so on.

<table>
<tr><th>Project Plan Section</th><th>Keywords</th></tr>
<tr><td>Goals:
By offering classes on the availability and use of information technology in the library, this project will:
1. assist the Spanish-speaking population in using information technology to find jobs;
2. assist the mature adult population to find and use health and medical information using information technology; and
3. inform new community members about information technology available in the library and how to use it.</td><td rowspan="3">Information technology
Technology
Computers
Resources
Services
Community, communities, community members
Spanish-speaking persons
Mature adults
Library, libraries
Employment
Jobs
Health or medical information
Class, classes
Instruction
Training
Education
Teach
Learning</td></tr>
<tr><td>Objectives:
1. An increase of 25% of the Spanish-speaking population will use information technology resources in the library to find jobs.
2. An increase of 25% of mature adult community members will use information technology in the library to answer their health and medical questions.
3. 50% of new community members will be aware of the library's information technology resources and how to use them.</td></tr>
<tr><td>Outcomes:
1. The ability of Spanish-speaking community members to find jobs will be increased due to their knowledge and use of information technology.
2. The ability of mature adult community members to research health-related questions using information technology will increase their ability to make informed medical choices.
3. New community members will be knowledgeable about information technology available in the library, and they will know how to use it to improve their quality of life.</td></tr>
<tr><td>Activities and Action Steps:
1. Develop a public awareness plan and marketing strategy.
2. Create a brochure.
3. Hold public awareness activities at local stores, fairs, and offices.
4. Design pre- and post-surveys.
5. Implement pre- and post-surveys.
6. Create advertisement.
7. Advertise information technology resources and services in local newspaper.
8. Put advertising inserts in water bills.</td><td>Public awareness
Marketing
Brochure
Advertisement
Curriculum
Water Department
Computer, computers
Classroom
Computer lab
Tests</td></tr>
</table>

Figure 6-1. Keyword Selection Worksheet Example

Activities and Action Steps:	
9. Offer incentives or prizes to winners of information technology "games."	
10. Track computer usage.	
11. Develop curriculum.	
12. Schedule classes/Reserve computer classroom.	
13. Advertise classes.	
14. Register people for classes.	
15. Teach classes.	
16. Design pre- and post-tests.	

Figure 6-1. Keyword Selection Worksheet Example (*Continued*)

DIFFERENT KINDS OF GRANTS

Before you begin your research, familiarize yourself with the terminology for different kinds of grants. If you understand what these kinds of grants are, you will save yourself from spending time researching a kind of grant that is not appropriate for your project.

Block Grant	A grant that the state or federal government allocates to fund a specific need. For example, the federal government allocates $2 million in a block grant to schools that provide after-school care for children in low-income neighborhoods.
Challenge Grant	A grant awarded to grant seekers if they reach a specific fund-raising goal.
Capital Grant	Funding for endowment purposes, construction, or equipment.
General Operating Support	Funding for the general purpose or work of an organization, for example, personnel, administration, and other expenses for an existing program.
Matching Grant	A grant that requires the grant seeker to provide a certain amount to fund the project, and the funder will provide the rest. For example, a 1:1 match would mean that the funder provides half and the grant seeker provides half of the cost of the project.
Project/Program Grant	Funding for specific initiative or new endeavor, not general-purpose.
Seed Grant	Funding designed to help start a new project or charitable activity or to help a new organization in its start-up phase.
Technology Grant	A grant that provides funding for a technology project.

Figure 6-2. Kinds of Grants

RESEARCHING GOVERNMENT RESOURCES

Catalog of Federal Domestic Assistance (CFDA)

There are many ways to navigate the CFDA Web site. One way is to go to www.cfda.gov, click on "Search for Assistance Programs," then "Find a Grant," "Education," and finally "Libraries and Technical Information Services." Web sites are periodically redesigned or reorganized, so if these links don't appear when you go to cfda.gov, do a search or look at the site map for the "Libraries" section.

In Figure 6-3 you will see a list of all federal grant programs in the category "Libraries and Technical Information Services." Beware—these are not all active grant opportunities. You will have to click through each program to the information on an agency's Web site for specific grant

CFDA
The Catalog of Federal Domestic Assistance

Home | FAQ | Privacy | About The CFDA Web Site

Grant Programs

Sub-Category	Programs
Libraries and Technical Information Services	10.217 - Higher Education Challenge Grants (B)
	10.226 - Secondary And Two-Year Postsecondary Agriculture Education Challenge Grants (B)
	45.130 - Promotion Of The Humanities_Challenge Grants (B)
	45.310 - State Library Program (A)
	45.311 - Native American And Native Hawaiian Library Services (B)
	45.312 - National Leadership Grants (B)
	45.313 - Librarians For The 21st Century (B)
	81.039 - National Energy Information Center (B)
	84.016 - Undergraduate International Studies And Foreign Language Programs (B)
	84.060 - Indian Education_Grants To Local Educational Agencies (A)
	84.144 - Migrant Education_Coordination Program (B)
	84.168 - Eisenhower Professional Development_Federal Activities (B)
	84.257 - National Institute For Literacy (B)
	84.303 - Technology Innovation Challenge Grants (B)
	84.304 - Civic Education - Cooperative Education Exchange Program (B)
	84.323 - Special Education_State Program Improvement Grants For Children With Disabilities (B)
	84.326 - Special Education_Technical Assistance And Dissemination To Improve Services And Results For Children With Disabilities (B)
	84.327 - Special Education_Technology And Media Services For Individuals With Disabilities (B)
	84.337 - International Education_Technological Innovation And Cooperation For Foreign Information Access (B)
	84.341 - Community Technology Centers (B)
	84.364 - Literacy Through School Libraries (B)
	93.379 - Grants For Graduate Training In Family Medicine (B)
	93.600 - Head Start (B)
	93.630 - Developmental Disabilities Basic Support And Advocacy Grants (A)
	93.879 - Medical Library Assistance (B)

Figure 6-3. CFDA Search Results Screen

availability and deadlines. The CFDA site is a good place to view an overall "big picture" of existing, federally funded grant programs in your area of interest. Here you will find formula grants that funnel funds through state agencies. If you see a potential opportunity that is a formula grant, you can follow through by going to your state agency to inquire about applying for these funds.

If you see a potential match that is not an active grant program, you can watch for an upcoming "Notice of Funding Availability" on the *Federal Register* Web site or periodically revisit the agency's Web site for new grant announcements. If you find a match that is active, fill out a Funding Research Worksheet, and you're in business!

See the Grants for Libraries Tool Kit and CD in this book for an example of a program description on the CFDA Web site.

You can narrow your search on the CFDA site by functional area, agency, and subagency, alphabetically by program title, by applicant eligibility, by beneficiary, by program deadline, by type of assistance, and more.

Federal Register

Grant opportunities usually appear in the *Federal Register* in the form of "Notices of Funding Availability" or "Notices Inviting Applications." Go to www.gpoaccess.gov/fr/index.html and select "Advanced Search." Check the appropriate volume box for current notices (3–6 months ago through today's date) and select "Notices." You can limit the inclusive dates to narrow your search; however, be careful with this. You don't want to limit yourself out of results. The periods of time between notice announcements and submission deadlines vary widely among federal agencies. Enter your broad keywords in the Search box, combining them with the word "funding." Read the "Search tips" for information on Boolean searching capabilities and truncation, for instance. See Figure 6-4.

Again, because this is a broad search to start, your results may require major sifting. The good news here is that you may catch something that wouldn't appear if you had performed a narrow search. The extra work upfront is sometimes worth it in the long run.

The results are shown in Figure 6-5. To view a sample *Federal Register* entry for [6], see the CD in this book. As you will see, the notice includes eligibility information, application submission information, application review information, and whom to contact if you have questions.

Grants.gov

Grants.gov is your best bet for an initial broad search. Click on "Search for Grant Opportunities" and type your broad term(s) in the keyword search box. Then click on "Start Search." Figure 6-7 shows the results.

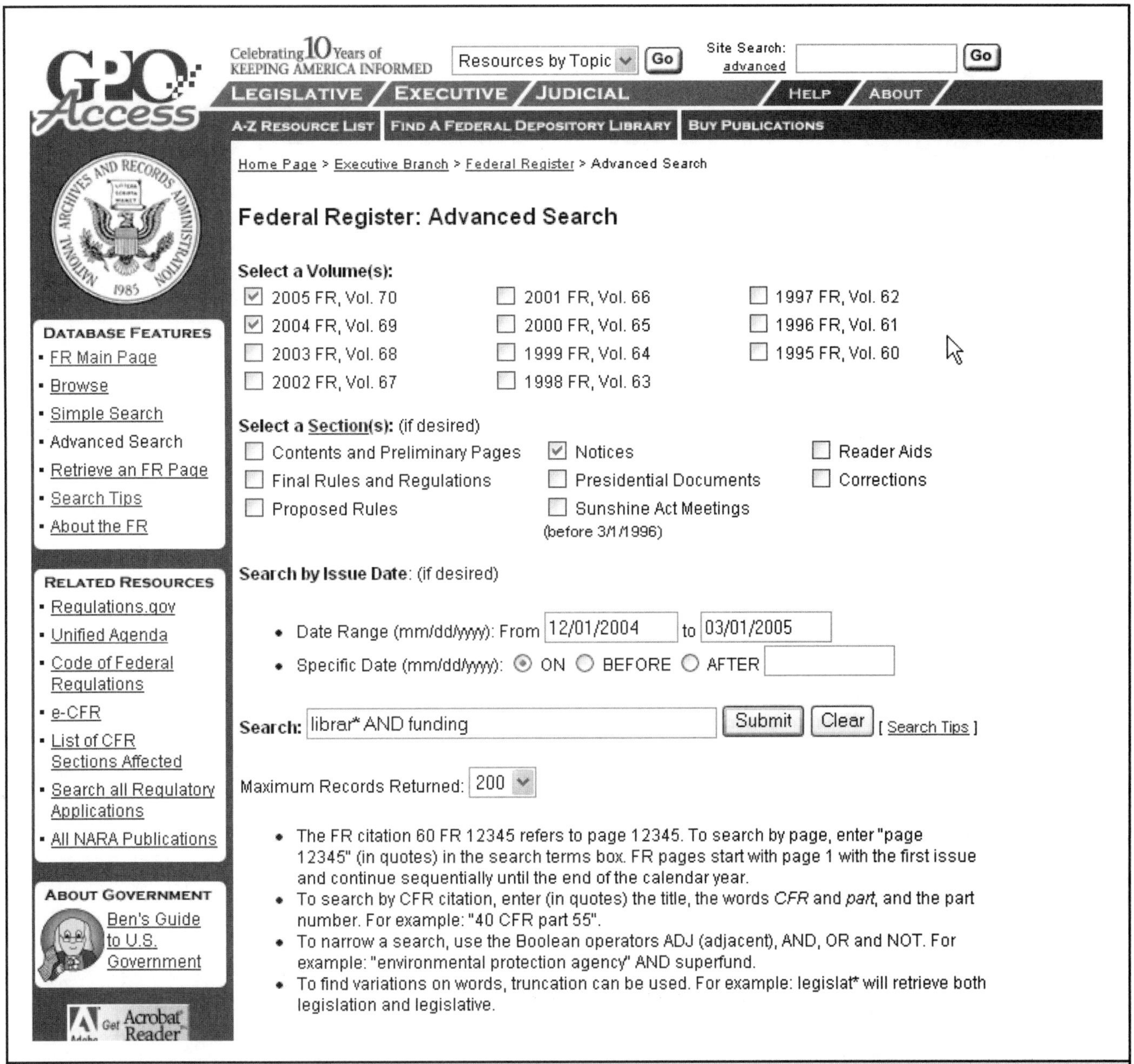

GPO Access

Celebrating 10 Years of KEEPING AMERICA INFORMED | Resources by Topic | Go | Site Search: advanced | Go

LEGISLATIVE / EXECUTIVE / JUDICIAL / HELP / ABOUT

A-Z RESOURCE LIST | FIND A FEDERAL DEPOSITORY LIBRARY | BUY PUBLICATIONS

Home Page > Executive Branch > Federal Register > Advanced Search

Federal Register: Advanced Search

Select a Volume(s):

- [x] 2005 FR, Vol. 70
- [x] 2004 FR, Vol. 69
- [ ] 2003 FR, Vol. 68
- [ ] 2002 FR, Vol. 67
- [ ] 2001 FR, Vol. 66
- [ ] 2000 FR, Vol. 65
- [ ] 1999 FR, Vol. 64
- [ ] 1998 FR, Vol. 63
- [ ] 1997 FR, Vol. 62
- [ ] 1996 FR, Vol. 61
- [ ] 1995 FR, Vol. 60

Select a Section(s): (if desired)

- [ ] Contents and Preliminary Pages
- [ ] Final Rules and Regulations
- [ ] Proposed Rules
- [x] Notices
- [ ] Presidential Documents
- [ ] Sunshine Act Meetings (before 3/1/1996)
- [ ] Reader Aids
- [ ] Corrections

Search by Issue Date: (if desired)

- Date Range (mm/dd/yyyy): From 12/01/2004 to 03/01/2005
- Specific Date (mm/dd/yyyy): ON BEFORE AFTER

Search: librar* AND funding | Submit | Clear | [Search Tips]

Maximum Records Returned: 200

- The FR citation 60 FR 12345 refers to page 12345. To search by page, enter "page 12345" (in quotes) in the search terms box. FR pages start with page 1 with the first issue and continue sequentially until the end of the calendar year.
- To search by CFR citation, enter (in quotes) the title, the words *CFR* and *part*, and the part number. For example: "40 CFR part 55".
- To narrow a search, use the Boolean operators ADJ (adjacent), AND, OR and NOT. For example: "environmental protection agency" AND superfund.
- To find variations on words, truncation can be used. For example: legislat* will retrieve both legislation and legislative.

DATABASE FEATURES
- FR Main Page
- Browse
- Simple Search
- Advanced Search
- Retrieve an FR Page
- Search Tips
- About the FR

RELATED RESOURCES
- Regulations.gov
- Unified Agenda
- Code of Federal Regulations
- e-CFR
- List of CFR Sections Affected
- Search all Regulatory Applications
- All NARA Publications

ABOUT GOVERNMENT
Ben's Guide to U.S. Government

Get Acrobat Reader

Figure 6-4. Federal Register Search Screen

From the search page, you may also select "Browse by Category" or "Browse by Agency" to do your broad search. When you browse by Agency, don't forget to look at the list of federal government agencies that fund libraries, clearinghouses, archives, and technical information services mentioned in Chapter 5, such as the Department of Education, Department of Health and Human Services, National Endowment for the Arts, National

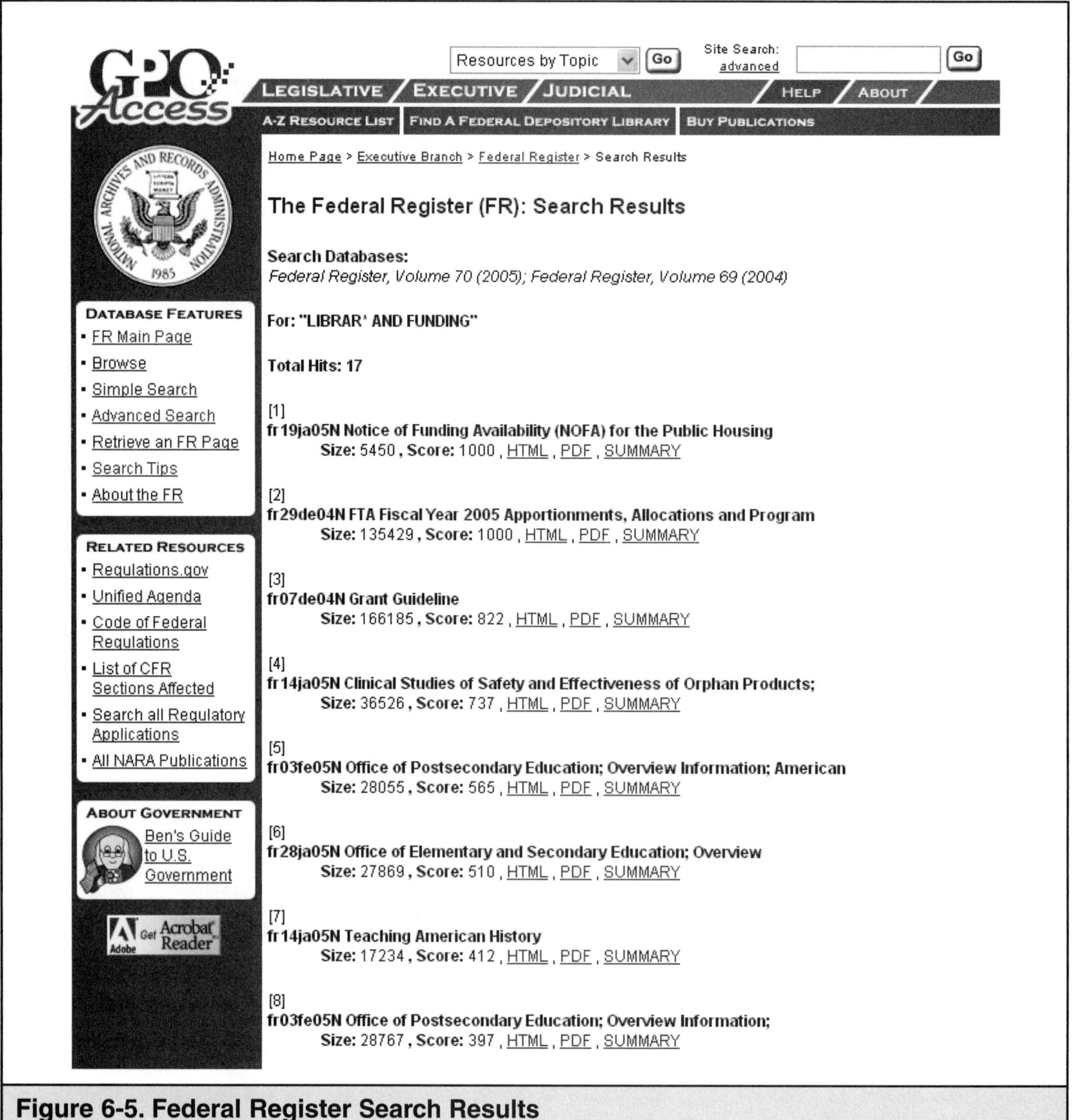

Figure 6-5. Federal Register Search Results

Grantors Applicants EBiz About Us Resources P.L. 106-107 Privacy FAQs Site Map HELP
GRANTS.GOV℠
Get Started | Find Grant Opportunities | Apply For Grants | Customer Support

FIND
Search Grant Opportunities
Receive Grant Opportunity Emails

QUICK LINKS
Access the most requested information and features.
Select A Topic

RESOURCES
Posted Grant Opportunities within last 7 days
Available Grant Application Packages
Types of Grants
Grant Making Agencies
Additional Grant Resources
Get Adobe Reader
Word Viewer

Home > Find Grant Opportunities > Search Grant Opportunities

Search Grant Opportunities

Basic Search | Browse by Category | Browse by Agency | Advanced Search — Search Tips

To perform a **basic search** for a grant, complete the "Keyword Search"; the "Search by Funding Opportunity Number"; **OR** the "Search by CFDA Number" field; and then click the "Start Search" button below.

Access Search Tips for helpful search strategies, or click the Help button in the upper right corner to get help with this screen.

Keyword Search: librar*
Search by Funding Opportunity Number:
Search by CFDA Number:
Start Search | Clear Form

Figure 6-6. Grants.gov Search Screen

Endowment for the Humanities, Institute of Museum and Library Services, and the National Institute for Literacy. Most of these agencies, such as the Institute of Museum and Library Services, have their own Web sites (Figure 6-8) where they post the availability of grants, including application and deadline information.

RESEARCHING FOUNDATION RESOURCES

For library-related projects, the *National Guide to Funding for Libraries and Information Services* is a good place to start your broad search for foundation grants. This Foundation Center publication is arranged by state; within each state, foundations are arranged alphabetically. Each foundation is assigned an entry number for indexing purposes. Each entry includes entry number, foundation name, address, contact information, establishment data, financial data, areas of giving, types of support, limitations, publications, application information, offices and trustees, staff, and recent grants. See sample entry (Figure 6-9).

These Foundation Center *National Guides* all follow a similar format,

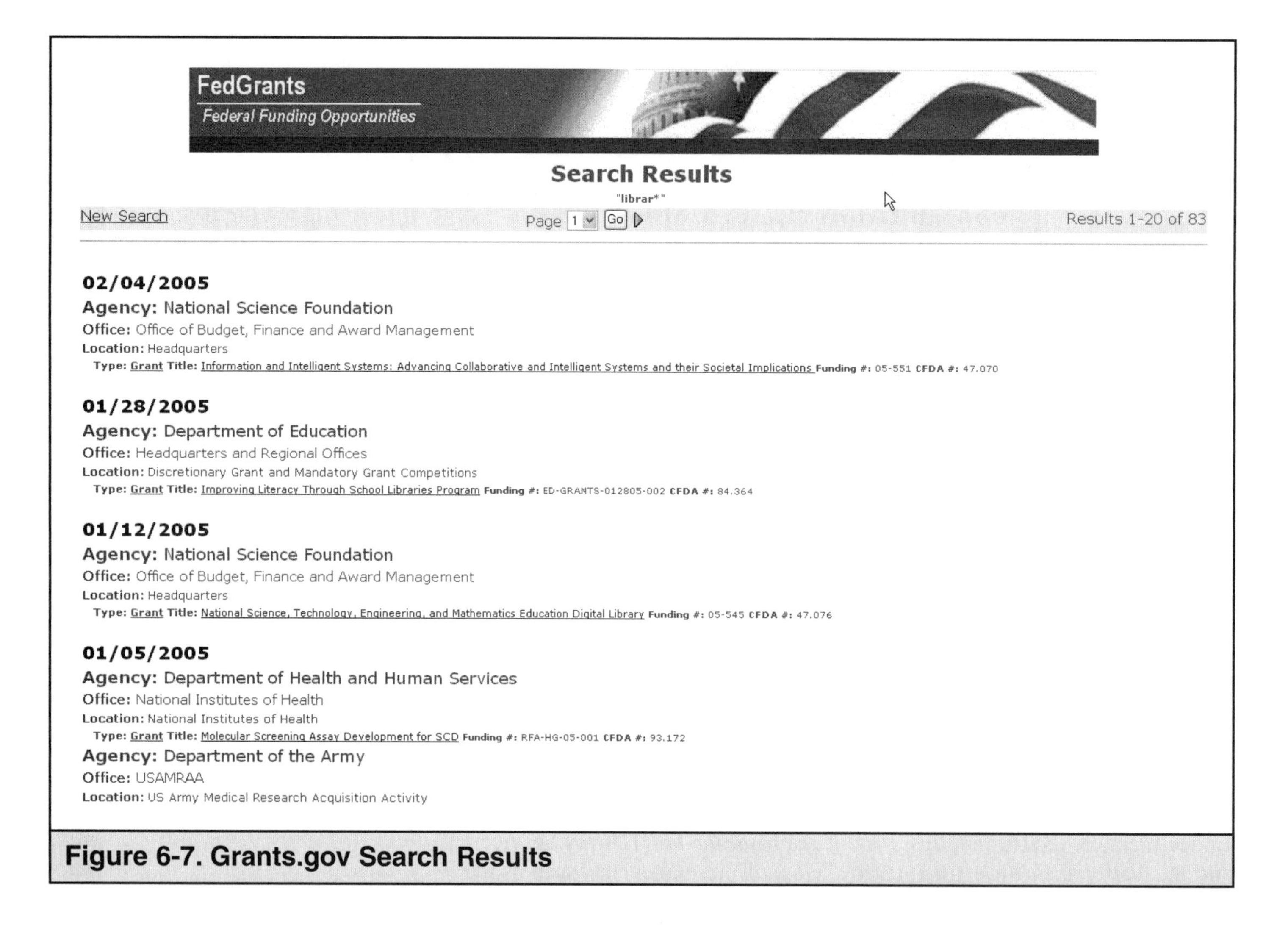

Figure 6-7. Grants.gov Search Results

which includes indexes by donors, officers, trustees, geographic location, types of support, and subject. Remember to look at other subject-specific directories that match your project, such as arts and culture, health, and education.

Narrow your search by referring to the *Foundation Directory* or the *Foundation 1000* for more in-depth information about a particular foundation. In *Grant$ for Libraries and Information Services* you will find descriptions of foundation grants of $10,000 or more awarded in the field of libraries and information services.

RESEARCHING CORPORATE RESOURCES

Many major corporations have set up their own foundations and corporate giving programs. The *National Directory of Corporate Giving* is a good

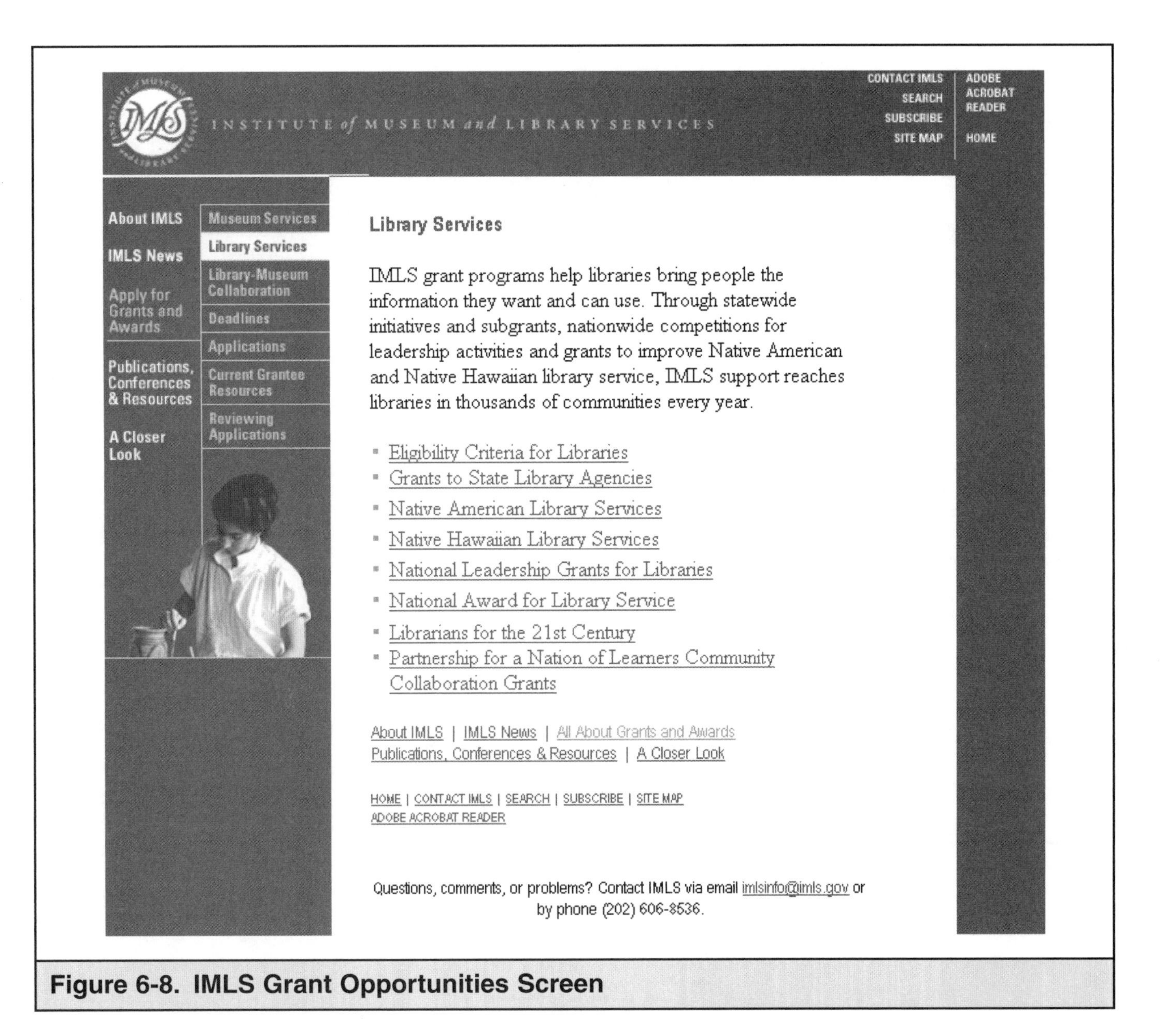

Figure 6-8. IMLS Grant Opportunities Screen

starting place as well as the Web sites for corporations that have operations facilities in your community.

1. When you visit www.mayco.com, you will see a link to "Community Involvement."
2. Follow this link to the 2003 Contributions List of $5,000 or more, where you can see a more current list of grants.
3. Then go to the Guidelines link, where you will find out how to apply.

Sample Entry

Entry number — Street address — Person to whom inquiries should be addressed — Establishment data — Areas of foundation giving — Types of grants and other types of support — Specific limitations on foundation giving by geographic area, subject focus, or types of support — Application information — Staff

Year-end date of accounting period — Assets at market value (M) or ledger value (L) — Total expenditures figure — Amount and number of grants paid — Separate information on amount and number of employee matching gifts, grants to individuals, or loans — Printed material available from the foundation — Officers and trustees or other governing bodies — Recent grants

681
The Champlin Foundations ▼
300 Centerville Rd, Ste. 300S
Warwick, RI 02886-0203 (401) 736-0370
Contact: David A. King, Exec. Dir.
FAX: (401) 736-7248; E-mail: champlinfdns@worldnet.att.net; URL: http://fdncenter.org/grantmaker/champlin

Trusts established in 1932, 1947, and 1975 in DE.
Donor(s): George S. Champlin,‡ Florence C. Hamilton,‡ Hope C. Neaves.‡
Grantmaker type: Independent foundation
Financial data (yr. ended 12/31/99): Assets, $502,288,387 (M); expenditures, $25,263,631; qualifying distributions, $22,884,344; giving activities include $22,798,134 for 310 grants (high: $2,000,000; low: $500; average: $15,000–$70,000).
Purpose and activities: Giving primarily for conservation; higher, secondary, and other education, including libraries; health and hospitals; cultural activities, including historic preservation; scientific activities; and social and family services, including programs for youth and the elderly.
Fields of interest: Arts/cultural programs; libraries/library science; education; environment; animal welfare; family planning; health care; human services; youth, services; science.
Types of support: Capital campaigns; building/renovation; equipment; land acquisition.
Limitations: Giving primarily in RI. No support for religious schools, books, films, videos, or plays. No grants to individuals, or for general support, program or operating budgets, matching gifts, special projects, research, publications, conferences, or continuing support; no loans.
Publications: Program policy statement.
Application information: No grants are awarded on a continuing basis, but applicants may qualify annually. Application form not required.
Initial approach: 1-page letter
Copies of proposal: 1
Deadline(s): Submit public school requests by May 31 if invited; submit all other requests between Mar. 1 and June 30; deadline June 30
Board meeting date(s): Nov.
Final notification: After Nov. meeting
Distribution Committee: David A. King, Exec. Dir.; John Gorham, Louis R. Hampton.
Number of staff: 3 full-time professional; 1 part-time professional; 1 full-time support; 1 part-time support.
Recent grants for library/information services:
681-1 Barrington Public Library, Barrington, RI, $62,850. For PCs, switch, tape check, edge repair system, DVD collection, music CD's, special needs equipment, large print books, window film and carpeting. 1999.
681-2 Brownell Library, Little Compton, RI, $10,850. For switches, computers, software and printers to complement CLAN equipment. 1999.

For a complete listing of data elements, see "How to Use the *National Guide to Funding for Libraries & Information Services*" in the Introduction. Please refer to the actual entry to view the information for this foundation in its entirety.

Symbols

- ▼ Identifies foundations for which in-depth descriptions have been prepared for inclusion in the Foundation Center's *Foundation 1000*.
- ‡ Indicates individual is deceased.
- (L) Ledger value of assets.
- (M) Market value of assets.
- * Officer is also a trustee or director.

Figure 6-9. Sample Entry from *National Guide to Funding for Libraries and Information Services*

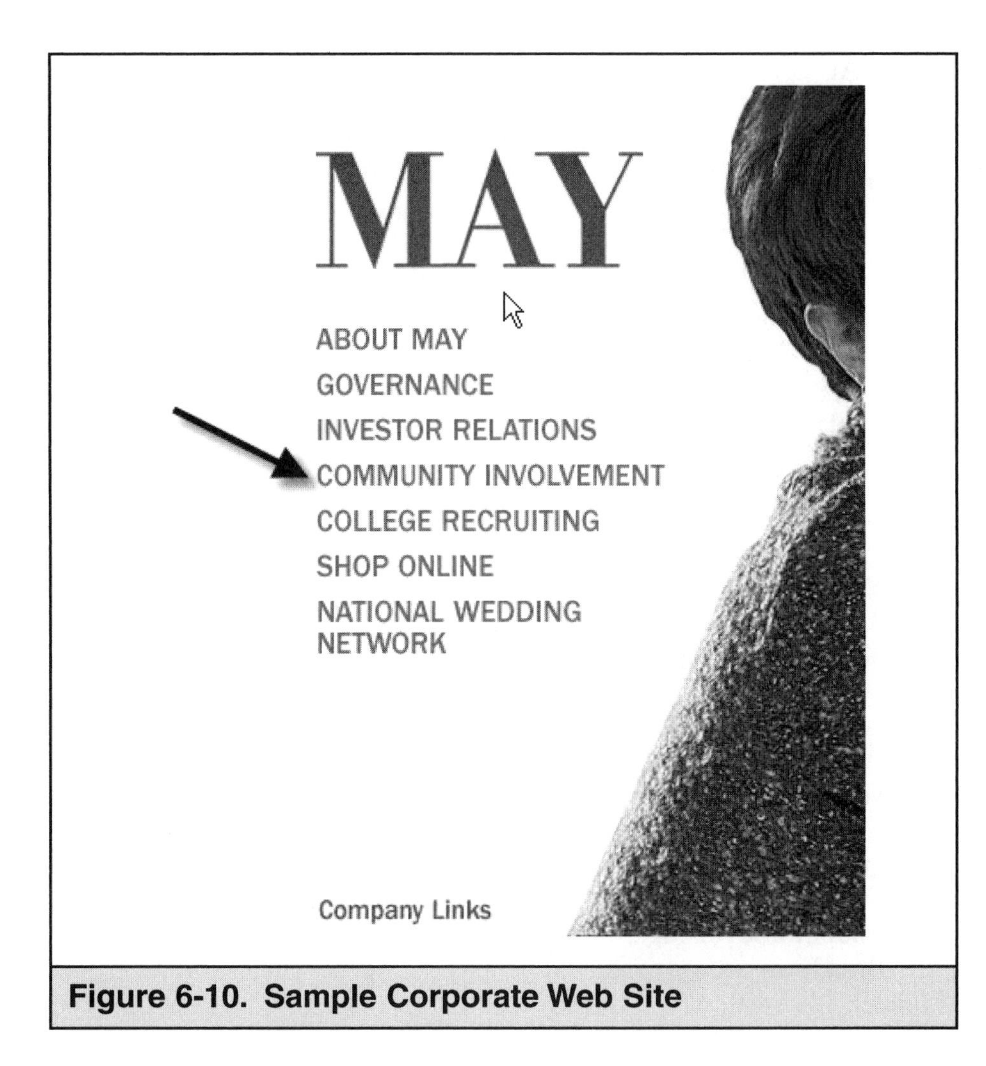

Figure 6-10. Sample Corporate Web Site

READ PUBLICATIONS, JOIN ELECTRONIC DISCUSSION GROUPS, BLOGS, AND USE ELECTRONIC ALERT SERVICES

Electronic Alert Services

At the Foundation Center Web site you can subscribe to the *RFP Bulletin* http://fdncenter.org/pnd/rfp/, which is published weekly. Each RFP listing provides a brief overview of a current funding opportunity offered by a foundation or other grant-making organization.

At Grants.gov you can sign up to receive grants announcements from the Federal Grants Notification Service. After subscribing, you will receive announcements of both new grants and modifications of existing grant announcements. Four registration options are available: all notices for selected notices based on funding opportunity number; all notices from selected agencies and categories of funding activities; all notices from selected interest and eligibility groups; all grant notices. Grants .gov also offers an option to view all grant opportunities posted in the last 7 days.

Periodicals

Chronicle of Philanthropy
Biweekly
www.philanthropy.com

Grants for Libraries Hotline
Quinlan Publishing Group
23 Drydock Ave.
Boston 02210-2387
www.quinlan.com

Grassroots Fundraising Journal
3781 Broadway
Oakland, CA 94011

Electronic Discussion Groups
Charity Channel Forums are online discussion groups related to funding: www.charitychannel.com.

Blogs
We've created a Web page especially for grant opportunities for libraries. It is updated regularly. Visit it at http://librarygrants.blogspot.com/.

LOCAL RESOURCES

Don't forget to look at local opportunities. Start with your local or state funding directory. Visit your local community foundation to use its library or collection of information on local corporations and foundations.

Talk to the people at your community foundation. Their business is to match funders with organizations like yours. Visit your community foundation's Web site for announcements of grant opportunities and application guidelines. Talk to friends and contacts that are associated with local entities that may fund projects like yours. Visit with your chamber of commerce and local clubs to tell them about your project. Look at a local corporation or foundation Web site for detailed information about its community involvement. Ask your board for help in connecting with potential funders in your community. Watch the local newspaper for articles about grants given to other nonprofits in your community and follow up with the funders. Join your local chapter of the Association of Fundraising Professionals.

Read your local nonprofit newsletters and your state library association newsletter or local public library association or special library association chapter newsletter for announcements of recently funded library projects in your area. Contact your colleagues at these libraries and ask how they did it, what project is their, what the process was, and with whom they did work at the funding source.

TALK WITH FUNDERS

"[The most important element of a successful grant is] good writing, careful needs assessment and figuring out what the grantor likes to fund." Becky Heil, Dubuque County Library, Farley, Iowa.

Throughout your research, as you work with your Funding Research Worksheets, you will be contacting funders to clarify questions and discuss their interest in your project—all the time developing a working relationship with the contact person. At this point in your research, you should feel comfortable calling any of the contacts on your "match" list should questions or concerns arise.

Now it is time to write your proposal.

7 CREATING AND SUBMITTING THE WINNING PROPOSAL

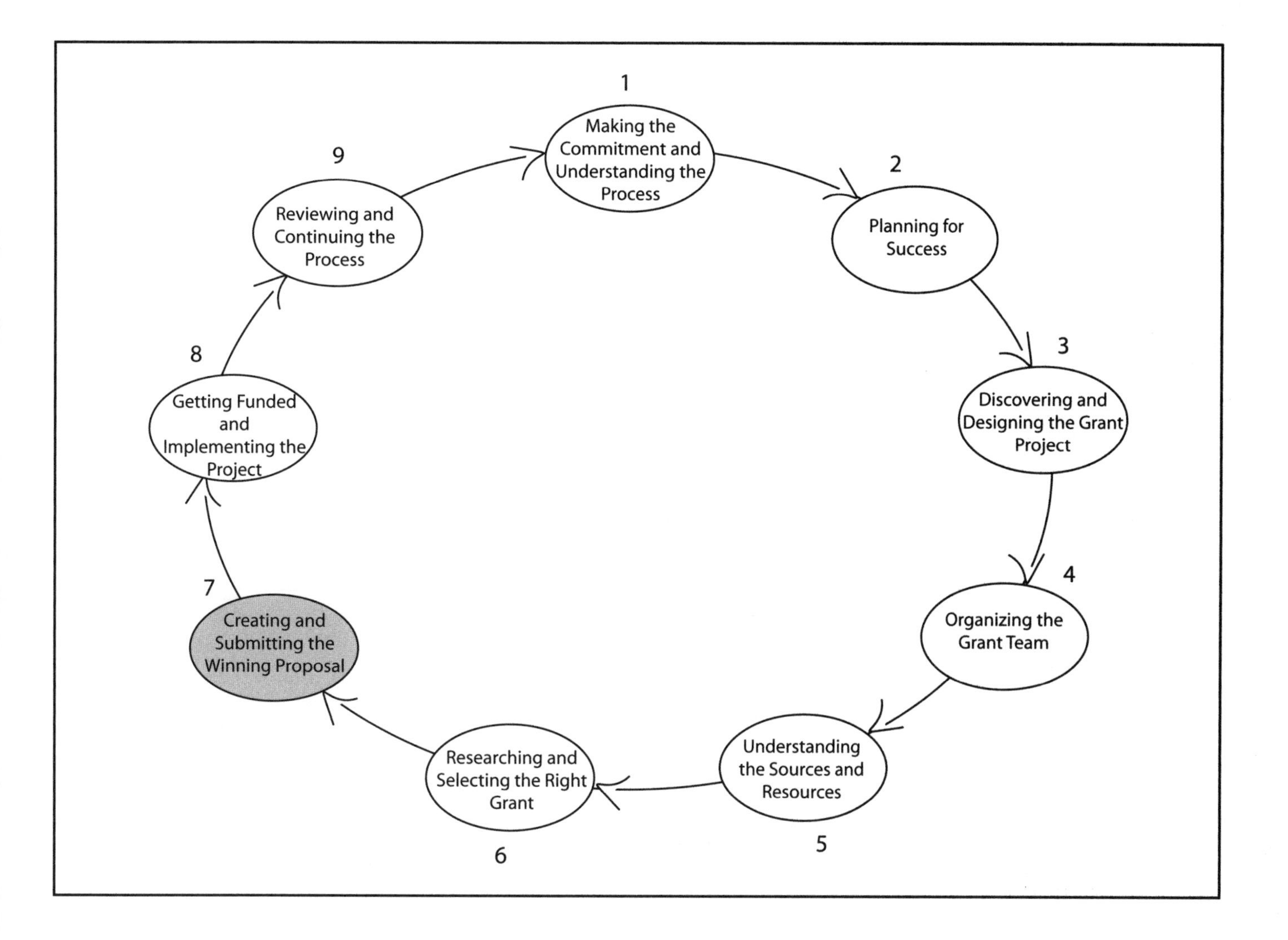

OVERVIEW

Writing the winning proposal requires good planning and organization. As we specified in earlier chapters, planning the project thoroughly is the single best thing you can do to ensure success. It is very important to realize that the beginning of the grant process doesn't start with a project. Just because you admire the senior center in a nearby town does not mean that it would fit into your community. Having a strategic plan, as the foundation of your project ensures it, supports your library's mission. Your proposal will use the plan as the road map to demonstrate that you know where you are going and how you will get there. Since your project is based on your library's plan, the funders will see that the project is tied to your mission and not just a haphazard daydream.

First read the entire grant application carefully, especially the qualifications and the evaluation criteria. You don't want to be almost finished writing a proposal when you realize that you do not qualify, that you've missed a deadline, that you needed to partner with the local health department, or that you must include services to immigrant populations. Highlight all of the questions you need to answer and make a list of the resources and materials you will need. Underline keywords or phrases you might want to incorporate into your proposal.

WRITING STYLE

Writing a proposal is different from other types of writing. Proposal writing is similar to sales or marketing work or even good storytelling. You are attempting to convince the funder to sponsor and support your idea and project. In your proposal, you are telling the story about the people in your community, the need that they have, and how your project, supported by the funder's grant, can make a positive and even life-changing impact in these people's lives. Creative storytelling techniques can be useful in demonstrating need, helping the funder see your community as real people with real problems. Your well-planned grant project with objectives and activities is the resolution to the need. Making your story come alive successfully is especially important in the Proposal Summary, as some grant reviewers may use only this one section of your grant to judge your entire proposal.

Display confidence and capability by approaching your project with the belief that it will be successful. Use language throughout your proposal that shows positive assurance. Demonstrate your ability to achieve the stated objectives. Your grant must show that you will be able to implement the project with success. Be persuasive but reinforce your claims with plans, as bravado alone will not impress a funder. Be specific and include your goals, measurable objectives, and outcomes. Proposals should also be concise. Elaborations should add depth and scope, insight, and interest. The proposal will be judged on content, not weight.

For a powerful and energetic proposal, do not use passive verbs, such as *was and were,* or static verbs such as *am, is, are, be, have, do, could, should, would.* Use active verbs instead, such as the following examples.

Active Verbs

achieve	coordinate	direct	identify	instruct	motivate
analyze	create	educate	illuminate	investigate	organize
assess	decide	elevate	illustrate	involve	plan
assist	define	engage	implement	lead	prepare
change	demonstrate	ensure	indicate	learn	promote
conclude	design	establish	inform	maintain	provide
connect	develop	evaluate	inspire	manage	validate

Be prepared to write one or more drafts, as you want your proposal to be concise and easily understood. You certainly don't want to have a grant rejected due to typographical errors. Let as many people as possible read your proposal and get their feedback. Especially helpful are those who are not connected to the library or the project. Even a family member could provide an interesting and helpful perspective. Just ask them to read your proposal for 15 minutes and tell you what they understood. This may be more time than most preliminary reviewers will give your proposal on the first read-through. They can also catch any use of library lingo or acronyms that might be confusing to a grant reviewer. If they didn't immediately see the value of what you want to achieve, rewrite it until it is clear. We've reviewed some grant proposals in which we were unable to discern exactly what funding the library was asking for. It should not be difficult to understand exactly how much you are requesting or for what purpose.

PROJECT PARTNERS AND COLLABORATORS

"Be sure to develop community support for your project. When ever possible, collaborate with another agency in planning and implementing your grant. There's a great deal more 'bang for your buck' when you work with someone else." Clermont County Public Library Success Story, see page 174.

Emphasize collaboration and partnerships throughout your proposal. Funders will admire that you are planning for sustainability and ensuring future community support. Collaborating with other organizations is also a beneficial way to share equipment, expertise, and resources. Many small nonprofits find great fulfillment in their partnerships with libraries, as often there are similar goals. Partnerships between libraries, schools, museums, religious groups, and community organizations are often successful.

APPLYING TO MULTIPLE FUNDERS

You may want to apply to more than one funder at a time. If you are submitting proposals to several different funders, you should indicate this in the proposal. For example, you might state, "In addition to your foundation, this proposal is being submitted to the Community Foundation and the Mr. Wealthy Benefactor Foundation" or "We have already received a grant of $30,000 from the Happy to Give Foundation and are requesting $15,000 from your organization, which is the balance required for the project." This will not be viewed negatively, as funders correctly consider that multiple funding sources can be a significant factor in the sustainability of projects. However, if you use the same grant proposal, make sure you customize it for each funder. Some funders have relayed that they have received proposals with other agencies' names on them. Not a very good first impression for your proposal!

REVIEWERS

As with any type of writing, it is important to keep your audience in mind—the individuals who will be reading and reviewing your proposal. More than one person will probably be evaluating your proposal. It may be a committee that reviews your proposal, with each individual reviewer scoring your proposal on established criteria. Some funders even distribute the individual sections of the proposal to different reviewers. For example, one reviewer may be focused on judging the specific project you propose to use for your grant, while a different reviewer will focus on examining the evaluation process you have specified. Some funders employ external proposal reviewers on a contract basis. These reviewers may be subject specialists, and they may be reading hundreds of grants.

Never assume any specific knowledge on the part of readers. Do not assume that they will know that libraries are commendable, or that you are automatically informed on your community's needs or that they will know what a reference librarian does or what a Summer Reading Program entails. Many grants are very competitive, which means that reviewers have a lot of proposals to read. Ensuring that your proposal is very clear and easy to comprehend will increase your chances of success.

CONTACTING THE FUNDER

Don't be apprehensive about contacting the funder if you have questions. Most charitable organizations have been created out of a desire to be part of the solution to societal problems. The reason they extend grants is to help fulfill their own missions. Funders want to give money away to meet their goals, it is their job, and they are there to help. Of course, be certain you've done your research first and that you're not asking a question already answered in their documentation. You don't want to bother a funder and become a nuisance, but if you call with a realistic inquiry, it will be welcomed. An added benefit is that the funder will be familiar with your proposal before it has been submitted. This is a good way to start building a communicative partnership with the funder. Building trust and identifying mutual goals are essential to successful grant work.

> "Work closely with staff of the granting agency. The first draft of our proposal was not fundable, but with the help of NEH [National Endowment for the Humanities] staff we were able to tailor a grant that met the needs of our library and the NEH." Clear Lake Public Library Success Story; see page 180.

QUESTIONS TO ASK FUNDERS CHECKLIST

____ Is my library eligible?

____ How are applications reviewed?

____ Are there specific screening criteria or a rubric used? Can we have a copy?

____ Can we submit a draft of the grant proposal before the final deadline for review?

____ If I briefly describe the project, would you provide suggestions or advice?

____ Are copies of successful grant proposals available?

____ Can we include our strategic plan or other supporting documentation in an appendix?

____ May we include a table of contents?

____ How and when are final decisions made?

____ Will we be notified that our grant proposal has been received?

SPECIFICATIONS

The content of the proposal should be tailored to the specifications found in the grant guidelines. This will include details such as the number of pages allowed, necessary forms, and formatting particulars. Each detail is important. If a funder receives thousands of grants, it is easy to whittle the number of applicants by rejecting those who do not comply with instructions. For example, some funders specify that proposals should not be bound, as they may need to make copies for multiple reviewers. So before you spend the extra time and funds to produce a beautifully packaged manuscript, be sure you are fulfilling the funder's specified requests.

Also, submit the required number of copies. And if the funder has specified the arrangement of the sections of the grant proposal, don't change the order, even though it makes more sense to you to do so. Match the names of the section headings in your proposal to the section headings provided in the instructions. This will allow the reviewer to easily determine that all required information is included. Reviewers should never have to search for needed information. The proposal should be neat, organized, and professional. Single-space the document unless specified otherwise. Make a checklist of the specifications so that you ensure that you've met them. A sample is included at the end of this chapter.

TYPES OF PROPOSALS

THE LETTER OF INTENT OR INQUIRY LETTER

This is a two- to three-page summary that gives a brief description of the project, the amount requested, the need, and a brief organizational overview. Funders sometimes ask for a letter of intent to be sent to them so that they can quickly decide whether it is a project that they would like to fund. If the funder accepts your letter of intent, then you will probably be asked to submit a longer, more detailed proposal. This letter should focus on how the project aligns with the funder's mission and goals. It should describe the needs and then outline the project. It should be written very succinctly, clear enough for the funder to read it quickly and make a decision as to whether he or she would like more information.

THE RFP OR APPLICATION

This is the typical grant proposal and is sometimes called a Request for Proposal (RFP) or a grant application. There are examples of corporate, government, foundation, and common grant applications included on the CD-ROM. Some funders will provide forms, while others will give guidelines or even have an online application process. There will be differing priorities and deadlines and variant approaches to the funding process. The good news is that although there are differences, most funders are essentially asking for the same information. They just may use different wording or prefer a different order. This means that once you've written one quality grant proposal, the subsequent proposals will be less challenging and will not require the same intensive background work as the first. There are also common application forms that are shared by some organizations, usually in a specific geographic area.

ONLINE PROPOSALS

Many funders, especially government organizations, are requiring proposals to be submitted online. The National Science Foundation requires all proposals to be submitted online through the FastLane system. There are usually detailed instructions with FAQs and contact information for questions related to electronic submissions. Some sites have forms that you can download to your computer, fill out, and then upload to submit. Others have only an electronic form that must be completed while connected to the Internet. For those, we've found it best to first create the proposal in a word processor; then you can easily cut and paste into the Web form. There have been proposals lost in the Ethernet, so always make sure you have a backup copy.

KEY PROPOSAL COMPONENTS

There are many ways to organize proposals. A Request for Proposal (RFP) will stipulate the requirements, and some are more detailed than others. Read the guidelines for specifications about required information and how it should be arranged. Most grant proposals are usually fifteen pages or less. Government grants may require that you fill out lengthy forms. The Grants for Libraries Tool Kit contains a Grant Proposal Template on page 220 that includes all the common components. You can also access this template on the CD-ROM and fill it out with your library's information. Also included in the tool kit are sample successful grant proposals from libraries of different types from across the United States and an Example Grant Proposal from our fictitious library, Exemplar on the companion CDROM. Following are the most standard grant proposal components, many of which you've already written as part of your project planning.

Title Sheet
Cover Letter
Table of Contents
Proposal Summary
Organizational Overview
Statement of Needs
Project Description
Approach/Methodology
Budget Request
Evaluation Process
Appendix

TITLE SHEET

This is your opportunity to display creativity and develop an ingenious title for your project or program—something that the grant reviewer will remember. However, don't let this be a stumbling block; if you are not particularly inspired, a title that is descriptive and informative is perfectly acceptable as well. You should also include the name of the funder to whom you are directing the proposal, the name and address of the submitting library, and the date.

COVER LETTER

This is a basic letter outlining your proposal. This cover letter sets the tone for your proposal and should therefore be convincing. It should be easy to read, interesting, and comprehensive. Anyone reading this cover letter should be able to quickly determine exactly what your organization does, the purpose or reason for your request, and the amount of the request.

Keep it to one page and use your organization's letterhead. The header should include the date, the name of the contact person at the funding organization, the name and address of the funding organization, the title of your grant, and the date.

Include:

- Pleasure in submitting grant in order to serve your target audience
- Names of Grant Project Partners
- Grant Project Title
- One to two sentences from your Statement of Needs
- One to two sentences from your Project Description, including outcomes
- Two to three sentences from your Organizational Overview
- Funding Requested and any in-kind, matching, or outside grant funds
- Any planning and involvement of the target audience completed

Conclude by offering to provide additional information, if any is needed. The library director or another authority should sign the cover letter.

TABLE OF CONTENTS

Just like in a book, this will help organize your proposal and make it easy for reviewers to locate necessary information. In large foundations, different reviewers may be responsible for analyzing different parts of your proposal, so make sure each section can be comprehended independently. If it is not specified in the guidelines that you should include a table of contents, this may be one of the questions you should ask the funder.

PROPOSAL SUMMARY

Although this section appears at the beginning of the proposal, it should probably be written last. This ensures that it contains all the information included in the proposal. The summary will essentially be a condensed form of your entire proposal. There should not be anything in your summary that is not in your proposal. It is your infomercial, your 3-minute advertisement. This summary serves as the first impression and can be critical to the success of the proposal. It may be carefully scrutinized to determine if the rest of the proposal should even be considered, so it needs to be able to stand on its own.

The Grant Proposal Template in the Grants for Libraries Tool Kit on page 220 and on the CD-ROM contains a basic outline.

Include:

- Library's Exact Legal Name and Full Mailing Address
- Contact Information for the Library Director and the Grant Coordinator
- Project Title
- Project Description (one sentence from your Project Planning Worksheet)
- Amount Requested
- Project Funding from Other Sources
- Total Project Budget
- Project Budget Time Period
- Grant Abstract

In the Grant Abstract, you should be succinct, sell your idea, and make your point precisely. In 500 words or less, you should present your whole case: what you want to do, why it's important, why you will succeed, and how much it will cost. It should be immediately clear why your project is unique and so compelling that the funder will want to immediately read your entire proposal. Be sure to avoid any library jargon that may be unclear or unfamiliar to the reviewer. This abstract should tie into the funder's mission and display the impact of your project and how the project will help fulfill the funder's goals.

Include:

- A few sentences summarizing the library's Organizational Overview, which will show why the library is the best choice for implementing the grant project.
- Any partners and how they are contributing.
- The Needs Statement, as well as the Target Audience.
- A few sentences from the Project Description detailing what the project entails and how it fulfills the needs.
- The Project Goals, Objectives, and/or Outcomes.
- A brief overview of the Evaluation Plan to be used.
- How the funder's mission aligns with your grant project.

ORGANIZATIONAL OVERVIEW

Before a funder will invest in a program, he or she must be certain that the funding will be managed by a capable, dependable, effective organization.

Your overview is one of the first areas a funder will use to judge the integrity of your organization. This is your opportunity to sell what you do. Libraries have an instant reputation of credibility and trust but remember that not everyone understands everything a library does, so don't be too general. Libraries are the center of communities, but to some people, they represent only books and reading.

Detail your history, mission, whom you serve, achievements, primary programs, current budget, leadership, board members, and key staff members. Brief success stories and human interest can be included but should be relevant to the project and to the funder's interests. Answer the questions, Who are we? and How are we qualified and Why should we be trusted? A funder needs to be able to deem your organization as trustworthy and reliant for a true partnership to develop. Having a strategic plan is another way to demonstrate that your organization is well managed. If an appendix of supporting material is allowed, including the plan can be beneficial.

Granting agencies want to make the best use of their funding and want to be assured that your project will be successful and help fulfill both your mission and theirs. If you've done your research, your organization should be a good match with the funder, so as they are reading your overview, they should immediately recognize similarities in mission, vision, and goals. Your goal in writing this section of your proposal is for the reviewers to think to themselves, Hey, they are just like us; we want to accomplish the same things!

STATEMENT OF NEEDS (PROBLEM STATEMENT)

In this section you will describe the current situation in your community and how your project will address it. There should be a compelling, logical reason why the proposal should be supported and is important. Start with the facts and then move on to the solution. This is not a list of wants but the need for your project that will bring about a change in your target audience. You will include your needs assessment and show what your community really does require. Support this assessment by including qualified research and evidence to justify the need. Use both statistics and local human interest stories for supporting examples. Include data that are historical, geographic, quantitative, and factual. Identify any other existing projects being implemented in your community that are related to the problem.

Avoid describing the need for your project as the problem. Not having enough computers at your library is not the problem. Rather, the problem is the increase of deaths due to preventable illness and lack of health literacy. Providing more consumer health materials and health-related programming on a free online health database is a better solution. Explain how you will attempt to fulfill the need. Define what you are going to do.

Don't focus on the state or the country's needs but the needs of your specific and unique community. The exact target population should be identified. Many funders are interested in knowing that the people who will benefit in the program are actually supportive of the grant. If the audience has had input and assisted with designing the program, make sure you include this information. Projects that are created without this involvement and input are less likely to be successful.

Then prove why the library has the ability to respond to the need you have identified. Link the fulfillment of the need to your library's mission.

Answer the questions:

Why this issue?
Why this target population?
Why this funder?
Why your library?

PROJECT DESCRIPTION

This section includes an overview of your project. It is a more in-depth narrative than the project summary. In the previous section you discussed the needs; now you will focus on the solutions. Acknowledge that you are aware of several solutions and that you have chosen the approach that will be most successful. State the advantages and any limitations of the solutions.

You should explain the significance of your project. Clarify how your work differs from, is related to, or extends earlier work. Back this up with research that proves it. Funders are more inclined toward a well-thought-out project that includes assurances of sustainability and appropriate use of the funds. Funders want to fund projects that will be successful, and these are often the indicators.

Don't assume that the reader is familiar with the subject. You could include articles in the appendix to support topics with which they may be unfamiliar. For example, if requesting a computer lab, you could include studies done on public access computing, the digital divide, and the number of people who use library computers. It is especially important to have someone outside of your organization review for you to make sure it is easy to comprehend the plans for your project.

Include information on your target population, specifically, the number to be served, how you will attract them to the project, and how you will involve them. You may have more than one target population. For example, a reading program may involve children and their parents.

Sustainability of projects can be the biggest obstacle. Funders realize this and are more likely to favor libraries that address this issue in their proposals. Having partners and supporters and showing that you are investigating other sources of funding for the future prove your project isn't short-term but a project that is worth investing in and supporting. Also include any ways that the project implementation would be able to leverage impact for other library goals or for other community needs.

Mention if research or planning has begun. This will enable the funder to see that you are prepared and committed to the implementation of the project. Some funders would rather support new activities and programs rather than existing ones. They would like to be connected to something original, exciting, groundbreaking. They want to see that their funding will make a difference.

Include:

- Project Significance (include one or two sentences developed from the Need Statement)
- Target Audience
- Project Goals
- Project Objectives
- Project Partners
- Plans for Sustainability and Leveraging Impact

APPROACH/METHODOLOGY

This section also requires a lot of detail. You have identified project activities from your goals and objectives. These activities will define how you are going to accomplish your project goals. In your timeline you will estimate the length of each phase of your project, from the day you receive your grant check through the months or even years of your project's duration. All resources should be specified, from printing costs to staffing needs. Specify any in-kind resources that your organization will provide for this project, as they will demonstrate existing support of the project. This may be portrayed through a calendar format with start and end dates, project activities, and outcomes listed. If you are unsure of specific dates, you can instead break the timeline into months, for example, months 1–2: recruit and hire temporary employees; months 3–4: form advisory committees; publish Web site. See Chapter 3 for more information on creating timelines and use the Project Timeline Template in the Grants for Libraries Tool Kit on page 211 and on the CD-ROM.

BUDGET REQUEST

Budgets are cost projections and should be very detailed. Some funders will provide mandatory budget forms that must be submitted with the proposal, while others are less specific. Costs should be reasonable with thorough explanations. Although it may be difficult to calculate some of the necessities, make a good effort. Taking the time to obtain estimates instead of guessing will not only keep your budget detailed but also ensure that you really have enough funds to cover what you want to do. You most likely want to involve your fiscal office or financial administrators at this point, as they may have a better awareness of costs. Include an outside evaluator if necessary to be certain your budget is correct. Incorrect balancing of the budget is one of the most common errors in grant proposals and can lead the funder to mistakenly conclude that your proposal may contain other inaccuracies as well.

Include other funding sources and efforts to supplement this grant request, including the financial commitment of your organization (often called in-kind contributions). This can include office space, computer labs or equipment, and personnel salaries. Few funders want to support an entire project. Like most nonprofits, libraries never have enough funding, so when a funder sees that a library is willing to dedicate a portion of its budget to a project, it demonstrates the importance and support of the initiative. This also proves your organization's commitment to the project and indications for future sustainability. Funders also value matching funds and support from other sources, so include partners' contributions as well.

Be flexible about your budget in case the funder chooses to negotiate costs. If the funder gives no specifications regarding the budget, you should make sure to include the following expenses: personnel expenses, direct project expenses, and administrative expenses.

Personnel Expenses This area consists of the salaries or a portion of salaries for everyone who will have a role working with the project. You may include payroll taxes and benefits, such as insurance. If you are hiring contractors who will be working specifically only on this project, you can include either the flat fee or hourly wage you will be paying them.

Direct Project Expenses These are expenses that occur as a result of the project. They may include travel (related to the project), photocopies, postage fees, supplies, advertising, marketing, space rentals (in addition to existing space), equipment, fees for outside evaluators, and publications.

Administrative/Overhead These are costs that would be part of your annual budget, regardless of whether your library implements the grant project. This would include the cost of the library building, utilities, phone and other telecommunication costs, insurance, taxes, security systems, and maintenance costs. Some funders will not cover overhead costs, while others will specify a flat percentage acceptable for inclusion. Depending on the funder, personnel costs may be included as overhead as well.

For help writing and organizing your grant budget, use the Budget Templates in the Grants for Libraries Tool Kit on pages 212–213 and the CD-ROM.

EVALUATION PROCESS

Evaluation is basically a method to examine, monitor, and determine the effectiveness of a project or activity. Evaluation aids in determining project success and helping to communicate that success to the funders and to your community. It is important to know what the funders expect from you when it comes to evaluation. Most funders are very interested in ensuring that the funding and resources that they provided were used for a successful purpose. Evaluating your project and sharing that information are another way to sustain the partnership you have developed with your funder.

Funders do not always use the same vocabulary when it comes to outcomes and objectives. The definitions for goals, outcomes, objectives, and activities can vary widely by funder. What one funder considers an outcome another may consider an objective. If a funder uses an example in the grant guidelines, use it as a model to form the goals, outcomes, and objectives for your proposal, even if that means changing the wording from your original project plan. If a funder specifies in the grant guidelines that outcome-based evaluation is required, then you must make sure your evaluation plan encompasses this kind of results measurement. If you are not sure about their use of terms or evaluation requirements, call the funder and ask. Remember that you are trying to identify a desired change and measure that change, and regardless of what the funder calls it, you probably have the same intent, even if you don't use the same terminology.

Using your project's goals, outcomes, objectives to measure progress and success will help your project keep on-track through implementation and evaluation. The Project Evaluation Plan introduced in Chapter 3 will be helpful in writing this component of your proposal. Use the Evaluation Plan Template in the Grants for Libraries Tool Kit on page 214 or on the CD-ROM. Make sure you also review the Key Considerations for Writing an Evaluation Plan on page 77.

APPENDIX

Find out if supporting materials are desired or allowed. Supporting materials are often arranged in an appendix. These materials may endorse the project and the applicant, provide mission statements and certifications, add information about project personnel, consultants, and board members, or include tables and charts related to statistics. Some funders will ask for financial statements, annual budgets, an Internal Revenue Service (IRS) letter confirming that your organization is tax-exempt, or additional articles or subject matter information.

Endorsements from supporting or partnering organizations may be included. Find support for your proposal from partners, other types of libraries, politicians, professionals, local government agencies, or public officials. The State Librarian or the State Library Association president may be willing to write a letter of support. Endorsements are especially important for federal funding.

Policies about the inclusion of supporting materials differ widely among funders. Whether to allow them usually depends upon how materials contribute to a proposal's evaluation. Restrictions are often based on volume, bias, and relevance. Be prepared to invest the time to collect resources, document capability, update a résumé, and obtain letters or reports.

If a curriculum vitae (CV) or resume of participating staff members is requested, make sure to include:

- Education: degrees, years awarded, fields of study, institutions, locations.
- Professional work experience: position, institution and location, dates of employment.
- Honors and awards.
- Relevant publications.
- Qualifications and responsibilities associated with the grant.

AUTHORIZED SIGNATURES

Authorized signatures are usually required. Proposals may be rejected for lack of a specified signature. Be sure to allow the time to acquire all needed signatures. The last thing you want to find out is that a necessary signatory is on vacation the week your proposal is due.

GRANT PROPOSAL CHECKLIST

Here are some major criteria against which your proposal may be judged. Read through your application repeatedly and ask whether the answers to the following questions are clear, even to a nonlibrarian.

____ Does the proposal address a well-formulated problem or need?

____ Is it a real need of your community, or are you just trying to find a reason to justify a project you think would be fun to implement?

____ Is it an important problem, whose solution will have useful effects?

____ Is special funding necessary to solve the problem, or could it be solved using existing library resources?

____ Is there a good idea on which to base the project work? The proposal must explain the idea in sufficient detail to convince the reader that the idea has significant substance and should explain why there is reason to believe that it is indeed a good idea.

____ Does the proposal explain clearly what work will be done? Does it explain what results are expected and how they will be evaluated? How would it be possible to judge whether the work was successful?

____ Is there evidence that the library knows about the work that others have done on the problem?

____ Does the library have a good track record with grants, and will the library leadership be committed to implementation of this grant project?

SUBMITTING YOUR APPLICATION

Now that you have written the proposal, you are ready to submit your application, but first, make a checklist and go through it carefully, item by item, to make sure that you have followed all the directions and guidelines. You want to double-check that you have included everything the funder requested.

You don't want your application disqualified on a technicality, for instance, if you single-spaced when the funder specified that the application must be double-spaced; if you included brochures about your library programs in the appendix when they clearly stated not to include an appendix; or if you overlooked the lobbying form and forgot to include it in a federal application. After all this hard work, you don't want your application to be tossed into the trash for reasons like these. This really happens! You may think that this is silly and that they should just overlook such little details. But following the guidelines can be one of the most important steps toward success.

Funders eliminate applications that don't comply with their guidelines all the time. It makes their jobs easier—they will have fewer applications to read. This practice also eliminates candidates who don't follow directions. Usually funders have many more worthy applications than they can possibly fund. They don't have the time to deal with applications that don't comply with the instructions. Also, they don't want to give money to an organization that cannot follow directions. So, if you want the funder to read your proposal, follow the instructions and use the checklist.

The first thing we recommended you should have done with your application guidelines was to highlight all the questions you needed to answer and all the materials you needed to include. Add these items to the Submission Checklist. The Grant Submission Checklist is also available in the Grants for Libraries Tool Kit on page 232 and as a file on the CD-ROM.

GRANT SUBMISSION CHECKLIST

____ The funder is interested in receiving my proposal.

____ This proposal reflects the funder's areas of interest.

____ We have followed the instructions and guidelines of the funder's specifications.

____ Our proposal meets the page/word limits.

____ The font type and size are correct.

____ The margin size is correct.

____ The line spacing is correct.

____ We have used the specified type of paper.

____ We did not bind unless we were told we could.

____ The correct number of copies and the original were sent; we also retained a copy.

____ We included letters of support.

____ We have the specified signatures.

____ The proposal components are titled and compiled in the order specified.

  ____ Title Sheet
  ____ Cover Letter
  ____ Table of Contents
  ____ Proposal Summary

- ____ Organizational Overview
- ____ Statement of Needs
- ____ Project Description
- ____ Approach/Methodology
- ____ Budget Request
- ____ Evaluation Process
- ____ Appendix

____ The cover letter explains the project and states the total cost of the project, the amount expected from other sources, and the amount requested.

____ The project description specifies the need that will be met and how people will benefit.

____ The project description tells the whole story of your project in clear, understandable language.

____ The objectives are measurable.

____ The methodology explains how the objectives will be met.

____ The evaluation plan measures the degree to which the objectives are met.

____ The project includes partners and reflects community involvement.

____ The budget is reasonable.

____ The calculations are correct.

____ The project is sustainable.

____ There is adequate staff in the proposal to do the project.

____ There are adequate resources to do the project.

____ Your organization has the capacity to do the project.

____ There is no jargon or acronyms.

____ If there are attachments, you have confirmed that the funder allows them.

____ The proposal has been proofed by an impartial person.

____ The proposal is clear and easy to understand by someone outside the grant team.

____ Copies of the proposal were made for partners and supporters.

____ Letters of agreement from partners are included (provided funder allows them).

____ Letters from supporters are included (provided funder allows them).

____ We have met the deadline.

____ The proposal looks professional.

Now, carefully go through your application with your checklist and check off every item as you make sure it is in place. Once everything is checked, you may seal the envelope and head for the post office.

____ The proposal was submitted.

____ We have a dated receipt or confirmation that the proposal was submitted.

FOLLOW-UP

Now, take a deep breath and congratulate yourselves for a job well done!

Wait one week and then contact the funding source to make sure that they received your proposal. Confirm that you are the contact person for your proposal and double-check that they have your correct phone number and e-mail. Let them know that you want to be notified about the status, evaluation, and outcome of your proposal.

It is important to request feedback about your proposal's strengths and weaknesses, although this information is sometimes unavailable, especially with a large volume of submissions. This information may also be useful if you choose to approach the same or different funder again with your idea.

8 GETTING FUNDED AND IMPLEMENTING THE PROJECT

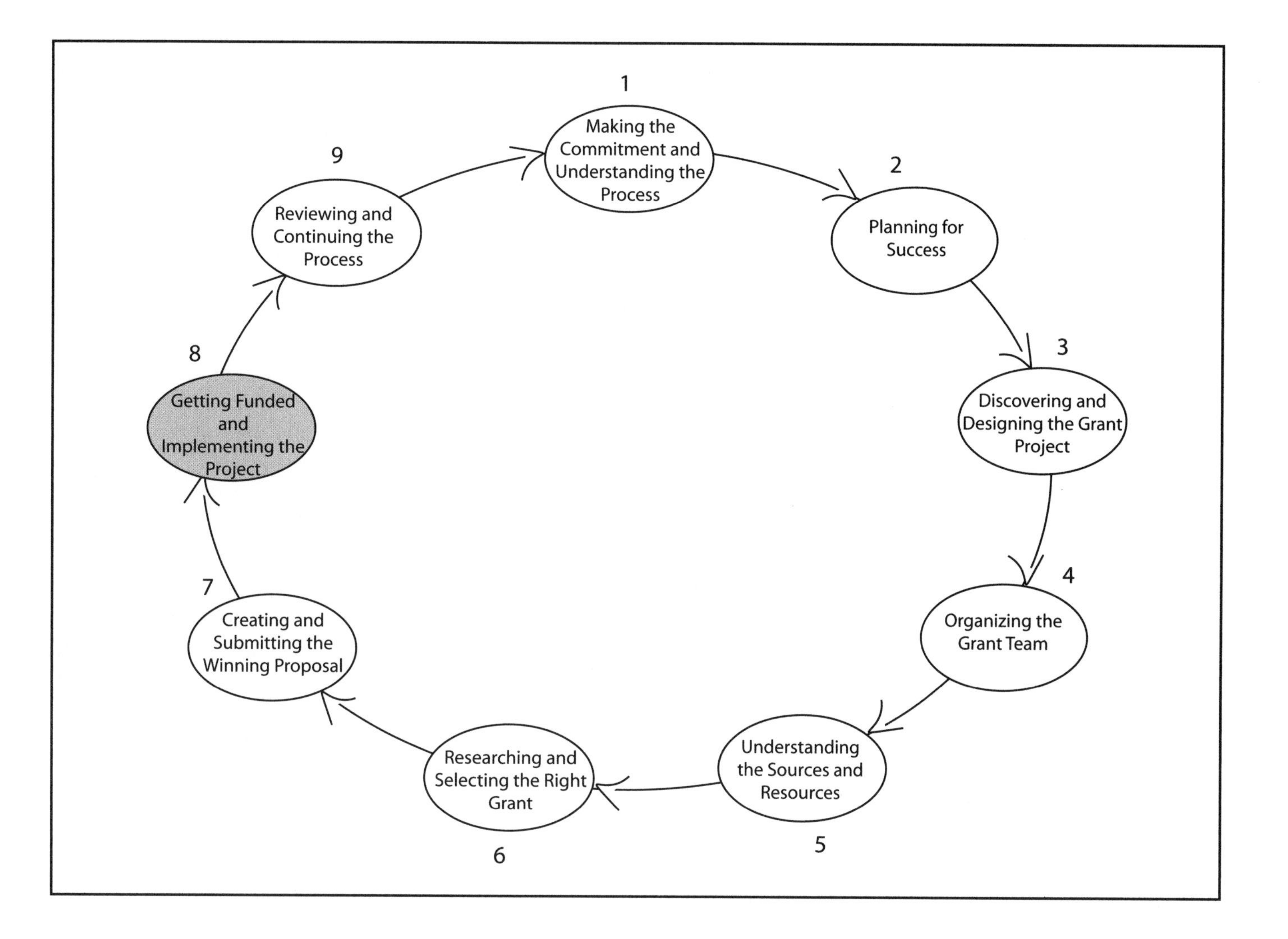

AFTER YOU SUBMIT YOUR APPLICATION

The process that funders use to evaluate proposals is as varied as there are numbers of funders. Some funders send proposals to reviewers who rate proposals based on a predetermined scoring system. Other rating systems may include review committees, government officials, a panel of experts, and community-based reviewers. The process could be a multiphase process where your proposal is first rated by an expert in the field of your project, such as literacy programs, and then by a foundation advisory board. If the process is not outlined in the grant guidelines, you should be able to find out this information by calling your contact at the funding agency. It sometimes helps to know their timeline, so you will know when to expect to hear from them as to whether or not your project has been funded. You don't need to be sitting on pins and needles right away if it will be 2 months before applicants will be notified.

Don't be surprised if your funder calls to ask questions during the process about something in your proposal. Reviewers may need clarification on something in your proposal. Getting a call like this is a good sign—it means that you are still in the running and that they are interested enough in your project to request more information. Keep your project and proposal files organized and close at hand so that you can answer quickly and effectively without rifling through drawers of files and piles of paper.

You may get a call about the budget or a specific activity or objective. You may get a list of questions that reviewers want you to answer prior to making their decision. Take care of these things promptly and follow up with the funder to make sure they received your responses, and that you have answered all questions to their satisfaction. Confirm with the funder that they have all the information they need. This is your responsibility.

YOUR PROJECT GETS FUNDED

There are various ways a funder may notify you that they have decided to fund your project. You could receive a letter, an e-mail, or a phone call.

The first thing to do after notification of funding is to thank your funder! Write a brief letter or note on behalf of the grant team expressing your thanks for the funder's support of your project, ensuring the funder that you are excited about implementing the project.

Inform your team about their success, congratulate them for a job well done, and honor their hard work by celebrating. Don't forget to include your partners and supporters. It doesn't have to be a major deal or cost a lot of money. Have cake and ice cream during an afternoon break. Decorate with crepe paper streamers. It is acknowledging the people and their efforts that is most important.

After you have verified with the funder that you may make the announcement, let the community know about your success. Send a press release to the local paper and media and to library publications. This is a good time to call for volunteers if your project will require them. People will be excited about becoming involved in the project at this stage.

There may be a grant contract for you to sign that stipulates the conditions of the grant. Be aware that the amount you are awarded may not be the amount you requested. The scope of work the funder is funding may not exactly match the scope of work you proposed. Reporting requirements may not be what you had expected. Make sure you understand the terms of the grant contract and the work the funder expects you to do for the funds they are awarding to you.

Review your budget, especially if it has been a long time between submitting your proposal and the notification of your award. Recheck things like salaries, technology and equipment costs, rent, and other dollar amounts that may have fluctuated since you submitted your proposal. Contact the funder immediately to talk about these changes. They may ask you to readjust items within your budget, totaling the same dollar amount. In other words, they may fund your project only for the amount you requested even if actual costs have risen. Or they may be in a position to fund the entire project, including higher cost adjustments.

Be sure that you are comfortable with what is in the grant contract and that it makes sense to you, especially if it differs from your proposed project and budget. To make the agreement, your authorizing agent will most likely need to sign the grant contract. Then return the signed contract to the funder. Once all parties have agreed to the terms, celebrate!

WHAT TO DO WHEN YOUR PROPOSAL IS NOT FUNDED

If your project is not funded, contact the program officer and ask for feedback on your proposal. When proposal reviewers read proposals, they take notes and write comments. These comments are often compiled for a final review that determines which projects are funded and which ones are not. These comments will be valuable to you as you write your next proposal.

They will often tell you where you can make improvements, where you did not make yourself clear, and where you were successful.

Remember to put these comments and the denial of funding in perspective. You may have written an outstanding proposal by most standards. If the funder had the resources to fund only a fraction of proposals submitted, even some excellent proposals had to be denied. The same proposal, submitted to a funder with more resources, might have been funded.

Proposal reviewers are humans, just like you and me, who come with their own biases, preferences, and opinions. Judging grant proposals is by nature a subjective activity. The same proposal read by a different team of reviewers may have been funded.

This is not to say that your proposal doesn't require some work. Read the reviewers' comments and get opinions from people you know who are not involved with your library or the project you have proposed. Sometimes an impartial reader can see things that you cannot because you are so close to it. Don't forget to do this as part of preparing your next proposal.

The Most Common Reasons Grants Are Turned Down

- **The project does not match the purpose of the award, or the applicant does not meet the funder's priorities.** Research the funder's priorities and interests thoroughly before applying. Pay special attention to the purpose of the award.
- **The applicant is not located in the funder's geographic area of funding.** Read the guidelines carefully and do thorough research before applying.
- **The proposal does not follow the format prescribed in the guidelines.** Read the application information and proposal instructions very carefully and follow them exactly. Then read them again. Before you mail your proposal, read the instructions one last time to make sure you have followed all the requirements.
- **The proposal is poorly written and difficult to understand.** Have friends and experienced people critique the grant before you submit it. Get help writing the proposal if you need it.
- **The proposed budget/grant request is not within our funding range.** Look at average size of grants of the funder.
- **The funder doesn't know who you are or if you are credible.** Set up an interview before submitting the proposal and have board members and other funded organizations help you establish a relationship to give you

credibility. Write an Organizational Overview that clearly explains who you are.

- **The proposal doesn't seem urgent. The funder is not sure it will have an impact.** Study the priorities and have a skilled writer do this section so it gets the attention of the funder. Your aim is to stress the importance of your project but not to sound as if you are in crisis.
- **The budget is unrealistic or inaccurate.** Never guess at the cost of items in your budget. Do not rely on sales or limited time offers for an accurate price. When it comes time to purchase the equipment, that sale price may no longer be available. Do not forget supplies like paper, pens, toner, and reproduction when preparing your budget if such items are available. Be realistic about the programs and budgets. Promise only what can realistically be delivered for the amount requested.
- **There is no evidence of support or cooperation from potential project partners.** Make sure your proposal clearly shows that you have support from other organizations and that they are involved in your project. You should include a letter of support from all partnering organizations. It needs to be obvious to the reviewer that the partnering organizations are aware of the project and have agreed to participate.
- **The proposal does not contain a clear and relevant evaluation plan.** You have designed a fantastic project, but how will you determine whether the project was a success? Evaluation is a critical component of any proposal.
- **The funder has allocated all the money for this grant cycle.** Don't take this personally. It is a fact of life. Try the next grant cycle. Next time, submit at least a month before the deadline to give ample opportunity for questions and a site visit.
- **There is not enough evidence that the program will become self-sufficient and sustain itself after the grant is completed.** Add a section to the proposal on your plans for self-sufficiency and develop a long-term strategy.

Adapted from *California Grants Guide*, Grant Guides Plus 2000.

Even if your application is denied, don't give up. It is not uncommon, especially in the federal arena, for funders to receive more money after funding the first round. This means that they must go to the next level of proposals—those that just missed getting funded the first time. If this happens to you, you must be ready to think and act quickly.

Therefore, after you have been turned down, and you are looking for other funding, you may get a call from the funder to whom you originally submitted your proposal asking if you are still seeking funding for your project. Even if you have received other funding for your project in the meantime, there is surely a second phase to your project or a similar project you have planned for the future that could use funding. Talk to the funder about the possibilities. Most funders who are interested in your proposal will be open to reconfiguring your project, talking about your project's current funding needs, or discussing other related projects you have planned for the future.

TAKING THE NEXT STEPS: IMPLEMENTING THE PROJECT

CONTACTING THE FUNDER AND TALKING TO YOUR PROGRAM OFFICER

After celebrating your success, call your program officer and introduce yourself, if you haven't already spoken with them. Confirm that the funder has the contact person's name, correct phone, fax, and e-mail. Make yourself available to this person. Ask any questions you may have and begin to develop a relationship with them. Tell them to call if they have any questions or concerns. The program officer can be very helpful to you as you begin project implementation and throughout your project.

START YOUR PROJECT EVALUATION

It is important to implement the evaluation process for your project as soon as you receive funding. Of course, you already thoroughly planned your evaluation methodology when you planned your project; however, after being funded and before your project is implemented, you must establish a baseline or starting point against which you will measure your successes. This may mean doing an assessment of current knowledge among the specific beneficiaries of your project or the state of technology in your library prior to the start of your project. You may need to do a preproject survey or an updated needs assessment to establish an accurate baseline. Your community needs assessment may have taken place months ago, and recent changes must be taken into account. Where you start depends on the nature of your project. Reread your objectives and the evaluation methods described in your proposal and start working on this right away.

UNDERSTAND YOUR REPORTING REQUIREMENTS

Make sure to familiarize yourself with your funder's report-writing requirements so that you are gathering the right information, you are ready to prepare your reports when they are due, and you get them to the funder on time.

The evaluation of a project should be based on the original purpose of the project and should indicate the extent to which this purpose was achieved. If you didn't accomplish all the grant objectives, it does not necessarily mean the project was a failure. Valuable lessons may have been learned or the population served may have been positively affected in other ways than those planned. The evaluation should outline any unexpected results or consequences and should also specify how the grant will affect future projects.

If you based your grant evaluation plan on Outcome Based Evaluation (OBE), as discussed in Chapter 3, the grant outcomes should be used to evaluate the impact on the population served. Include any information gained from your evaluation plan, such as data collected from focus groups or surveys or statistical data. Evaluations are also enhanced with the inclusion of qualitative data such as stories that illustrate specific examples of individuals benefiting from the project.

The evaluation also needs to report how the grant money was used. This report should correspond with the budget originally outlined in the grant request. Any deviations from the budget in the grant request should be explained.

Here is a sample of some of the information asked for on a grant evaluation or progress report:

Grantee Organization Name

Grant Number

Project Name

Evaluation Due Date

Original Project Purpose

Population Served

Extent Purpose Achieved (elaborate on whether you were able to accomplish what you'd planned, whether the need was addressed)

Summary of Outcomes/Results Achieved as a Result of the Grant

Report of Expenditures (in comparison to the original grant budget)

Future Plans for the Grant Project
Lessons Learned/Impact on Future Projects
Telling the Story (qualitative data)
Publications or Presentations Connected to the Grant
Honors or Awards Received as a Result of the Grant

SETTING UP TO IMPLEMENT YOUR PROJECT

Now you are ready to begin implementation of your project. If you need to hire staff, post or advertise the positions as soon as possible. In some organizations this takes time, so you will want to take care of this right away.

After the positions are advertised, make a list of the equipment, technology, materials, supplies, and any other items you need to purchase. This may already be detailed in your grant budget. There may be purchasing procedures in your library that may be time-intensive. Don't delay beginning these steps. Confirm that the costs in your budget are still accurate. Perhaps the price of computers or printers has gone down. If you do have leftover funds from your grant award, make sure you let your funder know and get approval to use the funds to support your project in other ways.

Designate a work space for project personnel, if necessary, and update the project timeline to include each detailed each step in implementation.

Your next step, covered in more detail in Chapter 9, is to review the grant cycle process you have just completed in order to identify what you could do to improve and also to note the things that did work well.

9 REVIEWING AND CONTINUING THE PROCESS

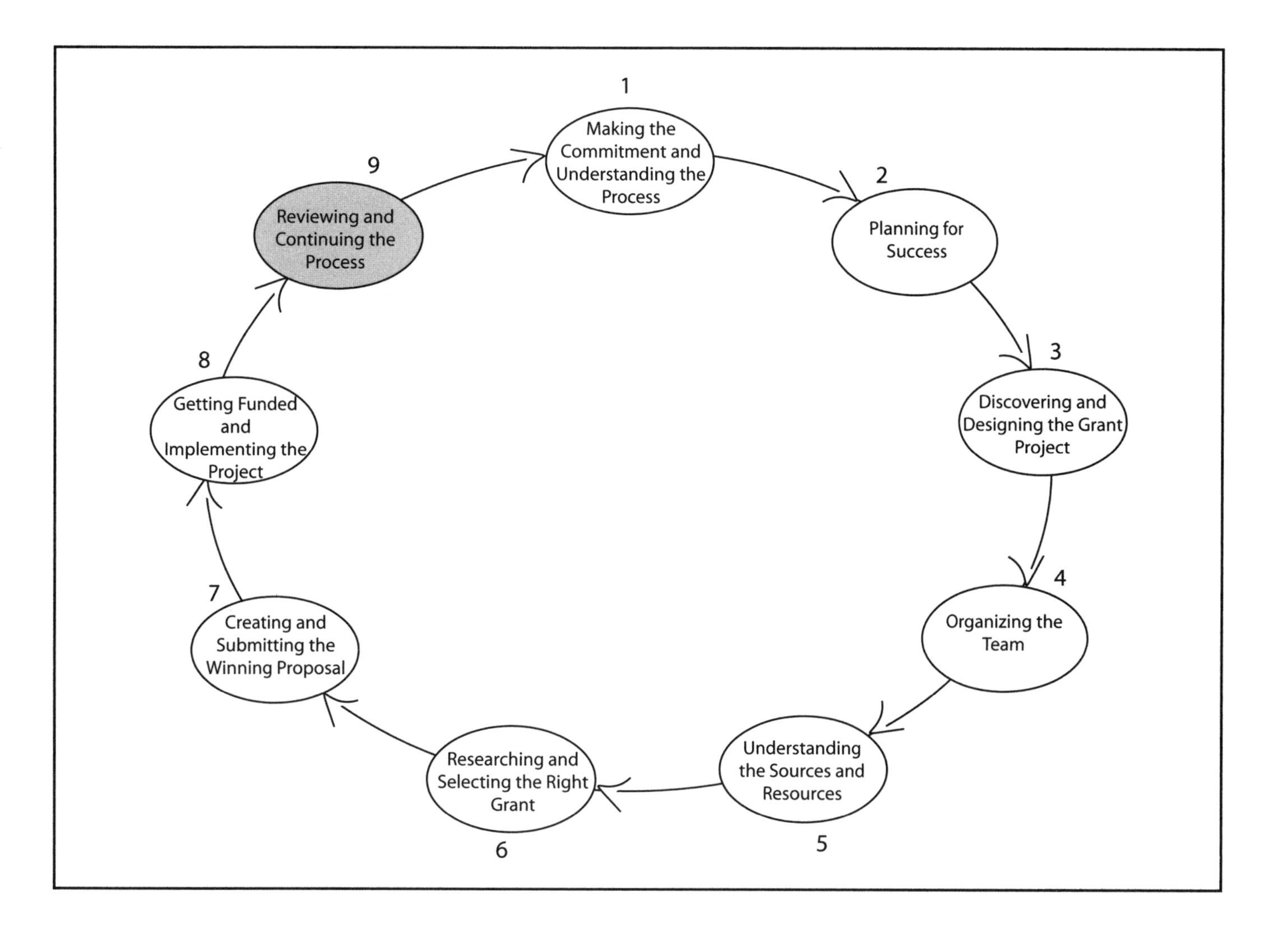

Congratulations on completing your first round of the grant process cycle!

If you have had success in acquiring funding for a project this first time around, you are now getting ready for project implementation. Or you may still be seeking your first successful grant. Either way, this is the time for you to review the process and to continue the process to seek additional grants.

DEBRIEF AND REVIEW

First, take some time to meet with your project planning team and your grant team to debrief. Often, it takes going through the entire process before our team members and we really understand how the process works or what the results will be. How did it go?

____ Did we remain true to the strategic plan?

____ Did we define the right projects?

____ Is there anything we overlooked?

____ Did we forget to include someone?

____ Did we delegate well?

____ Was everything completed on time?

____ Did we have enough time to get the authorizing signatures?

____ Were we rushing off to mail the proposal 5 minutes before the post office closed?

The good news here is that we can learn and make improvements for continuing from here. This process is never done; there is no last step. Whatever we can learn at any stage in the process can only help us to do better the next time around.

After reviewing, continue with the grant process. There may be some steps that you can go through quickly now that you have your strategic plan in place and you have discovered and designed several projects. Remember, when you have an updated plan or discover new community needs, you must build them into your project designs. Continue to do the research and update your proposal components.

Following are some things you can do to facilitate continuing the process.

PARTICIPATE IN ONGOING PROFESSIONAL DEVELOPMENT

- Attend workshops on researching grant opportunities given by your local community foundation.

- Attend overviews offered by foundations where they explain their profiles, interests, and preferences; funding opportunities they offer; and application help they offer for those who are interested in applying.
- Attend proposal-writing workshops given by your community foundation, State Humanities Council, or regional library system.
- The Foundation Center offers courses on proposal writing, grant seeking on the Web, evaluating funding prospects, proposal budgets, and more: www.fdncenter.org/.
- Foundation Center online tutorials include Guide to Funding Research, Proposal Budgeting Basics, and Proposal Writing Short Course: www.fdncenter.org/learn/classroom/.
- The Grantsmanship Center offers an intensive 5-day Grantsmanship Training Program in various locations across the United States: www.tgci.com/training/tprogram.asp.
- Your state library may offer workshops or guidance on grant research or writing or how to apply for LSTA and other funds.
- Federal agencies often offer free regional proposal-writing workshops and/or informational sessions on upcoming opportunities. They cover ways to write a proposal for the agency and how to be more competitive. These workshops and sessions are usually held nationwide.
- Go to grant workshops at your state library association conference, regional library association conference, or national library conferences such as the American Library Association (ALA) or Internet Librarian.

FOSTER PARTNERSHIPS

The best time to create and nurture partnerships is when you are not under pressure to write a grant or under a tight application deadline. It is best to work on these relationships on an ongoing basis, as a matter of course. Make a point of meeting people outside your organization, leaders in the community, and agencies or businesses that are doing activities that relate to what you would like to do to meet community needs. Get out of the four walls of your library and attend community meetings, join community groups, volunteer to give talks on the library to local groups, or visit local schools. Talk about your new ideas and plans to others in the community.

Build funder relationships. If you have received a grant, recognize the funder by using their name and logo, distribute press releases, and spread the word in your newsletter of Web articles about the funder of your project. Invite the funder to special events and give them recognition at your annual award program, for instance. Make sure to thank your funders and keep them updated about the progress of your project or about special accomplishments related to the project they funded. Send them copies of articles about your project and publicity materials.

Be visible. Speak at civic club meetings and other community organization events about your goals, the community needs you would like to address, and prospective projects. Volunteer to help with your partner's or potential partner's fund-raising events or create an e-mail distribution list of your accomplishments.

SUBSCRIBE TO CURRENT AWARENESS SERVICES, ELECTRONIC NEWSLETTERS, AND ONLINE DISCUSSION GROUPS

Electronic Newsletters/Alerts from Potential Granting Agencies Include:

Primary Source. The IMLS monthly e-mail newsletter links you to current agency news, grant deadlines and announcement dates, new publications, and highlights of funded projects: www.imls.gov/utility/subscribe.htm.

NEH Connect!, NEH's electronic newsletter: www.neh.gov/news/nehconnect.html.

RFP Bulletin from the Foundation Center: http://fdncenter.org/pnd/rfp/index.jhtmlgrants.gov alerts.

Federal Grants Notification Service: www.grants.gov/Find#receive.

If you are at a university, subscribe to SMARTS, the e-mail notification from the SPIN grant database, through your University Research Office.

Online Discussion Groups

Grants@charitychannel.com is a forum for online discussions about all aspects of grants and proposal writing. There is a nominal fee for joining: http://charitychannel.com/publish/templates/?a=1125&z=72.

SEARCH THE WEB AND VISIT BLOGS

The authors have created a Web page especially for grant opportunities for libraries. It is updated regularly. Visit it at http://librarygrants.blogspot.com/. Search the Web regularly and visit sites of federal agencies, foundations, and corporations that fund library projects.

JOIN GROUPS AND ASSOCIATIONS

Join your state or local chapter of the Association of Fundraising Professionals. You will meet others in your community who are fund-raisers and proposal writers, and you will be invited to association meetings, which may include workshops or talks about grants and proposal writing. You will have the opportunity to network and develop a supportive group with others who are searching for grants and securing the funds: www.afpnet.org/country.cfm?cntry=USA&folder_id=932.

KEEP UP-TO-DATE WITH YOUR STRATEGIC PLAN AND PROJECT PLAN

You always want your grant process to be aligned with your library's plan. Be aware of any updates or changes in your plan and build them into your project plans. Also, when your organization has developed a new plan, you may need to spend more time in the planning stages than in the years when you are working with a plan that is in place.

10 ANSWERING FIVE ESSENTIAL QUESTIONS

As this book explains, the most important aspect of grant seeking is thorough development and planning before you write a proposal. Funders often attest that they get many proposals that are full of great ideas. It's the practical implementation plan with clear goals and objectives that is often missing. Critical to obtaining funding are these important requisites: (1) organizational capacity; (2) fulfillment of a community need; (3) sustainability; (4) relationship building; and (5) evaluation. Your library must be able to meet these five criteria in order to be successful. Use these questions to evaluate your grant project's potential for success.

DOES YOUR LIBRARY HAVE THE CAPACITY TO IMPLEMENT AND SUPPORT THIS PROJECT?

Be certain that your library can follow through and achieve the results intended for your project; otherwise, you should not be accepting a grant. Funders call this "organizational capacity." They need to be sure that your library is competent and that the leadership can be trusted to carry out their intentions and truly deliver what has been promised.

Your organization must be invested in the project. Two of the most precious resources of any library are its funds and its staff. If a library is willing to dedicate a portion of those discretionary funds and staff hours to the proposed project, this signals a legitimate priority, rather than just a scheme for chasing grant dollars. Get agreement to the project from relevant staff and administrators. Be certain you know who will apply for the grant and also who will make it happen. You should have the actual names and support of the staff members who will carry out the project, file any required reports, and ensure that the funds are spent as planned. This will ensure not only grant compliance but also a successful project.

HOW WILL THIS GRANT MAKE AN IMPACT?

Your project should be not just a good idea but a true need in your community. This grant should make a difference, and you need to demonstrate how it will do so in your proposal. What are the concrete benefits to your community? You should identify a target audience that is an appropriate population to benefit. Libraries serve diverse populations, and this is attractive to funders, as it often matches their purpose as well. You should include the target audience in the project planning to ensure that your library is doing the project with the people you will be helping, not to them. Funders want to know that the people who will benefit from the project have provided input and assisted with designing the project.

On a large scale of impact, your project will have the power to affect public opinion and policy and transform your community. Even if your scope is not this extensive, the project should still have outcome potential for more than a few people. For example, a reading program for toddlers that serves only a few families will not have a broad impact on your community.

IS YOUR PROJECT SUSTAINABLE?

If projects live only as long as a funder is willing to give money to them, then it is highly unlikely that the project is even what your community wants or needs. But continuity does not just happen. Long-range funding strategies must be planned from the start. No funder wants to see a program die out after their grant money is depleted; they want to ensure that your library can sustain the program, whether through partnerships, leveraging, or reallocation. You have to make sure that any project you begin can either be fully completed within the time frame allowed or is sustainable after the allotted time with or without additional funds.

Also, continuation of the project should not be dependent on a single factor likely to change, such as a project director who is working around the clock to keep the project going, a limited pool of volunteers who can't keep up the pace, or a single donor whose only connection to the project is financial.

Sustainability can be a difficult issue to address. You must have the vision to picture ways that project activities can be maintained. This may mean that funding from other sources has to be secured to cover the costs of these activities. A long-term plan to sustain the project should be developed. While it is acceptable for this plan to include partial reliance on future grant awards, it should identify some steady sources of income if at all possible. Perhaps your library can continue some project maintenance expenses such as computer equipment, meeting room space, or even staff. If your project involves the hiring of temporary staff members, is it possible to build these positions into your budget so that these will become permanent positions?

Another way to sustain a grant project is to expand the activities to other areas over the course of a few years. Perhaps the activities could take place in different geographic areas of the community or with different populations.

As you address sustainability, keep in mind that it is important to let funders know that you will be working on this from the beginning of the project period. Do not let sustainability issues wait until the end of the project, or else you may find it is too late. Finally, if for legitimate reasons your project is time-limited, make sure that you explain this to the readers in your proposal so that it is clear.

DO YOU HAVE REAL RELATIONSHIPS WITH FUNDERS AND PARTNERS?

You must research all potential funders and find that perfect fit. Your goals and theirs should fit together like pieces of a puzzle. You should be clear about what the funder is trying to achieve, what the funder expects of your library, and what will be required throughout the grant cycle. But to truly build effective partnerships that endure, libraries need to cultivate strong relationships with funders. This means working together on an ongoing basis to share ideas and approaches to problems. The relationship requires mutual trust, honesty, and clarity, which take time and effort to achieve.

Frequent communications, establishing personal connections, and finding creative ways to reach out to donors are all ways to build real relationships. You need to have more contact with a funder than just sending the proposal and final report. Send them newsletters, periodic updates, and invitations to events, so that you aren't contacting them only when you need funds. If your library gets an award, or your grant project has recently produced something noteworthy, send them a clipping or reprint with a handwritten note. Build relationships with both current and potential donors.

Collaborations are a great way to leverage resources, share expertise, and apportion costs to tackle complex challenges. Whether you have a small staff or a large staff, partners can also help increase your library's organizational capacity. Determine whether there are other groups in your community that share your vision and goals. Begin collaborating with those individuals or groups before you apply for grants. Any partners that you can find in your community, such as public agencies, businesses, or service groups, can help add validity to your proposal. Programs that are designed in isolation from the community they serve are inclined to fail.

HOW WILL YOU KNOW THAT YOU'VE BEEN SUCCESSFUL?

An effective proposal describes a program for change, not a list of wants. There must be a detailed plan that describes exactly where you are going and how you will get there. Be specific about broad goals, measurable objectives, and quantified outcomes and outputs. Otherwise you will never know if you truly made a difference. Often libraries do programming such as summer reading or computer classes but never really know if reading skill levels are increased or if adults are promoted at their jobs due to increased technology knowledge. Wouldn't those be great things to know and share with your funders, board, community, and other stakeholders?

Not only must your goals be achievable, but they must be measurable. Don't wait until the end of the grant to see if you got it right. You'll want to report your incremental achievements as you go along. What will you do, and by when will you do it? Benchmarks that are realistic, performed monthly and quarterly, and involve both quantitative and qualitative measurements are very important. Often knowing if you've been successful starts with knowing where you started from. Evaluations and surveys should be conducted prior to project start dates and then repeated yearly or at project end.

11 LIBRARY GRANT SUCCESS STORIES

INTRODUCTION

If you need a little help with brainstorming creative ideas for your project or you want advice from other librarians who have completed successful grant projects, here are some inspiring success stories from libraries around the country.

In response to our request for grant success stories on various electronic discussion lists and newsletters, we received many excellent submissions. We selected stories that illustrate best practices and represent a wide spectrum of project ideas, library types, and grant sources. By reading these examples, you will see how real-life successful projects are developed, funded, and implemented. You will understand the power of partnerships in making a grant project successful. You will receive valuable advice from numerous experienced librarians who know what to do and what to avoid—all *before* you embark on your own grant process.

Our deepest thanks go to our library colleagues who submitted their success stories for inclusion in *Grants for Libraries*. We appreciate your willingness to share your stories and advice to help others in becoming successful, too.

Listening to the Desert: Living in Harmony with Xeriscape Landscaping

Project Title	**Listening to the Desert: Living in Harmony with Xeriscape Landscaping**
Library	**Glendale Public Library** 5959 W. Brown St. Glendale, AZ 85302
Submitted by	Rodeane Widom, City of Glendale Library Director
Size of Collection	582,549
Population	228,210
Grant Amount	$41,576
Funder	Library Services and Technology Act (LSTA)

Grant Project Description

This grant was developed to encourage homeowners to conserve water by incorporating low water-use plants in their landscaping. The six-month project started with 18 free educational gardening classes held at all three Glendale Public Library facilities. The classes included "how-to" instruction covering various facets of Xeriscape landscaping taught by experts. Additional print and non-print resources were added to the collection so that patrons could take information home.

Glendale's Main Library is the site of a demonstration xeriscape botanical garden. A self-guided audio tour was created for the garden as part of the grant. State-of-the-art listening wands were purchased so that patrons can wander the grounds and learn about the various plants "up close and personal." Each person also received a map that has numbers marking the stops. The garden stops are marked with new signs, which display the wand icon. A plant booklet featuring information on plants and a history of the garden was produced from grant funding and is distributed free of charge at the library as well. A web site with detailed information on plants in

the library's garden was developed. By all of these means, it is hoped that homeowners will switch from turf to xeriscape landscaping.

What made your proposal/ project successful?	The success of the project rested with the numerous partnerships formed with other organizations also interested in promoting xeriscape practices. The list of partners included the city's Water Conservation Office, Glendale Community College, Historic Sahuaro Ranch Park, the Desert Botanical Garden, and the University of Arizona Cooperative Extension Office. Each entity advertised programs and provided their own particular expertise to strengthen it.
Would you do anything differently?	No.
What was the most difficult part of the grant process?	Coordination with all of the various partners was challenging.
Do you have any advice for other grant seekers?	Work with experts in the field because they give the project added credibility.
What do you think is the most important element of a successful grant?	Very extensive promotion and publicity of all facets of the project.
How many people worked on your grant application? Were they all library staff?	Approximately 15 people. About half of the people were not library staff.
Did you collaborate with an unusual partner?	The list of partners included the city's Water Conservation Office, Glendale Community College, Historic Sahuaro Ranch Park, the Desert Botanical Garden, and the University of Arizona Cooperative Extension Office.
Did your library reach diverse audiences through grant projects?	Homeowners in varying types of neighborhoods and students at a variety of institutions were reached.
Has your library found an unusual funding source?	There was a wide variety of in-kind cost sharing by various departments of the city such as the Cable Television Division and the Water Conservation Division. Each of the project partners provided expertise, such as the audio production done by Glendale Community College.
Did you implement innovative programming using grant funds?	We did include many different ways of education—creative and varied classes; printed materials; and the audio wands.

This project won a Governor's Pride in Arizona Award for Water Conservation at the Arizona Clean and Beautiful Conference in 2004!

Bridging the Gap

Project Title	**Bridging the Gap**
Library	**Athens Regional Library System** 2025 Baxter St. Athens, GA 30606
Submitted by	Kathryn S. Ames, Director, Athens Regional Library System: kames@arlsmail.org
Size of Collection	325,000 [system]
Population	197,000
Grant Amount	$250,030
Funder	Institute of Museum and Library Services (IMLS)

Grant Project Description

This demonstration project enables the library and our museum partner to establish a facility in a Hispanic neighborhood, to offer educational programs including Plaza Comunitaria [Mexicans may obtain a high school diploma via distance ed], story hours, art programs and exhibits, and other traditional educational programs.

Photograph is provided by Stacey O. Ferrelle.

What made your proposal/project successful?	In addition to our museum partner, we have many community partners, including the transit system which is providing free bus passes.
Would you do anything differently?	So far, this is working very well!

What was the most difficult part of the grant process?	Simply keeping things together—making sure we had partnership agreements, keeping everyone informed of progress and needs, and building a web report form.
Do you have any advice for other grant seekers?	We used the PLA Planning Process and the forms from Managing for Results to keep the planning team on track. Starting by analyzing community needs, having representation from target group, and moving through the process is an excellent way to keep things moving!
What do you think is the most important element of a successful grant?	Painting the picture very clearly of what you hope to accomplish!
How many people worked on your grant application? Were they all library staff?	6 people—3 library, 3 museum. PLUS we had assistance from our partners who made many suggestions
Did you collaborate with an unusual partner?	Our partners included the University of GA Office of International Public Service and Outreach, the UGA Carribean and Latin American Studies Office, the public transit system, Oasis—a Catholic outreach ministry in the neighborhood, Catholic Social Services, the PTO of the school the children attend, ESL program directors, Georgia Office of Public Library Service [for T-1 connections] and of course, the Lyndon House Arts Center [the museum].
Did your library reach diverse audiences through grant projects?	Our intent is to reach the 400 families residing within the target area.
Has your library found an unusual funding source?	We are still building on this. The Mexican Consulate has been very helpful in enabling us to become a Plaza Comunitaria site in Athens. We are working to build more local support.
Did you implement innovative programming using grant funds?	We have received several LSTA grants in the past to provide innovative programs to this target group. The IMLS grant was an outgrowth of those successes. We also are using grant funds to provide Spanish classes for staff.

Slammin' Jammin' Poetry

Project Title	**Slammin' Jammin' Poetry**
Library	**Des Plaines Public Library** 1501 Ellinwood St. Des Plaines, IL 60016
Submitted by	Margie Borris
Size of Collection	300,027
Population	57,000
Grant Amount	$31,122
Funder	LSTA Illinois State Library
Grant Project Description	The library hired professional poets who specialize in teaching young people to read, write, perform and enjoy poetry. Additionally, the grant included fieldtrips to a writing workshop/open mic night and a regional teen poetry slam. Two separate series of eight workshops were held, one for middle school students and one for high school students. Teachers and school librarians were also invited to participate. At the end, each group held a poetry performance for National Poetry Month (April) and produced a book of their collective works.

Photograph provided by Des Plains Public Library Staff.

What made your proposal/ project successful?	The professional poets were the secret to the success of the program. They all specialized in working with students from select grade levels. They entertained and inspired the students.
Would you do anything differently?	We would limit the number of students participating. The middle school program was so successful that an average of 40 students attended each week. A group of 20–30 is more manageable. We would also allow more

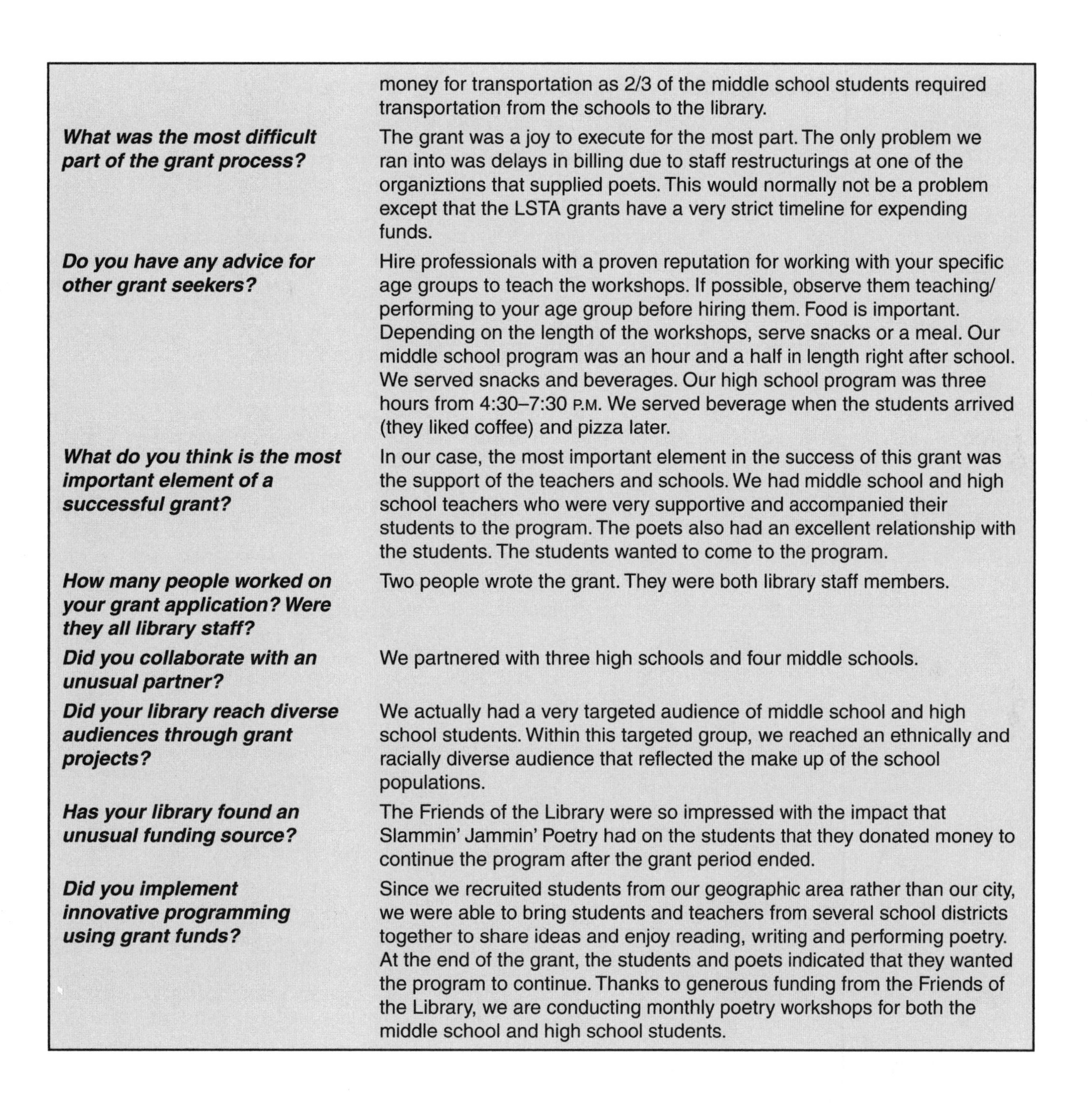

	money for transportation as 2/3 of the middle school students required transportation from the schools to the library.
What was the most difficult part of the grant process?	The grant was a joy to execute for the most part. The only problem we ran into was delays in billing due to staff restructurings at one of the organiztions that supplied poets. This would normally not be a problem except that the LSTA grants have a very strict timeline for expending funds.
Do you have any advice for other grant seekers?	Hire professionals with a proven reputation for working with your specific age groups to teach the workshops. If possible, observe them teaching/ performing to your age group before hiring them. Food is important. Depending on the length of the workshops, serve snacks or a meal. Our middle school program was an hour and a half in length right after school. We served snacks and beverages. Our high school program was three hours from 4:30–7:30 P.M. We served beverage when the students arrived (they liked coffee) and pizza later.
What do you think is the most important element of a successful grant?	In our case, the most important element in the success of this grant was the support of the teachers and schools. We had middle school and high school teachers who were very supportive and accompanied their students to the program. The poets also had an excellent relationship with the students. The students wanted to come to the program.
How many people worked on your grant application? Were they all library staff?	Two people wrote the grant. They were both library staff members.
Did you collaborate with an unusual partner?	We partnered with three high schools and four middle schools.
Did your library reach diverse audiences through grant projects?	We actually had a very targeted audience of middle school and high school students. Within this targeted group, we reached an ethnically and racially diverse audience that reflected the make up of the school populations.
Has your library found an unusual funding source?	The Friends of the Library were so impressed with the impact that Slammin' Jammin' Poetry had on the students that they donated money to continue the program after the grant period ended.
Did you implement innovative programming using grant funds?	Since we recruited students from our geographic area rather than our city, we were able to bring students and teachers from several school districts together to share ideas and enjoy reading, writing and performing poetry. At the end of the grant, the students and poets indicated that they wanted the program to continue. Thanks to generous funding from the Friends of the Library, we are conducting monthly poetry workshops for both the middle school and high school students.

Laurelton Library Youth Empowerment Initiative

Project Title	**Laurelton Library Youth Empowerment Initiative**
Library	**Queens Borough Public Library, Laurelton Branch Library** 134-26 225 St. Laurelton, NY 11413
Submitted by	Maureen T. O'Connor, Director, Programs and Branch Libraries
Size of Collection	71,489
Population	28,339
Grant Amount	$268,008 ($470,000 over 3 years)
Funder	New York State Division of Criminal Justice Services

Grant Project Description

The purpose of the Laurelton Library Youth Empowerment Initiative is to provide a positive atmosphere at a neighborhood library where youth age 7–15 participate in activities that help them succeed in school and prepare for the future. Over the past three years, the Laurelton Branch has gone from a hang out encouraging delinquent behavior to a model program of youth development and community cooperation. When the grant proposal was submitted, young people were congregating in large numbers at the Laurelton Branch Library. The Branch began experiencing increases in disorderly conduct, theft and property damage. This type of activity disrupted the comfort of the library environment for other customers, who would clear out during after-school hours.

Photograph provided by the Queens Borough Public Library.

Juvenile Justice funding provided the opportunity to turn the youth toward more positive pursuits that raised their self-esteem and increased their ability to cope in the world. The grant provided a full-time youth counselor, part-time social worker, a portable computer center, homework assistance and numerous programs to meet the needs of these young people. As word of the program spread, daily attendance and library usage at the branch increased dramatically, and word spread among elected officials, police, city agencies and civic associations who began or increased support of the program.

The great success of the Juvenile Justice grant was the impetus for further change through the positive developments that took place at the branch and within the community. In June 2004, the Branch was redesigned and renovated to provide much-needed space. The multi-purpose room of the branch was expanded and there is now a new Teen Area. These renovations have made a significant difference in the way the community and even library staff view their library.

What made your proposal/ project successful? QBPL [Queens Borough Public Library] Board of Trustees, administration and staff were committed to making a change at the Laurelton Branch. A great deal of this program's

	success is attributable to the flexibility and cooperation of staff, particularly at the branch library level.
What was the most difficult part of the grant process?	The project had to change the behavior of young people in the library, but it also had to address the way library staff was reacting to those youth. The project could only be effective when library staff learned how to react positively to youth in the library. All of the staff took part in Everybody Serves Youth training. The training demonstrates how to positively interact with youth and understand their developmental needs so their informational goals could be positively met.
Do you have any advice for other grant seekers?	Think outside of the box and look at other, less traditional funding sources for libraries and library programs. Queens Library knew that out-of-the-ordinary action was needed to create change.
What do you think is the most important element of a successful grant?	The staff who implement the grant project. Success hinges on their cooperation, professionalism and enthusiasm. Also institutional support for the project.
How many people worked on your grant application? Were they all library staff?	All were Queens Library staff. The director of the Library's Investigation and Security Department and the head of the Programs and Services Department spearheaded the proposal. Other staff, particularly Young Adult Services, provided valuable input.
Did you collaborate with an unusual partner?	The Juvenile Justice Advisory Council is an integral part of this program. Bimonthly meetings are attended by representatives from the local police precinct, the Queens District Attorneys office, elected officials, concerned citizens, social service agencies and library staff. The Youth Counselor fosters relationships with community and social service organizations, particularly the Southeast Queens Neighborhood Network (SQNN), and the NYC [New York City] Administration for Children's Services and Department for Youth and Community Development. Partnerships such as these have led to innovative programming for the greater community.
Did your library reach diverse audiences through grant projects?	The Juvenile Justice grant is designated to have a direct impact on the lives of young people, ages 7 to 15 in Laurelton, Queens, and their parents/caregivers. The area has a high truancy rate and is 83% above the city-wide average per school for students involved in NY Police Department Incidents.
Has your library found an unusual funding source?	According to the New York State Division of Criminal Justice Services, Queens Library was the first public library of its kind to receive such funding.
Did you implement innovative programming using grant funds?	The Laurelton Branch's Youth Counselor brings in a variety of programs designed to attract and keep the youngsters interest. These range from what to do if you are stopped by the police to discussions of health and hygiene issues. High school and college preparatory programs are also included in the offerings. On a weekly basis, technology-related programming utilizes the laptop computer lab. The social worker implemented conversations about issues important to young people.

Forever Free: Abraham Lincoln's Journey to Emancipation

Project Title	**Forever Free: Abraham Lincoln's Journey to Emancipation**
Library	**Highland Park Public Library** 494 Laurel Ave. Highland Park, IL 60035
Submitted by	Julia A. Johnas and Susan Dennison
Size of Collection	218,382
Population	30,073
Grant Amount	$1,000
Funder	National Endowment for the Humanities (NEH)
Grant Project Description	This grant supported a traveling panel exhibit that reexamined Lincoln's efforts to abolish slavery. Funds were used to host an exhibit reception, lectures, and a variety of music, drama, and activity programs for adults and children.

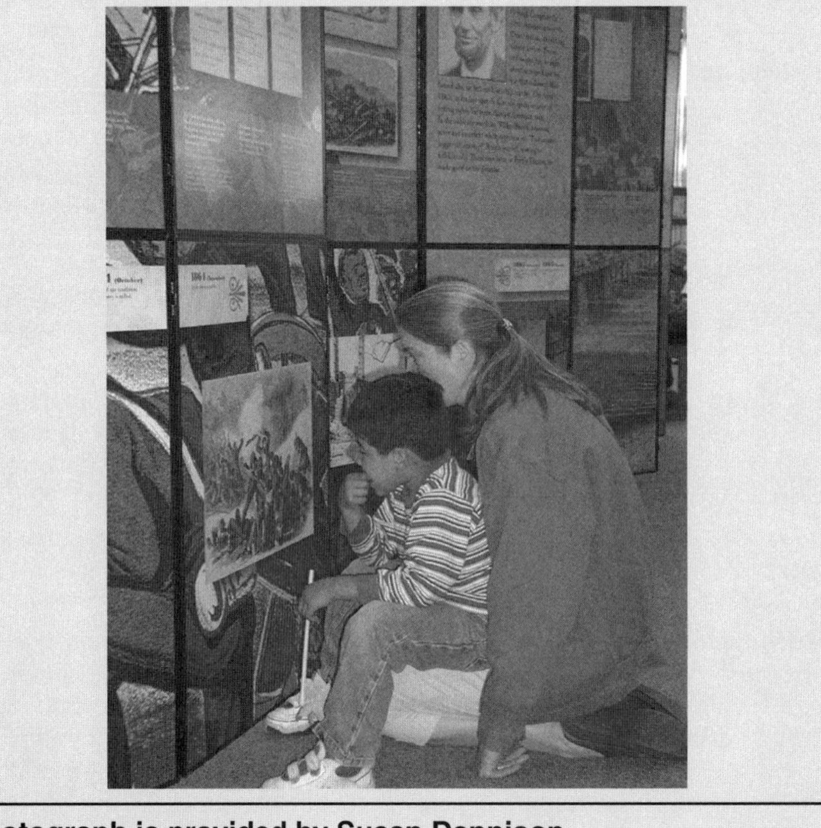

Photograph is provided by Susan Dennison.

What made your proposal/ project successful?	We developed a varied and exciting series of programs and mounted an extensive publicity campaign. We had great support from community

	partners and significant financial support from corporate sponsors. We received over $26,000 in funds and around $3,000 through in-kind donations.
Would you do anything differently?	We had such success that it's difficult to reconsider anything. Perhaps we would have targeted some of our publicity more specifically and would have purchased advertising for some events.
What was the most difficult part of the grant process?	Anticipating expenses and developing a budget was complicated. We had the good fortune of corporate sponsorship funds to supplement the grant, so we were able to carry out all the activities and have a surplus of funds! After the grant was received, we had some difficulty allowing enough staff time to carry out publicity and planning activities.
Do you have any advice for other grant seekers?	Have a well thought-out project. Identify the audience. Have a good marketing plan. Get community partners when appropriate. Look for matching funds or in-kind contributions. Provide plenty of staff support.
What do you think is the most important element of a successful grant?	A well planned project that indicates to the funder that it can be carried out with success—all the things mentioned in the advice for other grant seekers.
How many people worked on your grant application? Were they all library staff?	3, all Library staff
Did you collaborate with an unusual partner?	We attached letters of support to the grant application from our city government, school districts, Historical Society and from individuals who agreed to present programs—a Lincoln actor, a scholar, the owner of the Abraham Lincoln Book Shop, Inc. in Chicago and from a local music association (the Ravinia Festival).
Did your library reach diverse audiences through grant projects?	We have targeted teens with some grants. We have received grant funds to develop foreign language collections for recent immigrants.
Did you implement innovative programming using grant funds?	Yes, we had an extensive schedule of events during the six weeks of the exhibit. Storytelling, music, a Civil War encampment, a 40-piece Civil War reenactment band, film discussions, lectures by nationally known scholars, Lincoln actors, a performance by the Chicago Symphony Orchestra. We began event planning 9 months before the exhibit opened! Exhibit events were the exclusive focus for Library programming and marketing staff for several months in advance of the exhibit.
Has your library found an unusual funding source?	For the first time in its history, our Library solicited corporate sponsorship. Funding came in amounts from $1,000 to $5,000 from local businesses.

A Collage of Cooperation

Project Title	**A Collage of Cooperation**
Library	**Clermont County Public Library** 326 Broadway St. Batavia, OH 45103
Submitted by	Leslie A. Massey
Population	180,000+
Grant Amount	$350
Funder	Ezra Jack Keats Foundation
Grant Project Description	The Owensville Branch Youth Services staff worked with the local Kindergarten classes to do an eight week program that focused on the art of collage. Each week they would highlight a different children's book illustrator that used collage, then work with the children to make collage pictures using the same techniques. The final projects were highlighted at an open house at the branch library.
What made your proposal/ project successful?	The large amount of cooperation the staff received from the kindergarten teachers and the school. Also the number of volunteers from The Clermont County Board of Mental Retardation and Developmental Disabilities (MRDD) school that helped to prepare materials for the project. Schools in the Owensville Service Area had cut art classes for the children, so this project was particularly needed.
Would you do anything differently?	No, it was an excellent project start to finish. We would perhaps, run the art exhibit differently. Perhaps rotating it through the library system.
What was the most difficult part of the grant process?	The application form was fairly short, and information had to be written and re-written to fit the format. The waiting period on the grant also made planning chancy, since the time between the grant award and when the project would start was only about 1 month.
Do you have any advice for other grant seekers?	Be sure to develop community support for your project. When ever possible, collaborate with another agency in planning and implementing your grant. There's a great deal more "bang for your buck" when you work with someone else.
What do you think is the most important element of a successful grant?	Understanding the grantors' requirements and being sure that your proposal fits their interests.
How many people worked on your grant application? Were they all library staff?	3, all library staff
Did you collaborate with an unusual partner?	For this particular grant we partnered with the local elementary school, the Friends of the Owensville Branch and the local MRDD school.
Did your library reach diverse audiences through grant projects?	Many of the children did not have library cards, and as a result of this project, not only they, but also their parents began positive relationships with the library. Many of the parents of our MRDD school volunteers also attended the open house to see the projects their children had helped prepare.

Has your library found an unusual funding source?	For this grant, we applied to the Ezra Jack Keats Foundation. This is not necessarily an unusual funding source, as we have used them once before for a grant.
Did you implement innovative programming using grant funds?	The programming we did with the Kindergarten class was so successful, that we committed to offering it again next year out of our programming budget. We also decided to offer a shorter version of it to the local MRDD school in the community.

Improving Student Success through Strengthening Library Collections, Archives, and Information Competence

Project Title	**Improving Student Success through Strengthening Library Collections, Archives, and Information Competence**
Library	**Oviatt Library** **California State University** 18111 Nordhoff St. Northridge, CA 91330-8327
Submitted by	Kathy Dabbour, Project Director, HSI [Hispanic-Serving Institutions] Program Grant
Size of Collection	1,274,351
Population	30,000 students; 3,000 faculty & staff
Grant Amount	$1.6 million over 5 years
Funder	U.S. Dept. of Education, Title V Developing Hispanic-Serving Institutions Program
Grant Project Description	The goal of the grant is to increase students' library use and information competence by increasing the library's collection of materials related to the Latino/Chicano experience. We believe that providing library material relevant to Latino/Chicano students' lives and experiences, combined with education about how to use these resources will help students be more successful in their academic pursuits and ultimately help CSUN [California State University, Northridge] increase graduation rates. In achieving this goal, we will: 1. Increase Latino students' library use and research skills by expanding the Library's collection of books, journals, electronic resources, media, and teacher curriculum materials related to Latino history, social sciences, and culture. 2. Acquire, digitize and improve accessibility of primary archival materials related to Latino individuals and organizations of the San Fernando Valley area and other areas within Los Angeles. Archives offer a wealth of primary research materials. Student use of these collections contributes to the depth of cited resources and the quality of students' research projects. 3. Measure the impact of instruction by librarians on student information competence skills—one of the goals of the University's general education program. Information competence, which is the set of skills needed to find, evaluate, use, and produce information in today's many formats, is essential for student success.
What made your proposal/ project successful?	The U.S. Dept. of Education's Title V Hispanic-Serving Institutions (HSI) program is one of only a handful of federal grants inclusive of academic libraries. Under federal guidelines, Hispanic Serving Institutions are those with at least a 25 percent undergraduate FTE Latino enrollment, with at least half of those students considered low-income. California State University, Northridge (CSUN) appears to be unique in regards to this federal program in that its activities are exclusive to the library. Other HSI

	grant recipients either did not include their libraries, or involved their libraries as part of a more extensive campus endeavor. Under the broad scope of the program, CSUN was able to obtain funding to increase its materials budget and hire additional personnel.
Would you do anything differently?	Possibly broaden the scope of book/database purchases covered by grant monies to also include subjects that are needed by majors having a high Latino/Hispanic enrollment.
What was the most difficult part of the grant process?	Determining eligibility, gathering campus data to write the narrative.
Do you have any advice for other grant seekers?	Read the grant application and all related regulations carefully. You are probably the only expert on your campus for your grant. Don't expect your grants office to know the intimate details about every grant that is out there. Educate them early on about eligibility, allowable activities, indirect costs, etc.
What do you think is the most important element of a successful grant?	You have written your goals and objectives for a non-librarian audience and they are realistic.
How many people worked on your grant application? Were they all library staff?	1 author, with data/feedback from about 10 others. Yes, the author is a librarian and the rest are librarians/library staff, plus campus IR [Institutional Research] and grants office staff.
Did you collaborate with an unusual partner?	None, but we tried to do a collaborative grant with other Cal State University libraries, but they were not eligible.
Did your library reach diverse audiences through grant projects?	Hispanic/Latino/Chicano
Has your library found an unusual funding source?	I think so!
Did you implement innovative programming using grant funds?	I hope so!

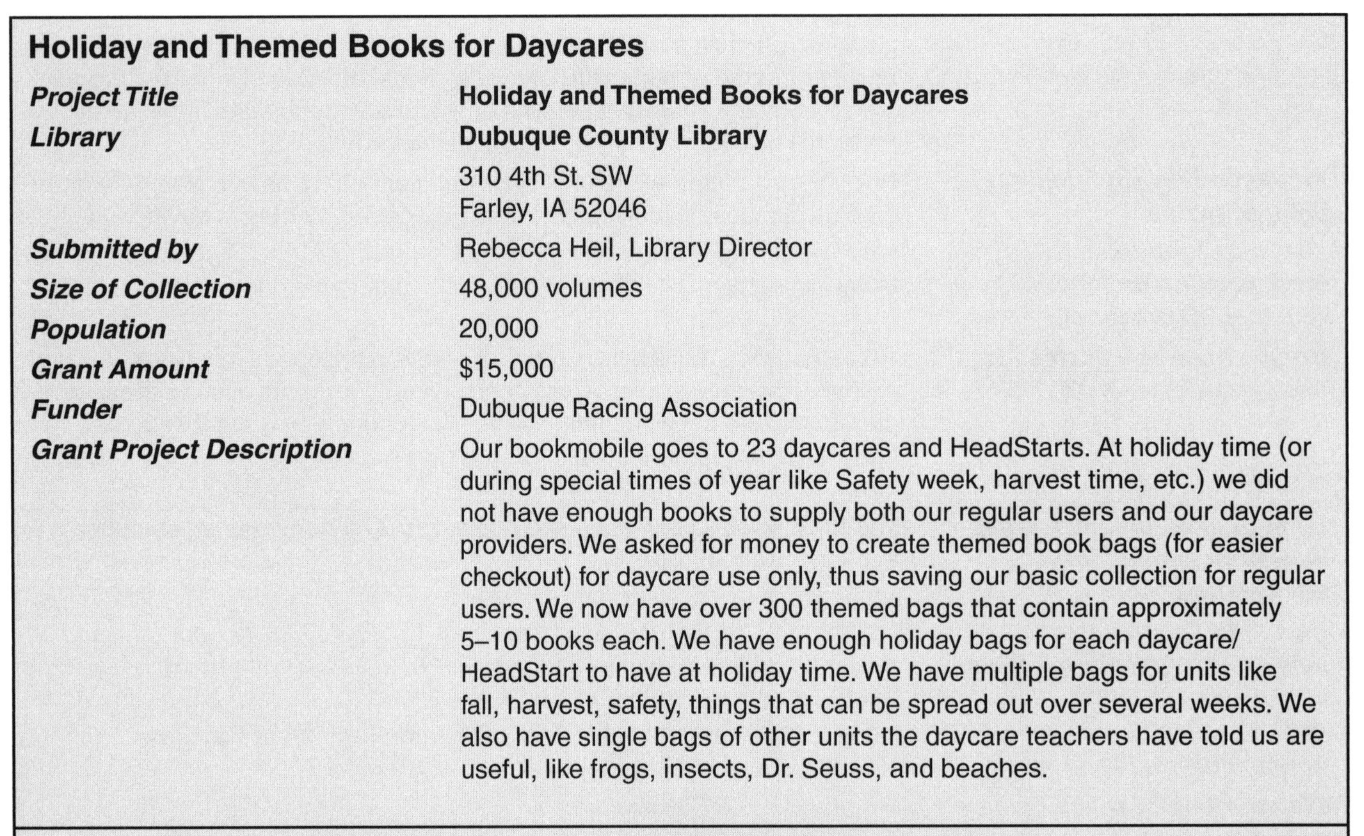

Holiday and Themed Books for Daycares

Project Title	**Holiday and Themed Books for Daycares**
Library	**Dubuque County Library** 310 4th St. SW Farley, IA 52046
Submitted by	Rebecca Heil, Library Director
Size of Collection	48,000 volumes
Population	20,000
Grant Amount	$15,000
Funder	Dubuque Racing Association
Grant Project Description	Our bookmobile goes to 23 daycares and HeadStarts. At holiday time (or during special times of year like Safety week, harvest time, etc.) we did not have enough books to supply both our regular users and our daycare providers. We asked for money to create themed book bags (for easier checkout) for daycare use only, thus saving our basic collection for regular users. We now have over 300 themed bags that contain approximately 5–10 books each. We have enough holiday bags for each daycare/ HeadStart to have at holiday time. We have multiple bags for units like fall, harvest, safety, things that can be spread out over several weeks. We also have single bags of other units the daycare teachers have told us are useful, like frogs, insects, Dr. Seuss, and beaches.

Small Wonders Day Care Kids on Bookmobile with Bags.

What made your proposal/ project successful?	We tried to focus on the need of the daycares/HeadStarts that weren't able to get the books they needed anywhere else. We had been providing them with some service, so this was a natural extension of what we already provided. We also focused on what their needs were, interviewing and surveying teachers about the units they planned and the types of materials they needed. Besides, everybody likes giving money to put books in preschoolers' hands!

What was the most difficult part of the grant process?	Although it seems ridiculous, the hardest thing was getting the money spent. We weren't able to start choosing books till very late, due to internal changes, so we were trying to buy several thousand children's books (specifically themed) in a very short time.
Do you have any advice for other grant seekers?	Never make it about what the library needs. Always point to the end user and how they will benefit.
What do you think is the most important element of a successful grant?	Good writing, careful needs assessment and figuring out what the grantor likes to fund.
How many people worked on your grant application? Were they all library staff?	1 wrote, 3 others did background.
Did you collaborate with an unusual partner?	The library staff members who worked directly with the daycares did a lot of the survey and interview work with the teachers.
Did your library reach diverse audiences through grant projects?	We do not have a lot of cultural diversity in our area, but the HeadStarts see many of the low income, minority preschoolers in the area. Our daycares generally serve any and all other preschoolers.
Has your library found an unusual funding source?	The Dubuque Racing Association is made up of two gambling ventures in our area. They have yearly grant cycles and are partial to libraries. They fund within a certain mileage circumference only and try to give money to schools, parks, fire stations, etc., particularly in small towns.
Did you implement innovative programming using grant funds?	Our ultimate goal was to provide some type of programming (on the bookmobile) along with the materials, but we were unable to find funding for the personnel component.

Two bags to show processing of bags.

Library Expansion and Renovation

Project Title	**Library Expansion and Renovation**
Library	**Clear Lake Public Library** 200 N. 4th St. Clear Lake, IA 50428
Submitted by	Jean Casey, Library Director
Size of Collection	51,000
Population	8,161
Grant Amount	$375,000
Funder	National Endowment for the Humanities
Grant Project Description	Library expansion and renovation to increase library services, programming and create local history archives.
What made your proposal/ project successful?	There was a close match of our project with the goals of the NEH's Library and Museum program to strengthen humanities resources and programming in our community, and to create the historical archive for a community where none existed.
Would you do anything differently?	No, the process went very well.
What was the most difficult part of the grant process?	Fundraising for 3-1 local match.
Do you have any advice for other grant seekers?	Work closely with staff of the granting agency. The first draft of our proposal was not fundable, but with the help of NEH staff we were able to tailor a grant that met the needs of our library and the NEH.
What do you think is the most important element of a successful grant?	Working closely with funder so that your project meets their program criteria.
How many people worked on your grant application? Were they all library staff?	Two. The Library Director and library board member with fundraising experience.
Did you collaborate with an unusual partner?	We had an excellent capital campaign committee to work on achieving the match for the grant. Included in the match was a funding commitment from our local municipality.
Did your library reach diverse audiences through grant projects?	A strengthened humanities collection was especially significant for students, including distance learners. The entire community benefits from an enhanced local history collection.
Has your library found an unusual funding source?	Serendipitous finding of this source. We went to visit Decorah Public Library to look at their building after they completed a renovation and

	expansion similar to what we planned. The discovery of the NEH grant was a by-product of this visit.
Did you implement innovative programming using grant funds?	A very active local history committee is now soliciting materials for and organizing the historical archive.

Perspectives: Inside/Outside

Project Title	**Perspectives: Inside/Outside**
Library	**Haines Borough Public Library** P.O. Box 1089 Haines, AK 99827
Submitted by	L. S. Moyer
Size of Collection	30,000
Population	2,450
Grant Amount	$6,500 plus in-kind donations
Funder	Alaska Humanities Forum ($2,500); Friends of Haines Borough Public Library ($4,000)
Grant Project Description	Perspectives: Inside/Outside was a year-long series that offered programs on different humanities-based subjects to the community at the Haines Borough Public Library. Speakers from inside and outside the community presented programs on such topics as Native Art, Archeology, and Culture; World Music; Writing and Literature; Comparative Religion; Civic Engagement; and more. Activities ranged from lectures and discussions to writing seminars, musical performances, demonstrations of a craft, children and teen programs, and hypothetical exercises in community planning. The goals of this program were to create a model program that could be replicated by other communities; to serve a constituency beyond our year-round resident population; to use the library as a vehicle to bring

Local musician Len Feldman and visiting artist John Walsh play reels and jigs for a packed library. Photograph is provided by Dan Coleman.

	a humanities series to Haines to offer information and encourage discussion about the topics in an atmosphere of tolerance for diversity of opinion; and to create at least six children and youth programs that shared the practice and study of human values.
What made your proposal/ project successful?	This program allowed the library to reach out to the community in a new way. The programs exposed people to the art, religion, cultural traditions, philosophies, music, food, and myths and stories of other people, as well as offered practical programs about how to start a non-profit organization, involve youth in civic activities, and plan communities. One of the highlights was the attendance and response of the program Islam and the Islamic World by World Religions Professor Kristin Helwig Hansen. As a result of this year-long series, people who had never used the library are now library advocates and have become library cardholders.
Would you do anything differently?	For the most part, the programs were thoughtful and directed to our community. However, we offered a program on community planning which should have been organized as an afternoon seminar rather than a one-hour lecture. Also, the number of hours (10/month) were not adequate for the amount of time it took to coordinate 2–3 programs per month.
What was the most difficult part of the grant process?	This grant required a lot of supporting documentation from each of the scholars as well as letters of support and took a lot more time to collect than anticipated.
Do you have any advice for other grant seekers?	State your goals clearly and then show how you will achieve those goals step by step. Have all support documentation in order.
What do you think is the most important element of a successful grant?	Stating the goals clearly and showing how they will be achieved step by step. Having the right people in place to implement the grant.
How many people worked on your grant application? Were they all library staff?	A total of three people worked on the grant. Two staff people and one professional grant writer.
Did you collaborate with an unusual partner?	We partnered with different programs at the library to create some of the programs such as Library Youth Afterschool Program and The Dragonfly Project: A Technology Awareness Program. We also asked the Haines Arts Council and the Lynn Canal Community Players to do programs.
Did your library reach diverse audiences through grant projects?	The programs reached out to all factions of our community: Native, non-Native, seasonal people, visitors, college and high school educated, professional and blue-collar, young and old, all income levels, and all political parties.
Has your library found an unusual funding source?	The Alaska Humanities Forum supports a variety of humanities-based projects throughout the state.
Did you implement innovative programming using grant funds?	For a small, rural town, providing a year-long series of humanities programs at the Library was a new experience—and very well received.

The Maine Experience

Project Title	**The Maine Experience**
Library	**Lawrence Junior High Library Media Center** 7 School St. Fairfield, ME 04937
Submitted by	Kathy Scott, Library Media Specialist
Size of Collection	10,000 books + AV materials
Population	450 7th and 8th graders and teachers
Grant Amount	$3,500
Funder	Coburn Classical Institute
Grant Project Description	A dedicated team of 8th graders selected books relating to a Maine topic, read and then researched it, then brought it alive by on-site field work and video journalism, creating an informative DVD to share through our Area Resource Center (audio-visuals for teachers and libraries).
What made your proposal/ project successful?	Flexibility: the books and topics were chosen after the students, and reflected their interests. Planning behind the scenes: as co-teachers, we researched possible field locations and planned for contingencies to insure success.
Would you do anything differently?	Start earlier in the year (we finished the last day of school).

Photograph is provided by Susan Morris.

What was the most difficult part of the grant process?	Coordinating with the Coast Guard to board their ship, *Abbie Burgess,* and tackling the logistics of transporting students to a remote off shore island to the lighthouse.
Do you have any advice for other grant seekers?	Look locally in untapped places for funding, then do your homework before applying.
What do you think is the most important element of a successful grant?	That it has a genuine and relevant focus, near and dear to the mission of the fund-holders.
How many people worked on your grant application? Were they all library staff?	2, librarian and video-volunteer/co-teacher.
Did you collaborate with an unusual partner?	Maine Public Television supplied a producer to instruct us in field location video journalism; the Coast Guard gave us a tour of a buoy-tender; the Rockland Library hosted the Puffin Project representative from Monhegan Island who shared information and video footage about the site of our research; Hardy Boat cruises helped us with fares and scheduling; the Rockland Historical Society opened its doors and hosted an information session on 1860s Maine coast history.
Did your library reach diverse audiences through grant projects?	Elementary and middle school students who viewed the DVD, the 8th graders who participated, and various interested adults.
Has your library found an unusual funding source?	Yes, the Coburn Classical Institute is made up of alumni of a private school (now gone) wishing to re-create an atmosphere of concentrated academic excitement and aspirations toward college by offering small teacher : student ratios in special learning situations.
Did you implement innovative programming using grant funds?	Yes. We read and delved into the biography of a young girl who tended a remote lighthouse alone in the setting of 1860s Maine, traveled to on-site locations (however remote) and filmed, then edited and produced a historical DVD.

Training and Equipment Enhancement

Project Title	**Training and Equipment Enhancement**
Library	**Northeastern University Libraries** 360 Huntington Ave. Boston, MA 02115
Submitted by	Debra Mandel
Size of Collection	968,000 volumes; 2,291,913 microforms; 7,626 serial subscriptions; 28,590 licensed electronic journals; 160,542 government publications; 21,957 audio, video, and software items.
Population	Supports the NU [Northeastern University] university community, members of the Boston Library Consortium, and the Boston public.
Grant Amount	$20,979.
Funder	Massachusetts Board of Library Commissioners (an LSTA FY2003 Mini-Grant).
Grant Project Description	The key goal of this project is to better serve members of the NU community with disabilities in the following ways: improve access to library information resources; remove barriers that impede that access; increase awareness about Library services for people with disabilities; and expand training to staff and to patrons with disabilities.

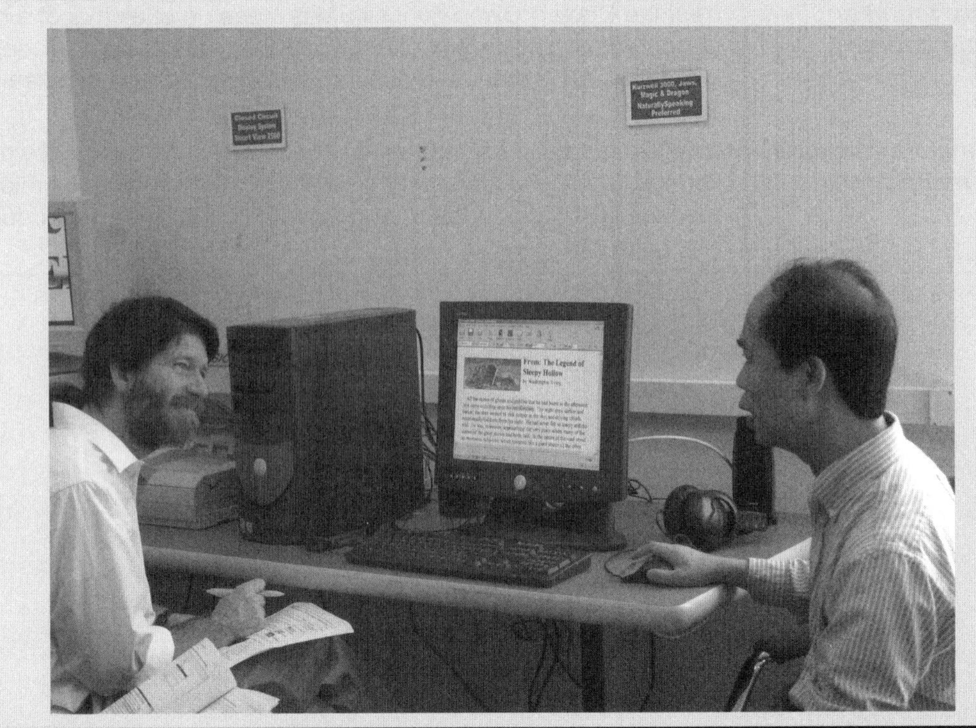

David Backer, principal of the new studio (left) with Computer Services Specialist Karl Lee (right), at Northeastern University Libraries. Courtesy of Northeastern University Libraries.

What made your proposal/ project successful?	Excellent collaboration between the Library and the Mass. Board of Library Commissioners; a productive and passionate cross-departmental Assistive Technology committee which included students and a representative from the University's Disability Resource Center; an excellent partnership and training with corporate vendor; supportive library staff; positive feedback from public.
Would you do anything differently?	No.
What was the most difficult part of the grant process?	Learning the complexities of the software and developing helpful training instructions.
Do you have any advice for other grant seekers?	Stick to deadlines, be realistic about what goals you can achieve in relation to staff, facility, additional resources needed. Do a thorough needs assessment.
What do you think is the most important element of a successful grant?	Good follow through, and teamwork.
How many people worked on your grant application? Were they all library staff?	Six people worked on our grant—four library staff, the Head of the Disability Resource Center, and a consultant from the Mass. Board of Library Commissioners.
Did you collaborate with an unusual partner?	We collaborated successfully with the Libraries' Staff Development and Publicity and Programming Committees; with the Mass. Board of Library Commissioners, the University's Disability Resource Center; our vendor, Adaptive Technology Consulting; and the Massachusetts Commission for the Blind.
Did your library reach diverse audiences through grant projects?	We reached patrons who are blind, visually impaired, learning disabled, deaf or hearing impaired, and patrons with mobility impairments.
Has your library found an unusual funding source?	No, it was a federal grant distributed to library state agencies nationwide.
Did you implement innovative programming using grant funds?	Yes, we had two open houses for the public which included hands-on demonstrations and guest speakers. After training sessions, Assistive Technology Committee members initiated various training programs for library staff and increased training to patrons.

New Literary Borders & Boundaries: A Semi-Permeable Layer?

Project Title	**New Literary Borders & Boundaries: A Semi-Permeable Layer?**
Library	**Harriet Cheney Cowles Memorial Library** **Whitworth College** 300 W. Hawthorne Rd., MS 0901 Spokane, WA 99251-0901
Submitted by	Tami Echavarria Robinson, Associate Professor/Coordinator of Instructional Services, Whitworth College Library
Size of Collection	195,000
Population	Academic community and Spokane area library community.

Graphic by Sue Chism, Graphic Designer, Office of College Communications, Whitworth College.

Grant Amount	$2750.
Funder	ALA Live! @your Library, National Endowment for the Arts, Wallace-Reader's Digest Funds, John S. and James L. Knight Foundation.
Grant Project Description	Program title: "New Literary Borders & Boundaries: A Semi-Permeable Layer?" was a multi-venue 2-day presentation by 3 minority authors (Alex Kuo, XuXi, Gloria Bird) which addressed discovery of self in literature and writing through migration, immigration and displacement. They described how coping with new environments and their search for new identity in a changing landscape caused them to examine their artistic creativity when confronted with new borders and boundaries.
What made your proposal/ project successful?	Collaboration between Whitworth College Library and English Dept. and invitation to area librarians including them in the discussion.
Would you do anything differently?	In one case, make a different author choice.
What was the most difficult part of the grant process?	Starting to write a grant proposal in the first place.
Do you have any advice for other grant seekers?	Take some training such as a grants workshop if possible before starting.
What do you think is the most important element of a successful grant?	Knowing the language of grant writing and format.
How many people worked on your grant application? Were they all library staff?	Two people worked on the grant, a librarian and the college's Director of Sponsored Programs.
Did you collaborate with an unusual partner?	Collaboration for the program was between the Library and the English Dept., a librarian and an English professor.
Did your library reach diverse audiences through grant projects?	College students, area librarians, area students from schools and colleges, faculty, staff, the public.
Has your library found an unusual funding source?	An additional grant of $500.00 from the Washington Commission for the Humanities.
Did you implement innovative programming using grant funds?	Yes. It was the first time the library offered panel discussions, readings, authors to classes, discussions between authors and area librarians.

Preserving Littleton's Legacy

Project Title	**Preserving Littleton's Legacy**
Library	**Reuben Hoar Library** 41 Shattuck St. Littleton, MA 01460
Submitted by	Marjorie H. Oakes, Director, Reuben Hoar Library
Size of Collection	77,400
Population	8,000
Grant Amount	$4,150
Funder	Massachusetts Historical Records Advisory Board
Grant Project Description	Identify, index, and safeguard existing historical records and documents in the collections of nine institutions in Littleton, MA. The project will hire an archives consultant to survey all of the collections and make recommendations; present a workshop for staff of these institutions about professional archival methods; and construct a model for using historical records and primary sources to create a living-history program about a local individual. The project will hire a historian to research historical documents related to Hannah Dodge collaboratively with the staff at several institutions. The model, to be shared with other interested towns, will be also be used for researching other Littleton citizens.

Donna White portraying Hannah Perkins Dodge, the current Littleton Superintendent of Schools, Dr. Paul Livingston; at the Littleton Historical Society exhibition on Hannah P. Dodge and the Littleton Schools. Photograph is provided by the Littleton Historical Society.

What made your proposal/ project successful?	1. Our partnership with the Littleton Historical Society allowed us to hold a reception and exhibit featuring Miss Dodge and to conduct a tour of local sites associated with Miss Dodge. Historical Society members were key to providing hard-working volunteers in all phases of the project. 2. Using a living history interpreter to portray Miss Dodge made her come alive. She attended a Town Meeting, a School Committee meeting, classes for third graders, a Littleton Lyceum presentation, and the exhibit reception in costume. Now everyone in Littleton knows who Hannah Dodge was and many know about our historical records survey.
Would you do anything differently?	The Littleton Historical Society had considerable expense associated with the exhibit. We should have thought of a better way to fund these expenses which were cut from the MHRAB (Massachusetts Historical Records Advisory Board) grant application. We also would like to have paid our interpreter at a higher rate.
What was the most difficult part of the grant process?	We had trouble keeping up with all the interest the grant generated.
Do you have any advice for other grant seekers?	Collaborations spread the workload and multiply the ideas.
What do you think is the most important element of a successful grant?	A well thought-out proposal followed by overwhelming publicity.
How many people worked on your grant application? Were they all library staff?	6 worked on the grant, and 2 were library staff members.
Did you collaborate with an unusual partner?	Littleton Historical Society, Eagle Scout candidate who organized the cleaning and arrangement of some town records, and all town offices and local churches that participated in the document survey.
Did your library reach diverse audiences through grant projects?	Adults of all ages, town officials, Rotary Club, historical society members, third graders who enjoyed Miss Dodge's visit, scouts who visited the exhibit at the historical society and just today, members of the New England School Development Council who are researching women in New England Education.
Has your library found an unusual funding source?	The Littleton Historical Society received a grant of $300 from the Littleton Cultural Council to support the costs of the exhibit.
Did you implement innovative programming using grant funds?	The grant generated the programming described above, but did not cover the expenses.

Neuro-Ophthalmology Virtual Education Library (NOVEL)

Project Title	**Neuro-Ophthalmology Virtual Education Library (NOVEL)**
Library	**Spencer S. Eccles Health Sciences Library** University of Utah 10 N 1900 E Salt Lake City, UT 84112-5890
Submitted by	Nancy Lombardo, Systems Librarian
Size of Collection	Monograph Volumes: 63,834; Journal Subscriptions: 2,358.
Population	Utah, the region, the world.
Grant Amount	~$450,000.
Funder	National Library of Medicine (NLM).
Grant Project Description	The library works with the North American Neuro-Ophthalmology Society (NANOS) to digitize materials relating to Neuro-ophthalmology, indexes the materials and creates user friendly interface to access them. Materials are free for all non-profit educational users.
What made your proposal/ project successful?	The unique content area was interesting and highly visual, making it a good sub-specialty for this type of resource. Also, the strong collaboration between library and national society gave the project a high probability of success.
Would you do anything differently?	No.
What was the most difficult part of the grant process?	Dealing with the forms and the various levels of bureaucracy.
Do you have any advice for other grant seekers?	Start early. Plan ahead. Have clear objectives that can be accomplished within the scope of the project.
What do you think is the most important element of a successful grant?	Defining a project that can be accomplished. It's easy to get carried away with a plan that is not manageable in the time frame of a grant.
How many people worked on your grant application? Were they all library staff?	3 or 4 people helped with the proposal, some were library staff, and others were members of NANOS.
Did you collaborate with an unusual partner?	The strength of this particular project was the collaboration between NANOS and the Eccles Library.
Did your library reach diverse audiences through grant projects?	This grant is aimed at Neuro-opthalmology professionals, residents, medical students, patients, neurologists, and ophthalmologists, which represents the broad sweep of all health related information.

Has your library found an unusual funding source?	No, NLM is a very traditional funding source.
Did you implement innovative programming using grant funds?	Yes, NOVEL is an innovative digital library.

NO Walls: A Community Technology Center

Project Title	**NO Walls: A Community Technology Center**
Library	**Resource Center** Center for Development and Disability University of New Mexico 2300 Menaul Blvd. NE Albuquerque, NM 87107
Submitted by	Pam MacKellar
Size of Collection	3,000
Population	500,000 total population; approximately 115,000 persons with disabilities
Grant Amount	$329,070 over 3 years
Funder	U.S. Department of Education
Grant Project Description	The goal of NO Walls was to demonstrate the effectiveness of training persons with disabilities, their families, service providers, caregivers, teachers and advocates on how to access information using computer technology. The outcomes were to increase the capacity of this population to make choices in their lives, enhance the capacity to provide services and supports for people with disabilities, and foster inclusive and collaborative communities which encourage participation across barriers. The grant funds created a technology center in an existing computer training lab in the Main Branch of the Albuquerque Public Library, built a project web site, trained people with disabilities to use computer technology, and instructed library staff on effectively serving people with disabilities.
What made your proposal/ project successful?	Collaboration with other community organizations to meet an identified need in the community. Utilizing an existing computer lab for the project. Including people with disabilities in the project implementation.
Would you do anything differently?	I would include people from the target population in the initial planning stages and throughout the entire project.
What was the most difficult part of the grant process?	The University's pre-award process including making sure the budget was error-free and the federal forms were signed by the appropriate authorized representatives by the deadline.
Do you have any advice for other grant seekers?	Develop ongoing partnerships with other community organizations. Include partners and representatives of the target population in project planning or as early in the process as possible.
What do you think is the most important element of a successful grant?	Meeting an unmet need in the community and developing a project that results in outcomes that improve the lives of the people it serves.
How many people worked on your grant application? Were they all library staff?	3 people worked on the grant proposal—one library staff, and two other staff members from the Center for Development and Disability.
Did you collaborate with an unusual partner?	The Center for Development and Disability collaborated with the Albuquerque/Bernalillo County Library System and Parents Reaching Out.

Did your library reach diverse audiences through grant projects?	We reached community members with a wide variety of disabilities and Albuquerque/Bernalillo County Library System library staff.
Has your library found an unusual funding source?	The U.S. Department of Education is not an unusual funding source for libraries.
Did you implement innovative programming using grant funds?	Yes, I think that NO Walls provided innovative instruction specifically about the use of technology for people with disabilities.

III THE GRANTS FOR LIBRARIES TOOL KIT AND CD-ROM

A. TOOLS FOR CHAPTER 1: MAKING THE COMMITMENT

Tool A-1: Worksheet: Grant Partnership Agreement

To be completed by the library and each individual partner.

Library Name & Contact Information:

Partner(s) Name & Contact Information:

Project Name:

Overview of Project: (include project description, and the goals, objectives, activities and outcomes of the project)

Goals of this Partnership:

Implementation Plan: (outline the roles and responsibilities regarding the management of this project)

Resources to be Provided: (include staff, funding, equipment, facilities, and by whom these will be provided)

Project Timeline: (include beginning and end dates of partnership, dates to review progress, dates related to the grant)

Impact of Partnership on each Partner: (overview of the gains and losses expected for each partner, including ownership of any products to be created with grant funds or shared funds)

Sustainability: (if project is to be sustained after the partnership ends, how will it be maintained?)

Services to be Provided: (include programs, services and activities, and party responsible)

Evaluation Process: (include any reports along with due dates and party responsible)

We agree to the validity of all of the above statements, and agree to fulfill the obligations specified. We further agree to each of the following:

- To implement the project as presented in the grant application
- To use funds or services received in accordance with the grant application and any applicable laws and regulations
- To provide all services at no charge to the target population
- To maintain honest communications with the partnering agency

Signatures:
Today's Date:

Tool A-2: Checklist: Making the Commitment: A Checklist for Committing to a Grant

The following questions will help you determine if your library can really make the commitment to apply for a grant.

Commit to Accountability

- ❑ Will the grant project definitely support your library's vision and mission?
- ❑ Will your library leadership support the project?
- ❑ Will the library director commit the necessary resources to the project/grant?
- ❑ Will the library staff have the time needed to complete the application process and to implement the project?
- ❑ Will the grant team have the necessary supplies, equipment, services and space?
- ❑ Can the library follow through on the promises made in the grant proposal?
- ❑ Will the library spend the funds as specified and keep accurate accounts?
- ❑ Will you make sure there are not other organizations in your community already doing your project and filling the need?
- ❑ Will all grant reports be filed on time?

Commit to Effective Communication

- ❑ Will your proposal be as clear, concise, and honest as possible?
- ❑ Will your goals, objectives and activities be clearly identified and understandable?
- ❑ Will you be able to convey that your library and the project are important?
- ❑ Will you ask for what you really need?
- ❑ Will all the library staff, board members, leadership, partners and volunteers be continually informed about the grant?
- ❑ Will you ask the funder if the library's grant project clearly fits their interests?
- ❑ Will you use all your contacts?

Commit to Meeting Community Needs

- ❑ Will your library identify the needs of your community?
- ❑ Will your analysis include enough information to educate and inspire the funder?
- ❑ Can statistics be used to quantify the problems identified?
- ❑ Can stories and cases be used regarding specific patrons or programs that illustrate the needs?
- ❑ Will your grant project focus on solutions to meeting community needs?
- ❑ Will you identify a target audience for your grant project and involve representatives in the planning process?

Commit to Planning

- ❑ Does your library have a strategic plan? Will you review it before writing your grant?
- ❑ Will you have a project plan that includes goals, objectives and activities and is based on your strategic plan?
- ❑ Will you set deadlines?
- ❑ Will you organize your materials (research, grant materials, etc)?
- ❑ Will you have a budgetary goal?
- ❑ Will you have a method to track tasks and contacts?

Commit to Partnerships

- ❑ Will you cultivate a strong relationship with your grant's funder?
- ❑ Will you develop the appropriate collaborations to leverage resources, share expertise and support the project?
- ❑ Will you determine what groups in your community share your library's vision and goals and approach them as partners?
- ❑ Will you invite community members to focus groups and planning sessions?
- ❑ Will you complete a partnership agreement outlining goals, responsibilities and benefits?

Commit to Evaluation

- ❑ Can your library clearly identify what success is in respect to the grant project?
- ❑ Will you have an evaluation plan or logic model to determine if your project has met its goals?
- ❑ Will you be able to identify what impact your project achieves; what difference the project makes?
- ❑ Will you identify outcomes for the project? Will your project have meaningful results that cause a change in people's behavior, attitudes, skills, condition or knowledge?
- ❑ Will you have a benchmark plan designed to measure each outcome?

Commit to Sustainability

- ❑ Will your project be completed?
- ❑ Will your project be supported by leadership after grant funds are depleted?
- ❑ Will you plan a funding strategy to continue your project after grant funds are depleted?
- ❑ Is your project reliant on a single person?
- ❑ If your project involves hiring new staff members, will their positions be maintained after the grant period ends?

Commit to Following the Grant Guidelines

- ❑ Will you check and double check all instructions?
- ❑ Will you answer all questions and complete any required narrative sections?
- ❑ Will you compile all attachments?
- ❑ Will you obtain all the required signatures?
- ❑ Will you submit the grant on time?

B. TOOLS FOR CHAPTER 2: PLANNING FOR SUCCESS

Tool B-1: Library Planning Checklist

- ❑ Have you developed a clear mission for your library?
- ❑ Have you clearly defined what the library does?
- ❑ Are your goals obtainable and supportive of your library's mission?
- ❑ Are your objectives clear, measurable and tied to goal achievement?
- ❑ Do you periodically evaluate your objectives to be certain progress is being made?
- ❑ Have you selected a strategy collecting data on your community and library?
- ❑ Are statistics compiled to allow easy retrieval of useful information?
- ❑ Are statistics kept that are seldom or never used?
- ❑ Can you list the strengths of your library?
- ❑ Are you aware of key weaknesses in your library?
- ❑ Are you involving your library staff and community members in the planning process?
- ❑ Did you communicate the final plan to staff, leadership, and community members and respond to their concerns?
- ❑ Is your timetable for implementation of your library's plan realistic?
- ❑ Have you designated specific dates for assessing progress toward goals?

Tool B-2: Links: Library Strategic Plans

Emery Unified School District. *Emery Unified School District Strategic Science Plan June 2003.* Emeryville, CA. Available at www.emeryusd.k12.ca.us/publicdocuments/eusd_science.htm.
Fayetteville Public Library. *Library Information.* Fayetteville, AR. Available at www.faylib.org/information/vision_mission.asp.
Las Vegas-Clark County Library District. *Strategic Plan, 2001–2006.* Las Vegas, NV. Available at www.lvccld.org/strategic_plan/index.htm.
The University of Texas at Austin. *The University of Texas at Austin Libraries Mission and Goals, 2004–2005.* Available at www.lib.utexas.edu/vprovost/mission.html.

C. TOOLS FOR CHAPTER 3: DISCOVERING AND DEFINING THE GRANT PROJECT

Tool C-1: Template: Strategic Plan Goals, Objectives, and Activities

Goals from Strategic Plan	Objectives from Strategic Plan	Activities from Strategic Plan
Goal 1	**Objective 1.1**	1. 2. 3. 4. 5.
	Objective 1.2	1. 2. 3. 4. 5.

<table>
<tr><td rowspan="3">Goal 2</td><td>Objective 2.1</td><td>1.
2.
3.
4.
5.</td></tr>
<tr><td>Objective 2.2</td><td>1.
2.
3.
4.
5.</td></tr>
<tr><td>Objective 2.3</td><td>1.
2.
3.
4.
5.</td></tr>
<tr><td rowspan="2">Goal 3</td><td>Objective 3.1</td><td>1.
2.
3.
4.
5.</td></tr>
<tr><td>Objective 3.2</td><td>1.
2.
3.</td></tr>
</table>

		4. 5.
	Objective 3.3	1. 2. 3. 4. 5.
Goal 4	**Objective 4.1**	1. 2. 3. 4. 5.
	Objective 4.2	1. 2. 3. 4. 5.
Goal 5	**Objective 5.1**	1. 2. 3. 4. 5.

	Objective 5.2	1. 2. 3. 4. 5.
	Objective 5.3	1. 2. 3. 4. 5.
Goal 6	**Objective 6.1**	1. 2. 3. 4. 5.
	Objective 6.2	1. 2. 3. 4. 5.
Goal 7	**Objective 7.1**	1. 2. 3.

		4. 5.
	Objective 7.2	1. 2. 3. 4. 5.

Tool C-2: Worksheet: Project Planning

1. Describe your project in one sentence. Include what you will do, where, why and with whom.	
2. List keywords that describe your project.	
3. Describe the need in your community or the problem your project will address.	

4. Identify target audience for the project.	
5. What are the goals of the project?	
6. What are the specific changes you expect to make in your community or among the beneficiaries of your project? Articulate objectives for the project.	
7. List the steps required to make the changes listed above. Develop activities or strategies required to reach an objective. How are you going to solve this problem?	
8. List the resources you will need to accomplish the steps. What resources do you already have?	

9. Cost.	
10. List your partners on this project. Who else is addressing this problem in our community? Who is likely to partner with us on this project?	
11. Describe how you will measure your success. How will things be different or what will the improvement be.	

Adapted from Project Profile/Planning Worksheet, JUST GRANTS! Arizona.

Tool C-3: Template: Project Action Steps

Project Objectives	Personnel	Action Steps

Tool C-4: Template: Project Timeline

Activity	Jan	Feb	Mar	Apr	May	June	July	Aug	Sept	Oct	Nov	Dec

Tool C-5: Template: Personnel Budget

Position	Salary	Benefits (%)	Total
TOTAL PERSONNEL COSTS			

Tool C-6: Template: Nonpersonnel Budget

ITEM	DESCRIPTION	COST
Marketing		
Equipment		
Copying Costs		
Supplies		
Space Rental		
Travel		
Other		
TOTAL NONPERSONNEL COSTS		

Tool C-7: Template: Evaluation Plan

Goal	Outcome	Objective	Evaluation Method	Timeline

D. TOOLS FOR CHAPTER 6: RESEARCHING AND SELECTING THE RIGHT GRANT

Tool D-1: Worksheet: Keyword Selection

Project Plan Section	Keywords
Goals: 1. 2. 3.	
Objectives: 1. 2. 3.	
Outcomes: 1. 2. 3.	
Activities and Action Steps: 1. 2. 3. 4. 5. 6. 7. 8. 9. 10.	

Tool D-2: Worksheet: Funder Summary

Funder Name	
Address	
Contact	
Funder's Financial Information	
Amount given last year	
Number of grants given	
Average amount awarded	
Funder's Interests and Criteria	
Purpose	
Fields of interest	
Type of support	
Eligibility	
Geographic area	
Limitations	
Application Information	
Approach	
Application form? Y N	Where found/format
Deadline	
Sources Used	
Directories/indexes and page/entry numbers	
Web sites	
990 PF	
Annual report	
Personal contact	
Notes	

Tool D-3: Links: Funding Resources for Libraries

Government Funding Resources

Federal

Catalog of Federal Domestic Assistance: www.cfda.gov.
Federal Register: www.gpoaccess.gov/fr/index.html.
Grants.gov: www.grants.gov.
USDA's Notices of Funding Availability: http://ocd1.usda.gov/nofa2.asp.

State, County, and City Government

State Libraries

Click on LSTA from your state library's home page:
www.ala.org/ala/washoff/WOissues/federallibprog/lsta/lstasts.htm.

State Humanities Councils, Arts Councils, Cultural Services Agencies, and Departments of Education:

Links to State Humanities Councils: www.neh.gov/whoweare/statecouncils.html.

Private Funding Resources

Foundations

Web sites of private foundations: http://fdncenter.org/funders/grantmaker/gws_priv/priv.html.
RFP Bulletin: http://fdncenter.org/pnd/rfp.

Community Foundations

Council of Foundation's Community Foundation Locator: www.cof.org/Locator/index.cfm?menuContainerID=34&crumb=2.
Community Foundations from Foundation Center: http://fdncenter.org/funders/grantmaker/gws_comm/comm.html.

Corporate

Corporate Funders from Foundation Center: http://fdncenter.org/funders/grantmaker/gws_corp/corp.html.

Local Funding Directories

State and Local Funding Directories: A Bibliography http://fdncenter.org/learn/topical/sl_dir.html.

Funding Resources for Libraries

Federal

U.S. Department of Agriculture Cooperative State, Research, Education, and Extension Service's unique: www.csrees.usda.gov/fo/funding.cfm.
U.S. Department of Education Grants and Contracts: www.ed.gov/fund/landing.jhtml?src=rt.
Office of Innovation and Improvement Funding Opportunities: www.ed.gov/about/offices/list/oii/funding.html.
Office of Elementary and Secondary Education: www.ed.gov/about/offices/list/oese/index.html.

Office of English Language Acquisition, Language Enhancement, and Academic Achievement for Limited English Proficient Students: www.ed.gov/about/offices/list/oela/index.html?src=oc.
Office of Postsecondary Education: www.ed.gov/about/offices/list/ope/index.html?src=oc.
Office of Special Education and Rehabilitative Services: www.ed.gov/about/offices/list/osers/index.html?src=oc.
Office of Vocational and Adult Education: www.ed.gov/about/offices/list/ovae/index.html?src=oc.
Department of Health and Human Services Administration for Children and Families: www.acf.hhs.gov/grants/index.html.
Health Resources and Services Administration: www.hrsa.gov/grants/default.htm.
National Library of Medicine: www.nlm.nih.gov/grants.html.
National Networks of Libraries of Medicine Regional Awards: http://nnlm.gov/projects/funding/.
Office of Juvenile Justice and Delinquency: http://ojjdp.ncjrs.org/funding/FundingList.asp.
National Endowment for the Arts: www.nea.gov/.
Institute of Museum and Library Services: www.imls.gov/grants/library/index.htm.
National Endowment for the Humanities: www.neh.fed.us.
National Historical Publications and Records Commission (NHPRC): www.archives.gov/grants/index.html.
National Institute for Literacy: www.nifl.gov/nifl/grants_contracts.html.

Professional Associations

ALA Grants and Fellowships: www.ala.org/Template.cfm?Section=grantfellowship.
ALA Awards and Scholarships: www.ala.org/Template.cfm?Section=awards.
American Association of School Librarians Funding Opportunities: www.ala.org/aasl/resources/funding.html.
SLA Scholarships and Grants: www.sla.org/content/learn/scholarship/index.cfm.

BLOG

Library Grants Blog
http://librarygrants.blogspot.com.

E. TOOLS FOR CHAPTER 7: CREATING AND SUBMITTING THE WINNING PROPOSAL

Tool E-1: Checklist: Questions for Funders

Is my library eligible?

How are applications reviewed?

Are there specific screening criteria or a rubric used? Can we have a copy?

Can we submit a draft of the grant proposal before the final deadline for review?

If I briefly describe the project, would you provide suggestions or advice?

Are copies of successful grant proposals available?

Can we include our long-range plan or other supporting documentation in an appendix?

May we include a table of contents?

How and when are final decisions made?

Will we be notified that our grant proposal has been received?

Tool E-2: Template: Grant Proposal

Library Name

Library Address

Library Address2

Library Telephone Number

Date

Grant Proposal submitted to:

Name of Prospective Funder

Grant Project Title

Date

Name, Title (Funder Contact Person)
Funder Name (Foundation, Government Agency, etc.)
Funder Address
Funder Address2

RE: Title of Grant

Dear: Insert Name of Funder Contact

Name of Library is pleased to submit this proposal for your review. We look forward to your partnership in our efforts to serve *Name of Your Community.*

Our much needed project, *Title of Project*, is a partnership among Insert name of Library and project partners. *Insert the one sentence Project Description from your Project Planning Worksheet.*

Insert the Needs Statement from your Project Planning Worksheet. Insert the Project Goals from your Project Planning Worksheet.

The *Name of Library* is committed to the success of this project. *Insert a statement of any outside funding that will be used towards the project.* Our request to *Name of Funder* is for *Total Amount of Funding Requested. Insert a statement regarding planning accomplished and/or involvement of target audience.*

Insert your Library Mission and a sentence or two from your Organizational Overview. Particularly demonstrate why the library is a viable grant candidate.

Thank you for your time and attention. We look forward to working together to build a better community. Please do not hesitate to contact us with any questions or requests for additional information.

Sincerely,

Name of Library Director, or other Authority
Title of Library Director, or other Authority

TABLE OF CONTENTS

I. Proposal Summary .... *Page Number*
II. Organizational Overview .... *Page Number*
III. Statement of Needs .... *Page Number*
IV. Project Description .... *Page Number*
V. Approach/Methodology .... *Page Number*
VI. Budget Request .... *Page Number*
VII. Evaluation Process .... *Page Number*
VIII. Appendix .... *Page Number*

PROPOSAL SUMMARY

Date of Application:

Name of Library (exact legal name)

Library's Full Mailing Address

Library Director: *Library Director's Full Name*
Library Director's Contact Information

Grant Coordinator: *Grant Coordinator's name, if not Director; include title*
Grant Coordinator's Contact Information

Project Title: *Project Title*

Project Description: *One sentence Project Description from Project Planning Worksheet*

Amount Requested: *$$*

Project Funding From Other Sources: *$$ Include in kind contributions from library, other grant funds*

Total Project Budget: *$$*

Project Budget Time Period: *Dates covered by project budget (June 1, 200x–May 31, 200x)*

Grant Abstract: *In 500 words or less condense the major points of each of the grant proposal components. You will want to write this section last, and definitely review it as the last step in editing your proposal.*

Include:

- A few sentences summarizing the library's Organizational Overview, which will show why the library is the best choice for implementing the grant project
- Any partners, and how they are contributing
- The Need Statement, as well as the target audience
- A few sentences from the Project Description detailing what the project entails and how it fulfills the needs
- The project goals, objectives and/or outcomes
- A brief overview of the evaluation methods to be used
- How the funder's mission aligns with your grant project

ORGANIZATIONAL OVERVIEW

Include a brief overview of the library's history, mission, qualifications, trustworthiness, community served, achievements & impact in community, primary programs, and current budget. Provide a sentence or two detailing the qualifications of key staff and library leadership/board. Include brief success stories if relevant to the project & funder.

STATEMENT OF NEEDS

Establish the existence and importance of the problem. This is a critical part of your proposal. A compelling need statement will motivate the funder to assist in the solution. Prove that the need is relevant to the funder. Why should they fund this project, why now and how will it benefit the library community?

The need should focus on those your library serves, not just the library. Support the need with evidence (research from statistics, experts, or census data; or information from the library's long range plan such as the community analysis or needs assessments). You may even include anecdotal substantiation such as a personal story of someone who needs this project, or input from focus groups.

Then prove why the library has the ability to respond to the need you have identified. Link the fulfillment of the need to your library's mission.

Answer the questions:

Why this issue?

Why this target population?

Why this funder?

Why your library?

PROJECT DESCRIPTION

This section includes an overview of your project. It is a more in-depth narrative than the project abstract. In the previous section you discussed the needs, now you will focus on the solutions. Briefly summarize the project and how it will be of benefit to the target population. Include the Project Goals, Project Objectives, and Project Partners. You may also include information on how the project will be sustained after the initial funding.

Include:

Project Significance (include one or two sentences developed from the Need Statement)
Target Audience
Project Goals
Project Objectives
Project Partners
Plans for Sustainability and Leveraging Impact

APPROACH/METHODOLOGY

How and when will the project be implemented? Describe the strategies and methods to be used and why they are the most effective solution to the need. Include Project Action Steps, and emphasize Project Partners and Collaborators. Include a timeline (example follows). Mention how the donor will be recognized.

Activity	Jan	Feb	Mar	Apr	May	June	July	Aug	Sept	Oct	Nov	Dec
List each grant activity in this column												

BUDGET REQUEST

PERSONNEL

Position	Salary	Benefits (%)	Total
Example: .20 FTE Library Assistant	$	$	$
Example: .15 FTE Reference Librarian	$	$	$
Complete according to Budget Template	$	$	$
	$	$	$1
TOTAL PERSONNEL COSTS	**$**	**$**	**$**

NON-PERSONNEL

CATEGORIES	TOTAL AMOUNT	AMOUNT FUNDED	AMOUNT REQUESTED
Marketing			
Insert any Subcategories (brochures, ads, etc.)	$$	$$	$$
Equipment			
Technology			
Supplies			
Postage Delivery			
Printing and Copying			
TOTAL NON-PERSONNEL COSTS:	$	$	$
TOTAL PERSONNEL COSTS:	$	$	$
TOTAL PROJECT BUDGET:	$	$	$

EVALUATION PROCESS

Provide a brief description of the evaluation plan for judging the success of the project. How will you measure success? How will you use the results? What reports will the donor receive and when?

Goal	Outcome	Objective	Evaluation Method	Time Period
1. Complete According to Project Evaluation Plan Template	*Complete According to Project Evaluation Template*	*Complete According to Project Evaluation Template*	*Complete According to Project Evaluation Template*	*Complete According to Project Evaluation Template*
2.				
3.				
4.				

APPENDIX

Some funders specify what should and should not be included in the appendices. If this is not specified in the grant guidelines, contact the funder to verify anything you wish to include that is not approved. Some examples of Appendix materials include: strategic plans, resumes or job descriptions of key personnel, organizational charts, letters of support, financial reports, the budget for the current year, lengthy charts and tables, IRS 501(c) (3) nonprofit determination letter; a recent library newsletter, or relevant newspaper clippings that demonstrate the library's applicable work.

Tool E-3: Checklist: Grant Proposal

Here are some major criteria against which your proposal may be judged. Read through your application repeatedly, and ask whether the answers to the questions below are clear, even to a non-librarian.

- ❑ Does the proposal address a well-formulated problem or need?
- ❑ Is it a real need of your community, or are you just trying to find a reason to justify a project you think would be fun to implement?
- ❑ Is it an important problem, whose solution will have useful effects?
- ❑ Is special funding necessary to solve the problem, or could it be solved using existing library resources?
- ❑ Is there a good idea on which to base the project work? The proposal must explain the idea in sufficient detail to convince the reader that the idea has significant substance, and should explain why there is reason to believe that it is indeed a good idea.
- ❑ Does the proposal explain clearly what work will be done? Does it explain what results are expected and how they will be evaluated? How would it be possible to judge whether the work was successful?
- ❑ Is there evidence that the library knows about the work that others have done on the problem?
- ❑ Does the library have a good track record with grants and will the library leadership be committed to implementation of this grant project?

Tool E-4: Checklist: Grant Submission

- ❑ The funder is interested in receiving my proposal.
- ❑ This proposal reflects the funder's areas of interest.
- ❑ We have followed the instructions and guidelines of the funder's specifications.
- ❑ Our proposal meets the page/word limits.
- ❑ The font type and size are correct.
- ❑ The margin size is correct.
- ❑ The line spacing is correct.
- ❑ We have used the specified type of paper.
- ❑ We did not bind unless we were told we could.
- ❑ The correct number of copies and the original were sent; we also retained a copy.
- ❑ We included letters of support.
- ❑ We have the specified signatures.
- ❑ The proposal components are titled and compiled in the order specified.
    - ❍ Title Sheet
    - ❍ Cover Letter
    - ❍ Table of Contents
    - ❍ Executive Summary
    - ❍ Organizational Overview
    - ❍ Statement of Needs
    - ❍ Project Description
    - ❍ Approach/Methodology
    - ❍ Budget Request
    - ❍ Evaluation Process
    - ❍ Appendix
- ❑ The cover letter explains the project and states the total cost of the project, the amount expected from other sources, and the amount requested.
- ❑ The project description specifies the need that will be met and how people will benefit.
- ❑ The project description tells the whole story of the project in clear, understandable language.
- ❑ The objectives are measurable.
- ❑ The methodology explains how the objectives will be met.
- ❑ The evaluation plan measures the degree to which the objectives are met.
- ❑ The project includes partners and reflects community involvement.
- ❑ The budget is reasonable.
- ❑ The calculations are correct.
- ❑ The project is sustainable.

- ❑ There is adequate staff in the proposal to do the project.
- ❑ There are adequate resources to do the project.
- ❑ Your organization has the capacity to do the project.
- ❑ There is no jargon.
- ❑ If there are attachments, you have confirmed that the funder allows them.
- ❑ The proposal has been proofed by an impartial person.
- ❑ The proposal is clear and easy to understand by someone outside the team.
- ❑ Copies of the proposal were made for partners and supporters.
- ❑ Letters of agreement from partners are included (provided funder allows them).
- ❑ Letters of support from supporters are included (provided funder allows them).
- ❑ We have met the deadline.
- ❑ The proposal looks professional.

Now, carefully go through your application with your checklist and check off every item as you make sure it is in place. Once everything is checked, you may seal the envelope and head for the post office.

- ❑ The proposal was submitted on __________.
- ❑ We have a dated receipt or confirmation that the proposal was submitted.

Tool E-5: Example RFPs and Grant Announcements

Tool E-6: Example of Grant Proposals

Tools E-5 and E-6 are available only on the companion CD-ROM because of their extensive length.

BIBLIOGRAPHY

Annual Register of Grant Support. Annual. New Providence, NJ: R. R. Bowker.

Bauer, D. G. 1999. *The "How To" Grants Manual: Successful Grantseeking Techniques for Obtaining Public and Private Grants*. Phoenix, AZ: American Council on Education and Oryx Press.

Berry, John. 2003. *Library of the Year: Las Vegas—Clark County Library District*. Available at http://libraryjournal.reviewsnews.com/index.asp?layout=articlePrint&articleID=CA302409.

Brown, Larissa Golden, Martin John Brown, and Judith E. Nichols. 2001. *Demystifying Grant Seeking: What You REALLY Need to Do to Get the Grants*. New York: Wiley.

Bryson, John. 2004. *Strategic Planning for Public and Nonprofit Organizations: A Guide to Strengthening and Sustaining Organizational Achievement*. 3rd ed. San Francisco: Jossey-Bass.

Burke, J. 2000. *I'll Grant You That: A Step-by-Step Guide to Finding Funds, Designing Winning Projects, and Writing Powerful Grant Proposals*. Portsmouth, NH: Heinemann.

Burns, M. E. 1993. *Proposal Writer's Guide*. New Haven, CT: Development and Technical Assistance Center.

Carlson, M. 2002. *Winning Grants Step by Step*. San Francisco: Jossey-Bass.

Catalog of Federal Domestic Assistance. Available at http://12.46.245.173/cfda/cfda.html.

Clarke, Cheryl A. 2001. *Storytelling for Grantseekers: The Guide to Creative Nonprofit Fundraising*. San Francisco: Jossey-Bass.

Constable, M. R. 1993. *Federal Grants and Services for Libraries: A Guide to Selected Programs*. Washington, DC: American Library Association.

Corporate Foundation Profiles. Annual. New York: Foundation Center.

Corporate Giving Directory. Annual. Rockville, MD: Taft Group.

Corporate Philanthropy Report. San Francisco: Public Management Institute.

FC Search. New York: Foundation Center. Available at www.fdncenter.org/.

Falkenstein, Jeffrey A., ed. 2001. *National Guide to Funding for Libraries and Information Services*. 6th ed. New York: Foundation Center.

Federal Register. Available at www.gpoaccess.gov/fr/index.html.

Florida Department of State, Division of Library and Information Services. 2000. *Workbook: Outcome Measurement of Library Programs.* Available at http://dlis.dos.state.fl.us/bld/Research_Office/OutcomeEvalWkbk.doc.

Forsberg, Kevin, Hal Mooz, and Howard Cotterman. *Visualizing Project Management*. New York: Wiley, 1996.

Foundation Center. 2005. *Proposal Writing Short Course.* Available at www.fdcenter.org/learn/shortcourse/prop1.html.

Foundation Center's User-Friendly Guide: A Grant-Seeker's Guide to Resources. 2002. New York: Foundation Center.

Foundation Center's Guide to Grant Seeking on the Web. 2000. New York: Foundation Center.

Foundation Directory. Annual. New York: Foundation Center.

Foundation Directory Online. Available at www.fdncenter.org/.

Foundation Grants Index. Annual. New York: Foundation Center.

Foundation Grants Index on CD-ROM. Semiannual. New York: Foundation Center.

Foundation 1000. Annual. New York: Foundation Center.

Foundation Reporter. Annual. Detroit: Taft Group.

Fundsnet. Available at www.fundsnetservices.com.

Geever, Jane C. 2004. *The Foundation Center's Guide to Proposal Writing.* 4th ed. New York: Foundation Center.

Gerding, Stephanie R. 2003. "Small Library, Big Fundraising: Community Support Is Way Above Par." *Computers in Libraries* 23, no. 2 (February):16.

Golden, S. L. 1997. *Secrets of Successful Grantsmanship: A Guerrilla Guide to Raising Money*. San Francisco: Jossey-Bass.

Grants for Libraries and Information Services. 2004. New York: Foundation Center.

Grants for Libraries Hotline. Available at www.quinlan.com/b_glb.html.

Grants Register. Biennial. New York: St. Martin's Press.

Grantsandfunding.com. Available at www.grantsandfunding.com.

Grantsmanship Center. Available at www.tgci.com.

Grantsmart. Available at www.grantsmart.org

Guide to US Foundations. Annual. New York: Foundation Center.

Guidestar. Available at www.guidestar.org.

Hale, P. D. 1997. *Writing Grant Proposals That Win*. Alexandria, VA: Capitol.

Hall, Mary S., and Susan Howlett. 2003. *Getting Funded: The Complete Guide to Writing Grant Proposals.* 4th ed. Portland, OR: Portland State University.

Hayes, L. C., ed. 1999. *Winning Strategies for Developing Grant Proposals*. Washington, DC: Government Information Services.

IMLS. *Introduction to Outcome Oriented Evaluation: Selected Resources*. Available at www.imls.gov/grants/current/crnt_bib.htm.

Introduction to Grant Funding. 1993. Sacramento: Nonprofit Resource Center, Sacramento Public Library. (Video).

Johnston, Michael. 1998. *The Fund Raiser's Guide to the Internet*. New York: John Wiley & Son.

McNamara, Carter. Ph.D. *Basic Guide to Program Evaluation*. Available at www.mapnp.org/library/evaluatn/fnl_eval.htm.

Michigan State University Research. Available at www.lib.msu.edu/harris23/grants/.

Miller, P. W. 2000. *Grant-Writing: Strategies for Developing Winning Proposals*. Peter Miller.

Miner, L. E. 1993. *Proposal Planning and Writing*. Phoenix, AZ: Oryx Press.

Mudd, Mollie, ed. 2000. *The Grantseeker's Handbook of Essential Internet Sites*. Gaithersburg, MD: Aspen.

National Directory of Corporate Giving. Annual. New York: Foundation Center.

Nelson, Sandra S. 2001. *The New Planning for Results: A Streamlined Approach*. Chicago: Public Library Association.

Nelson, Sandra S., Ellen Altman, and Diane Mayo. 2000. *Managing for Results: Effective Resource Allocation for Public Libraries*. Chicago: Public Library Association.

New, C. C. 1998. *Grantseeker's Toolkit: A Comprehensive Guide to Finding Funding*. New York: John Wiley.

Nugent, C. 2000. *The Grant-Writer's Start-Up Kit: A Beginner's Guide to Grant Proposals*. I. Successful Images (Video).

Outcomes Toolkit. Available at http://ibec.ischool.washington.edu/ibecCat.aspx?subCat=Outcome%20Toolkit&cat=Tools%20and%20Resources.

Peterson, Susan Lee. 2001. *The Grantwriter's Internet Companion: A Resource for Educators and Others Seeking Grants and Funding*. San Francisco: Jossey-Bass.

Philanthropy News Digest RFP Bulletin. Available at http://fdncenter.org/pnd/rfp.

Prospector's Choice. Available at www.gale.com/servlet/ItemDetailServlet?region=9&imprint=000&titleCode=CFGIS&type=4&id=600924.

Quick, James Aaron, and Cheryl Carter. 2000. *Grant Winner's Toolkit: Project Management and Evaluation*. New York: John Wiley.

RFP Bulletin. Available at http://fdncenter.org/pnd/rfp/.

Reif-Lehrer, L. 1989. *Going for the Gold: Some Do's and Don'ts for Grant Seekers*. Rockville, MD: National Institute on Alcohol Abuse and Alcoholism et al.

Reif-Lehrer, L. 1995. *Grant Application Writer's Handbook*. Boston: Jones and Bartlett.

Schladweiler, Kier, ed. 2001. *The Foundation Center's Guide to Grantseeking on the Web*. New York: Foundation Center.

State and Local Funding Directories: A Bibliography. Available at www.fdncenter.org/learn/topical/sl_dir.html.

State Library of Florida. 1999. *The Library Services and Technology Act Outcome Evaluation Plan*. Available at http://dlis.dos.state.fl.us/bld/Research_Office/Outcome_EvalPlan_final.doc.

Taft Group. 2002. *Big Book of Library Grant Money: Profiles of Private and Corporate Foundations and Direct Corporate Givers Receptive to Library Grant Proposals*. Chicago: American Library Association.

U.S. Census Bureau. *American Factfinder*. Available at http://factfinder.census.gov.

U.S. Census Bureau. *State & County Quick Facts*. Available at http://quickfacts.census.gov.

United Way of America. *United Way of America's Outcome Measurement Resource Network*. Available at http://national.unitedway.org/outcomes/.

GLOSSARY

501(c) (3): A section of the federal tax code that designates an organization as nonprofit by the Internal Revenue Service. Funders may require proof of your nonprofit status with your application.

990-PF: The federal reporting form that private grant-making foundations are required to submit every year to the Internal Revenue Service. 990-PFs document the foundation's financial activities during the year. These are public documents so you may use the information in them to learn about a foundation, their trustees, where their funds originate, their grant-making contributions, and to whom they awarded grants for the year.

Abstract: A short summary of a project including all pertinent activities, a summary of the objectives, and the expected results. The abstract is usually limited to one page.

Action Steps: The specific steps taken to accomplish a grant project.

Activities: The specific actions or strategies that will accomplish the long-range or strategic plan.

Annual Report: A report published yearly by a foundation or corporation describing its activities, including grants awarded. Annual reports may be simple or very elaborate. Corporations often use annual reports as a way to inform the community about their contributions and activities, and they may also serve as marketing tools.

Appendixes/Attachments: Supporting documentation that is submitted with your proposal. Requirements vary, so be sure to check the application guidelines carefully for what the funder wants to see. May include:

Letters of support
Letters of agreement
List of board members or trustees, with titles
Résumés
Budget
Library's mission statement

Library's most recent accomplishments

List of other sources of funding

Copy of your 501(c) (3)

Any additional information about your library that will help the funder determine your ability to succeed (press clippings, service brochures, statistics, staff awards, for example).

Application: The formal document that you submit to a potential funder from whom you are seeking funds.

Audit, Financial: An examination of an organization's financial documents by an outside expert. Financial audits are usually conducted at the end of the fiscal year. Your funder may require an audit of grant funds at the end of your project.

Audit, Program: A review of the successes of a funded program by the funding agency. A program audit may be mandatory or random, at the end of a project, or midstream. Also known as Monitoring.

Authorized Signature: The signature of the person who is responsible for your organization by law.

Beneficiary: A member of the target population that the grant benefits. For example, a community member attending a library program is the beneficiary of a grant received by the library.

Bricks and Mortar: Capital funds generally used for building renovation or construction.

Budget: An annual fiscal plan for an organization that contains an itemized list of revenues and expenses. A project budget is often included in a grant proposal and covers estimated funds needed for the entire grant project. The library's annual budget may also be included in the grant proposal appendix.

Capital/Building Grant: Funds that are used to purchase land and construct, renovate, or rehabilitate buildings and facilities. May also refer to major equipment purchases such as computer systems.

Challenge Grant: A grant that requires the grantee to come up with additional funds from other sources, usually within a specified period of time.

Community Foundation: A tax-exempt, nonprofit philanthropic organization comprising funds established by many donors for the charitable benefit of the residents in a defined geographic area or community.

Cooperating Collection: A member of the Foundation Center's network of libraries, community foundations, and other nonprofit agencies that provides a core collection of center publications in addition to a variety of additional materials and services in areas useful to grant seekers.

Corporate Foundation: A private foundation that amasses its grant funds from the contributions of a profit-making corporation. The corporate foundation is a legally separate organization from the parent corporation. Corporate foundations are subject to the rules and regulations that oversee all private foundations.

Corporate Giving Program: A grant-making program established and administered within a for-profit corporation. Some companies make grants through both a corporate giving program and a corporate foundation.

Demonstration Grant: A grant made to implement an innovative project or program. If successful, this kind of grant may serve as a model, to be duplicated by others.

Discretionary Grant: The category of federal or state grants for which individual libraries, community organizations, schools, and local governments are eligible to apply. Unlike the federal grant funds that are distributed through a pass-through agent like the state.

Donated Products: Any goods, products, equipment, or other tangible property that is donated to your library for its use and ownership. These may include food, paper goods, or office supplies, as well as furnishings, computer equipment, vehicles, and so on. Donated products are part of "in-kind" support and should be included in your budget, at fair-market value.

Drawdown: The method by which a grantee requests payment from the funding agency. Frequency of drawdowns (or draws) may be weekly or quarterly, or it may be a single lump sum payment at the end of the project.

DUNS Number: A unique 9-digit number issued by Dun and Bradstreet that is used to keep track of more than 70 million businesses worldwide. The federal government recently adopted a policy that requires organizations to provide a DUNS number in federal grant applications and proposals.

EIN: Employer Identification Number. This number is issued by the Internal Revenue Service and must be included in all government and some foundation grant applications.

Evaluation Plan: The steps you will take to measure your success so you can make adjustments and technical improvements as the project progresses.

Fiscal Year (FY): A 12-month accounting period that ends with the closing of the books.

Focus Group: A group of individuals gathered together to discuss an issue or give feedback. Focus groups may be used to determine the library community's needs or to evaluate the effectiveness of a grant project.

Formula Grants: Grants from the federal or state government to a lower level of government where a specific monetary amount is determined based on a formula—usually derived from a socioeconomic standard.

Foundation: A nonprofit organization that has its own funds/endowments and that is managed by its own trustees/directors and usually benefits educational, charitable, social, religious, or other activities. Types of foundations include community foundations, corporate foundations, family foundations, and private foundations.

Funder: The agency, organization, foundation, association, or governmental unit that awards grants. Also known as a funding agency, grant maker, grantor, or donor.

Funding Cycle: The schedule of events that starts with the announcement of the availability of funds followed by the deadline for submission of applications, review of applications, grant awards, contract documents, and release of funds.

Goal: The broad purpose of your project or program.

Grant: The sum of money given to support the project or program of an agency, organization, or individual. This is usually the result of a formal proposal submission and review process. Grants are given outright, with no conditions for repayment.

Grant Agreement: A contract entered into by the recipient of a grant and a funder. Based on the application submitted, the agreement commits the recipient to implement a specific project, within a certain time frame, for a specific amount of money.

Grant Coordinator: The individual responsible for all activities involved in the grant, including the planning, submission, evaluation, and follow-up.

Grant Proposal Components: The standard sections of a grant proposal. These vary according to each funder. Typical components include Title Sheet, Cover Letter, Table of Contents, Proposal Summary, Organizational Overview, Statement of Needs, Project Description, Approach/Methodology, Budget Request, Evaluation Process, and Appendix.

Grant Team: This team comprises representatives from library leadership, community advisers, grant researchers, grant writers, staff members who will plan and implement the grant, and subject matter experts.

Grantee: The recipient of grant funds. May also be referred to as fundee or donee.

Guidelines: A funder's goals, priorities, criteria, and procedures for applying for a grant.

IMLS: Institute of Museum and Library Services is a federal grant-making agency that promotes leadership, innovation, and a lifetime of learning by supporting museums and libraries in the United States. Created by the Museum and Library Services Act of 1996. (www.imls.gov)

In-kind Support: A noncash donation of labor, facilities, or equipment to carry out a project. Examples are products or equipment, volunteer services, office space or staff time, and library materials donated for your project. In-kind support should always be included in your budget at fair-market value.

Lead Agency: The agency with the primary responsibility for overseeing the funded project, including filing reports and fiscal management.

Letter of Inquiry: A brief letter to assess a potential funder's interest in considering a grant proposal. It should include background on your library; a brief description of your project; the total amount required to fund the project; the specific dollar amount you are requesting from the funder; the amount you have from other sources; and an explanation of why your proposal matches the funder's priorities and interests. If the funder is interested, they will invite you to submit a full proposal. Also referred to as a letter of intent.

Letter of Intent: A letter that the grant seeker sends before writing or submitting a grant proposal to a funder in order to ensure that the proposal will fit within the funder's guidelines and mission.

Letter of Support: A simple letter attached as an addendum to your proposal. This letter should be from an "expert" or supporter of your project who tells why he or she believes that your project should be funded.

Library Service Responses: Library Service Responses were created by the Public Library Association and are used in the planning process in *The New Planning for Results*. They are used to prioritize the activities most needed by the library's community. The thirteen Service Reponses are Basic Literacy, Business and Career Information, Commons, Community Referral,

Consumer Information, Cultural Awareness, Current Topics and Titles, Formal Learning Support, General Information, Government Information, Information Literacy, Lifelong Learning, and Local History & Genealogy.

LSTA: The Library Services and Technology Act (LSTA) of 1996, a section of the Museum and Library Services Act, provides funds to state library agencies using a population-based formula. State libraries may use the appropriation to support statewide initiatives and services; they may also distribute the funds through competitive subgrant competitions or cooperative agreements to public, academic, research, school, and special libraries in their state.

Matching Funds: The portion of the project costs that the grantee is responsible for providing. Examples of matching funds are funding from other sources, personnel, or in-kind donations.

Mission Statement: A broad statement of the role or purpose of the library, whom the library serves, and justification of its existence.

Narrative: The written portion of your grant. The story of who, what, where, when, why, and how.

Need Statement: The part of the grant in which you explain, using both qualitative and quantitative data, why you should be funded. Remember to outline your problems and give data to verify the problems.

Needs Assessment: A method of collecting information to determine how well the library is serving its community and what other services or resources it can provide in the future.

Nonprofit: Nonprofit status is accorded to charitable, tax-exempt organizations by the Internal Revenue Service (IRS) by applying directly to the IRS. A copy of the IRS letter of determination is proof of 501(c) (3) status and is often required by funders as part of your proposal package.

Objectives: The desired outcomes of your activities, or your success indicators. Objectives specify who, what, when, how much, and how they will be measured. Objectives are the criteria by which the effectiveness of your project will be determined.

Operating Expenses: The costs of keeping a library open. These are the expenses of internal and administrative operations, rather than costs for specific programs or services.

Outcomes: Expected results of a project, which can be used to measure its success.

Outcome-Based Evaluation (OBE): Sometimes called outcomes measurement, this is a systemic way to determine if a program has achieved its goals. Many government agencies are requiring that OBE be integrated into grant proposals to measure meaningful results that change people's attitudes, skills, knowledge, behavior, or condition.

PI: Principal investigator.

Partner: Another organization that is collaborating with you on your project.

***Planning for Results*:** The Public Library Association's library planning model. A core principle is community involvement in the planning process. Written by Sandra Nelson, the book includes case studies, work forms, and a tool kit to provide library staff with all of the tools they need to complete a successful strategic plan in less than five months.

Program Officer: A staff member of a funding agency who reviews grant proposals, processes applications, and knows the ins and outs of the funder's interests, guidelines, and application procedures. Most foundations do not have program officers. Common in federal agencies.

Project Director: The individual responsible for activities involved in the grant, including implementation, evaluation, and follow-up.

Project Grant*:* Funds given to support a specific, well-defined project, program, or set of activities designed to address a specific need or achieve a specific goal.

Project Team: Representatives from library leadership, community advisers, grant researchers, grant writers, staff members, and subject matter experts who will plan and implement the grant project.

Proposal: A written or electronic application submitted to a government agency, foundation, or corporation to request a grant. Requirements vary widely among funders regarding contents, length, format, and accompanying materials. Follow guidelines carefully.

Request for Proposals (RFP): The formal announcement issued by a grant maker declaring that it is seeking proposals for funding in specific topic or program areas. The RFP usually includes complete details on the kinds of services or programs the grant maker will consider; proposal guidelines; deadline; proposal review and evaluation criteria; and other information to help you in preparing your proposal.

Research Grant: A grant made to support a specific research project.

Seed Money: Funding to support a new project in its start-up stage. Sometimes seed money will be granted to keep a new program going in its infancy until a larger funding source is found. Also known as start-up money.

Site Visit: A visit made by the funder to the grantee at the location of the project or program. The purpose is to meet with staff and beneficiaries, to observe the project in action, and to determine if technical support is needed.

State Library: The official agencies charged with statewide library development and the administration of federal funds authorized by the Library Services and Technology Act. These agencies vary greatly and are located in various departments of state government and report to different authorities depending on the state. They are involved in various ways in the leadership of enhancing library service for all the residents of the state.

Sustainability: Refers to an organization's ability to keep a grant project going after the initial funding has been used.

Target Population: The people who will benefit from the project the grant is funding.

Timeline: A systematic method of planning the month-by-month grant activities that will be implemented.

INDEX

ABOUT THE AUTHORS

Stephanie K. Gerding is the Continuing Education Coordinator at Arizona State Library, Archives and Public Records in Phoenix. She manages a statewide training program, bringing nationally known speakers, teleconferences, Library Institutes, and many other events to Arizona libraries. She also consults with libraries and assists in grant reviews for the State Library's Library Services and Technology Act (LSTA) state-based program. Additionally, she teaches a graduate level online research class for North Central University, with distance learners from across the world.

Focusing her publications on training, technology, and fund-raising for libraries, Stephanie loves to share her experiences by writing. She is the "Bringing in the Money" columnist for the Public Library Association's *Public Libraries* and has been a newsletter editor for various library associations. She has in-depth knowledge and practical experience in fund-raising, including both sides of the fund-raising experience—writing and granting.

Having done a variety of training during her library career for all types of libraries (school, public, academic, and special), Stephanie has presented at national conferences and conducted training across the United States from Seattle to Miami, Maine to California, and many places in between. In 2000, Stephanie did training on library topics in South Africa, where she was a volunteer for World Library Partnership's Inform the World Program in Kwazulu-Natal.

Formerly a trainer for the Bill & Melinda Gates Foundation's U.S. Library Program, Stephanie worked with many public libraries, either traveling to their site or conducting weeklong train-the-trainer programs in Seattle. There, she learned that giving away large sums of money or computers isn't always easy. Stephanie has also managed a small technical library at Federal Express, worked for SIRSI as a traveling trainer, as a cataloger at an academic library, and also for the New Mexico State Library. Stephanie received her master's degree in library and information science at the University of Tennessee.

Pamela H. MacKellar holds a master's degree in library science from the State University of New York at Albany. She has over 20 years of experience in libraries, including over 10 years of management experience. Pam learned to write grant proposals "on the job" when she found herself managing a library that relied on contract and grant funding to stay in operation.

Pam has conceived, planned, generated funding for, and implemented new programs, including NO Walls: A Community Technology Center for People with Disabilities, which was funded with a $327,000 grant from the U.S. Department of Education. She has also had success in preparing winning proposals to the Institute of Museum and Library Services, the National Network of Libraries of Medicine-South Central Region, the Bill & Melinda Gates Foundation, the Beaumont Foundation, the Albuquerque Community Foundation, and the MacArthur Foundation.

Pam has attended the Grantsmanship Training Program, and she has taught a preconference session and a continuing education class on "Writing Grants for Technology Projects."